Making Dinner

Also available from Bloomsbury

Culinary Art and Anthropology, Joy Adapon
Kitchen Secrets, Frances Short
The Making of the Modern Kitchen, June Freeman
Cooking Technology, edited by Steffan Igor Ayora-Diaz

Making Dinner

How American Home Cooks Produce and Make Meaning Out of the Evening Meal

Roblyn Rawlins and David Livert

BLOOMSBURY ACADEMIC
LONDON • NEW YORK • OXFORD • NEW DELHI • SYDNEY

BLOOMSBURY ACADEMIC
Bloomsbury Publishing Plc
50 Bedford Square, London, WC1B 3DP, UK
1385 Broadway, New York, NY 10018, USA

BLOOMSBURY, BLOOMSBURY ACADEMIC and the Diana
logo are trademarks of Bloomsbury Publishing Plc

First published in Great Britain 2019
Paperback edition published 2020

Copyright © Roblyn Rawlins and David Livert, 2019

Roblyn Rawlins and David Livert have asserted their right under the Copyright,
Designs and Patents Act, 1988, to be identified as Authors of this work.

For legal purposes the Acknowledgments on p. vii constitute
an extension of this copyright page.

Cover design by Irene Martinez Costa
Cover image © PeopleImages/Getty Images

All rights reserved. No part of this publication may be reproduced or
transmitted in any form or by any means, electronic or mechanical,
including photocopying, recording, or any information storage or retrieval
system, without prior permission in writing from the publishers.

Bloomsbury Publishing Plc does not have any control over, or responsibility for,
any third-party websites referred to or in this book. All internet addresses given
in this book were correct at the time of going to press. The author and publisher
regret any inconvenience caused if addresses have changed or sites have
ceased to exist, but can accept no responsibility for any such changes.

A catalogue record for this book is available from the British Library.

Library of Congress Cataloging-in-Publication Data
Names: Rawlins, Roblyn, author. | Livert, David, author.
Title: Making dinner: how American home cooks produce and make meaning out
of the evening meal / Roblyn Rawlins and David Livert.
Description: London; New York: Bloomsbury Academic, 2019. |
Includes bibliographical references and index.
Identifiers: LCCN 2019001491 | ISBN 9781474252553 (hardback) |
ISBN 9781474252560 (ePpub) | ISBN 9781474252577 (ePDF)
Subjects: LCSH: Food habits—United States. | Dinners and dining—Social
aspects—United States. | Cooking, American—Social aspects.
Classification: LCC GT2853.U5 R38 2019 | DDC 394.1/20973—dc23
LC record available at https://lccn.loc.gov/2019001491

ISBN: HB: 978-1-4742-5255-3
PB: 978-1-3501-7669-0
ePDF: 978-1-4742-5257-7
ePub: 978-1-4742-5256-0

Typeset by Integra Software Services Pvt. Ltd.

To find out more about our authors and books visit
www.bloomsbury.com and sign up for our newsletters.

Contents

List of Tables vi
Acknowledgments vii

1 Making Dinner, Making Meaning: Cooking, Family, and the Self 1
2 The Basics of Making Dinner 31
3 Hoping, Feeling, and the Home Cook 53
4 Time and the Home Cook 79
5 Cooking and the Self 97
6 The Family-first Cook: "The Point of My Cooking Is to Nourish My Family and Make Others Happy" 111
7 The Traditional Cook: "Like My Mom Used to Make" 127
8 The Keen Cook: "I Love to Try New Things" 141
9 Making Dinner Matters 157

Appendix A: Interview Protocol 173
Appendix B: Cooking Journal 175
References 204
Index 215

Tables

1	Profile of the households in the study	8
2	Cooking skills reported by cooks	43
3	Cooking is most enjoyed…	55
4	Cooking is least enjoyed…	56
5	Cooking feels like a chore	57
6	Objectives for the evening meal	65

Acknowledgments

We must first thank the home cooks who so graciously gave their time and candor to help us understand how they go about doing cooking. It has truly been a pleasure and a privilege to learn about their cooking lives, and we hope we have done them justice in our representation here.

Roblyn acknowledges the intellectual and academic support and resources made possible through the generosity of the Faculty Resource Network (FRN) of New York University, which sponsored her in its Scholar-in-Residence Program during the fall semester of 2010. She thanks Debra Szybinski and Anne Ward of the FRN for their leadership of the program. Krishnendu Ray's care, critiques, and conversation as Roblyn's FRN Research Consultant were simply invaluable. She thanks Dean Richard Thompson of the College of New Rochelle for his support of her application to the Faculty Resource Network and the College of New Rochelle for Faculty Fund awards in support of this research. David acknowledges the support and resources of Pennsylvania State University, Lehigh Valley campus, particularly those of Kenneth Thigpen, Peter Behrens, Kevin Kelley, and Ilyse Resnick.

We thank the editorial team at Bloomsbury Academic for their professionalism, guidance, and patience, including Miriam Cantwell, Lucy Carroll, and Clara Herberg. We are especially grateful to Jennifer Schmidt for commissioning the work of a pair of first-time authors and first-time collaborators. We thank the anonymous reviewers for making our book better.

We are grateful to so many friends and colleagues who offered support, encouragement, and advice for our work, including Anne Reid, Liz Tighe, Ronni Greenwood, Pauline Cullen, Brian McKenzie, Megan Jesse, Bob del Grosso, Anne McBride, Amy Bass, Dan McCarthy, Nereida Seguro-Rico, Nick Smart, Kim Case, Julie Gallagher, and colleagues in the Association for the Study of Food and Society. A special thanks to Michael Pardus, who first brought us to the table, fed us, and inspired us.

We dedicate this book to our mothers, Caroline Rawlins and Marjorie Livert, in loving gratitude for the thousands of dinners they made for us: we can never think of home cooking without thinking of you. Finally, we are grateful to Sammy Livert, our greatest coauthored project, who did his best to keep his parents from finishing "The Book" but makes our family dinner table the best place we have ever eaten.

1

Making Dinner, Making Meaning: Cooking, Family, and the Self

Consider the following evening meals prepared for their families by two different home cooks, one in the Middle Atlantic and one in the Pacific Northwest region of the United States.

Melissa's Sunday dinner menu:　　Cheese
　　　　　　　　　　　　　　　　Pepperoni
　　　　　　　　　　　　　　　　Crackers
　　　　　　　　　　　　　　　　Fresh baby bell peppers

Peter's Wednesday dinner menu:　　Cheese
　　　　　　　　　　　　　　　　　Salami
　　　　　　　　　　　　　　　　　Bread
　　　　　　　　　　　　　　　　　Pickles
　　　　　　　　　　　　　　　　　Fresh fruit

In the cooking journals they completed as part of our research into the meaning and practice of home cooking in the contemporary United States, Melissa and Peter reflected upon their dinners of cheese and sausage. Each considered the meal to have been a success, and each enjoyed preparing dinner that evening.

Melissa is an art teacher who cooks for her husband and their eight-year-old and ten-year-old children. She is a home cook of the type that we describe as a drudge. She does not enjoy cooking yet nevertheless does it out of a sense of obligation so that her family can eat a home-cooked meal together. Often only Melissa and the children are together at the dinner table because her husband gets home from work later in the evening. He enjoys cooking more than she does and often does much of the preparation in the morning so that she "just has to throw it together" when it is time for dinner. In her interview, Melissa stated, "I hate cooking." In the cooking journal, when asked how much she enjoyed cooking on the nights she did so, her answers indicated that she didn't enjoy it and did it only out of necessity: "Not much, but necessary; not at all, but had to." However, after serving the dinner described above, Melissa noted in her journal that she did enjoy preparing the meal that evening: it was "great, no cooking!" She also thought that the dinner was a success because it was "easy" and "different."

Peter works in sales and cooks for his wife and their eight-year-old daughter. He is a home cook whom we assigned to the types of family-first cook and keen cook. As a family-first cook, his cooking practice is highly motivated by a sense of care for his family. He takes a lot of pleasure in preparing good meals they enjoy eating. He also is a keen cook who enjoys building his already above-average skills and knowledge about food and cooking. In his cooking journal, he labeled this menu a "French picnic." Peter explained that a friend of his daughter was the family's guest for dinner that evening and "she loves Paris, so we did it French style." He judged the meal to be a success: "They were very happy … it was well received and enjoyed by all." He enjoyed preparing and serving the meal, although he did note in his journal reflections that it was all prep work to make an attractive presentation and no actual cooking.

So we have two home cooks who enjoyed making two almost identical dinners, but the meanings they made out of those dinners were strikingly different. To begin, the social context of the meals differed: in one household, there was a guest for dinner. Peter, along with almost all the home cooks in our study, varies his cooking when hosting dinner guests. He typically sticks to a short list of standards when entertaining guests, with the addition of one or two "special" dishes selected to please particular guests. In this case, the guest was a Francophile young girl, so Peter prepared a meal that he thought would please her.

In addition to differences in the social context of the cheese and sausage dinner, Melissa's and Peter's personal orientations and approaches to cooking diverge, as do their cooking skills and knowledge. While each dinner was judged by the cook to be a success, these evaluations were based on very different orientations to and feelings about cooking and food. Peter's approach to making dinner as a family-first cook can be seen in his attribution of the meal as a success. He felt his "French picnic" was a success because his wife, his daughter, and her friend enjoyed eating it. As a family-first cook, what is most important to him in his daily task of making dinner is caring for his family, making them happy, and keeping them healthy by providing good food that they like to eat. As a keen cook, Peter's mediated knowledge of French cuisine and culture enabled him to make his dinner of cheese and sausage and accompaniments, which appealed to Melissa simply because it was easy and different, into a special "French picnic." In the pages that follow, we demonstrate the complex ways in which the meaning that home cooks attribute to their cooking and to the meals they prepare is shaped by the intersection of their self-identities, orientations, abilities and aspirations as home cooks and by the material, temporal, cultural and social contexts in which their cooking takes place.

We are not here primarily interested in the *product* of making dinner—the evening meal ready to be eaten—but in the *process* of making dinner: the decisions, the aspirations, the emotions, and the perceived outcomes experienced by home cooks as they go about their daily tasks of preparing the evening meal. Doing home cooking is a complex, fluid, contingent process that includes planning, provisioning, preparing, and finally serving and eating. Home cooks vary in how they think and feel about cooking and about themselves as cooks. These personal factors in turn shape how different cooks respond to the material, temporal, cultural, and social contexts in which they make dinner.

The study

The idea for this book began eight years ago on a sunny summer Sunday morning. We had been having a delightful time that weekend, hosting friends at our home on the banks of the Delaware River. The house party included a professionally trained chef, a professor of culinary arts, a food studies professor, an academic researcher, two kids, and ourselves, one a professor of sociology and one of social psychology. We had kayaked and canoed on the river, gone out for breakfast, played chess, harvested wild mushrooms (a gigantic haul of chanterelles), gone for walks, read, celebrated a birthday with homemade cake and cava, laughed, and talked. And we had cooked and eaten, very well indeed. Sunday morning plans included coffee and the *New York Times*. We were drawn in to the magazine section by Erwin Olaf's striking photograph of an upscale home kitchen whose cook had apparently suddenly abandoned the food and tools, now festooned in cobwebs and insects and falling into decay. Another photograph depicted a high-end refrigerator filled with boxes and cartons of take-out pizza and Chinese food. In the cover article, "Out of the Kitchen and Onto the Couch," acclaimed food writer, critic, and activist Michael Pollan took up the increasingly familiar lament of the "decline and fall of everyday home cooking" (Pollan, 2009a). Pollan quoted food-marketing researcher Harry Balzer, whose firm has been tracking home cooking since the late 1970s and who claims that the amount of time Americans spend cooking at home has decreased, while their use of already prepared foods has increased. Pollan juxtaposed these trends indicating a lack of interest in actually doing cooking with the increasing popularity of watching others cook on television. It was, like all of his work, at its base an impassioned screed against industrial food and eating without care, well written and provocative.

But although easy to swallow in its familiarity (isn't criticizing home cooks the comfort food of many a food writer?), what Pollan was serving up that morning didn't sit all that well with us. We know a lot of people who do cook at home, maybe not every night, and maybe using some prepared foods, but nevertheless they do cook. And we know people, family and dear friends among their number, for whom cooking at home—being a good home cook—is vital to their sense of who and what they are and whose cooking adds meaning and value to their lives. We also knew that there was not a great deal of empirical research into the practice and meaning of cooking at home in the contemporary United States. This book was launched that day by the river, drinking coffee, eating frittata and bacon, reading, and talking with friends.

What counts as cooking?

When we have presented this research in various venues, we have often started our presentations with a discussion of the salami and cheese dinners that we use to open this book. And we have always gotten responses along the lines of "but that's not cooking" or "that's not dinner." In *Deciphering a Meal*, the anthropologist Mary Douglas wrote, "I need to know what defines the categories of a meal at home" (1972: 62). Forty-five years later, what counts as family dinner and what counts as cooking is still a question without a simple answer. For example, the participants in Wolfson and colleagues' (2016) focus groups defined the practice of home cooking as falling along various points on a continuum from all scratch cooking to any food made at home. As Amy Trubek has recently noted, "the emergence and pervasiveness of the modern food industry in all corners of the United States has deeply complicated the apparently simple question of what is and is not home cooking" (Trubek et al. 2017: 298).

In our view, *if our home cooks reported they made dinner at home, they did.* We take our definitions of cooking, dinner, and related phenomena from the participants in our study. Our inquiry into home cooking starts by honoring the home cooks' "working knowledge of her [and his] everyday world" (Smith 1987: 154). Some of our home cooks did make distinctions between "actual" cooking—which they viewed as more technically difficult—and simple preparation of the evening meal, as Peter did when he wrote that his French picnic dinner was all prep and no actual cooking. Virginia, who works as a counselor and cooks for her husband and two young children, told us in her interview that she "cook[s] an actual dinner maybe two or three times a week." When asked what she meant by an actual dinner, she explained that this would entail "more preparation, no microwave, and we actually eat together." Kaye works as a staff assistant and prepares almost every meal that she and her husband and two young children eat at home. The family eats out only once a month. Kaye reports that about four times a week, she cooks "an actual meal, not just macaroni and leftovers." On a night when they decided to make a spontaneous evening trip after a long workday to see the spring flowering trees and needed to cook and eat dinner very quickly, the dinner menu at Jack and Jeremiah's house consisted of frozen veggie burgers for the parents and a frozen waffle and a banana for the toddler. Jack's reflection on the meal as noted in their cooking journal was that it was "hard to call it cooking—but it was fine."

When we speak of home cooking then, we mean the everyday task of preparing and providing food for the household or family, including planning, provisioning and preparing the evening meal, regardless of how much "actual" cooking is involved in the preparation of a given dinner. This definition is in line with that of Anne Murcott (1995): to cook is to do the household task of making and providing food, a task like shopping or doing the laundry. Frances Short in *Kitchen Secrets* defined cooks as "'people who cook,' whether for themselves and/or for others, frequently or infrequently, with great technical expertise or without" (2006: 75). Our approach to defining cooking is also informed by Luce Giard's (1998) notion of "doing-cooking," which includes planning for the meal, cooking abilities, and related conceptual tasks, and DeVault's (1991) concept of "feeding work," which includes the practical and logistical tasks of making dinner as well as its emotional and relational components. To do home cooking or make dinner as we conceptualize it is to perform all the tasks and activities that make up the work of feeding the family. Feeding work includes planning meals, learning about food and food preparation, deciding where to shop, shopping for food, monitoring the food supplies in the household, preparing the meals, serving the meals, cleaning up after the meal, storing the leftovers, and disposing of the waste (Carrington 1999). It also includes knowing and monitoring the emotional and dietary needs of those for whom the cook cooks.

What are cooking skills?

In the view of French anthropologist Luce Giard, "doing-cooking" or the "nourishing arts" "demands as much intelligence, imagination and memory as those [life activities] traditionally held as superior, such as music and weaving" (1998: 151). How do we conceptualize the skills and capabilities that home cooks employ in their daily task of provisioning, planning, and preparing the evening meal?

We utilize a person-centered rather than a task-centered approach to understanding the skills and capabilities involved in home cooking (Short 2006). A task-centered approach would see making dinner as a range of techniques used to prepare various dishes. However, all practical tasks, such as making dinner, require a combination of mechanical abilities; knowledge; and "tacit" perceptual, conceptual, and planning skills (Singleton 1978). Perceptual, conceptual, and planning skills enable a person to visualize the process of a task, plan and design it, and have the confidence to carry it out.

Our person-centered approach to cooking skills includes consideration of not only those mechanical and technical knowledges and skills the cook employs but also the conceptual, perceptual, organizational, and logistical skills used by the home cook to plan, provision, and prepare dinner. This approach acknowledges the emotional and relational capabilities that are central to the practice of home cooking as feeding the family, including the ability to evaluate and to meet others' perceived physical and emotional needs. The person-centered approach to home cooking skills also directs our attention to the circumstances or context in which making dinner takes place. Our approach considers home cooking skills from the perspective of the individual home cook in terms of actions required, contexts of decision-making, self-perceptions of such actions and decisions, and the reactions and responses of those who eat.

Our approach to thinking about cooking skills is informed by Short (2006) and Trubek (Trubek et al. 2017). In her study of British home cooks, Frances Short argued that the relationship between people's cooking skills and their cooking practices was not straightforward. She noted that research had paid little attention to people's attitudes toward cooking, their confidence in their cooking skills, and how they feel about the task of feeding their family. More recently, based upon a decade's worth of research into home cooking practice, Amy Trubek's research group has put forth a conceptual argument for considering a "food agency" paradigm in cooking research: understanding how individuals set and achieve their goals—from provisioning to planning to preparing—within complex individual, cultural and social contexts (2017: 297). They propose that this approach "considers how the actor [read: home cook] completing the work employs manual and cognitive skills as well as sensorial perceptions, while also navigating and shaping various societal structures (e.g., time, money, mobility, etc.) in the course of setting and meeting personal meal preparation goals" (2017: 298).

As Frances Short (2006) has argued, making a meal is a process that requires home cooks to engage in activities beyond the home kitchen. Amy Trubek and her colleagues (2017) similarly identify cooking as a skilled practice in relation to social and cultural contexts and constraints, rather than simply a set of mechanical and individualized skills. When we look at cooking with an emphasis on context, we see that the skills needed for successful home cooking include those of professional chefs—albeit likely to a different standard—but they also include organizational, planning, emotional, relational, caregiving, multitasking and time allocation knowledge and skills. A successful home cook may produce a dinner that is technically not perfect but nevertheless is just right for the occasion and is eaten happily by their family. The home cook's skill set includes the ability to fit cooking around other tasks and activities such as childcare, to use up leftovers, and to plan and prepare food to suit different tastes and dietary requirements and to suit different occasions in family life.

Methodological approach

Our study of home cooks employed a mixed-methods approach. Data were collected via personal interviews with the primary home cook(s) and cooking journals subsequently completed by that cook or anyone else who cooked the evening meal. These complementary methodologies provide insights into how cooks perceived and made meaning out of making dinner while also providing more quantitative data regarding the daily practice of making dinner. The interviews and journals included a variety of open-ended questions that provide rich qualitative data regarding the meanings associated with making dinner as well as detailed depictions of the daily challenge of preparing the meal. Closed-ended questions and scales in the cooking journals provided quantitative data regarding details of daily practice as well as home cooks' emotions, enjoyment, and motivations. Our use of qualitative data analysis is particularly suited for investigating social processes that have attracted little prior research attention, where the research is limited in depth or where a new point of view on familiar topics appears promising (Milliken 2010). The mixed-methods approach permitted us to explore our cooks' experiences in their local, contextualized setting and allowed the participants' voices to define key elements of the phenomenon under study (Rahman 2017).

The study's methodology was approved by the Institutional Review Board of Pennsylvania State University. Informed consent was acquired at the outset of the in-depth interviews.

Recruitment of the study's participants

Our participants consist of fifty-one home cooks in forty-two households across the United States. Two sampling approaches were employed to recruit participants for the study. A convenience sampling approach involved recruiting (mostly through e-mail lists) from the following sources: a local community-supported agriculture (CSA) farm, community hospital, staff at both authors' academic institutions, a Facebook page community of those interested in cooking, and the social networks of both authors. Snowball sampling was also employed: participants were asked during the in-depth interview to recommend others whom we could invite to participate in the study.

When initially contacting participants, we asked for volunteers who cooked the evening meal at home most of the time. Because we were interested in how home cooks balanced work and family responsibilities in light of these competing time demands and logistical challenges, we purposively sampled for home cooks who worked outside the home and for households with children. We specifically expressed that we were looking for all types of cooks, not just "good" cooks. In recruitment materials, we targeted home cooks with the goal of including those with a broad range of cooking skills. We described the study as "not only for gourmet cooks or for people who cook a particular style or type of food" and explained that we were "interested in learning from anyone who cooks at home … all types of cooks with all types of families and many different backgrounds and life experiences." Nevertheless, our sample is likely biased by self-selection: while we do have a few cooks who dislike cooking (the "drudges"), it is reasonable to expect that people who are interested or invested in cooking would be more likely to participate in the research.

Criterion-based sampling

We employed criterion-based selection techniques to select cooks who were employed full-time and who lived with family. Our goal was to sample for homogeneity in order to explore differences between home cooks who experience relatively similar structural constraints in planning, preparing, and serving the evening meal. This type of qualitative, criterion-based selection technique is appropriate to research which generalizes to theory rather than to populations (Moon, Dillon, and Sprenkle 1990). We wanted to understand the practice of making dinner among cooks who—while many did try to economize and reported being unable to afford everything they might want to cook—nevertheless had access to most of what is available in the foodscape of the contemporary United States.

It was also important to restrict our sample to food-secure households, those that have reliable access to a sufficient quantity of affordable, nutritious food (ers.usda.gov 2017). The challenges of deciding what to cook and how to cook it are strongly related to the amount and type and quality of food available to the cook. Food insecurity can limit the variety of food and the likelihood of trying new foods: the home cook may worry about "wasting" food if it goes uneaten. Reay Tannahill reminds us that "food flexibility (as a matter of choice) is usually a characteristic of affluent societies. The nearness of hunger breeds conservatism. Only the well-fed can afford to try something new because only they can afford to leave it on the plate if they dislike it" (1989: 393). Likewise, the availability of kitchen spaces that are well equipped and adequate to most cooking tasks is related to the amount of economic resources available. Food-secure households are generally able to choose virtually anything from the North American foodscape, as long as it is available locally or by delivery.

Profile of participating households

Table 1 depicts the forty-two households in the sample. (Respondent pseudonyms are used throughout the book.) Thirty-four households included children under eighteen years of age (three households had children over eighteen living at home). Of these, roughly half included young children under age eight. Among households with children under eighteen, 39 percent included one child, 42 percent two children, and the balance had three or more children. There were three single-mother households in our sample. There were ten households without children, including eight couples and two older single women who had cooked for their families earlier in their lives. Gay or lesbian couples made up five households, including two households with children. The ages of the cooks ranged from their twenties to their sixties.

Table 1 Profile of the households in the study

Primary cook(s)	Other adults	Children	Occupation	Self-reported ethnicities	Meal most representative of cook	Type of cook
Alice (40s) Michael (40s)		Ages 7 & 9	Librarian/librarian	German, Austrian	Alice: Tofu fried rice, roasted veggie tarte tartin Michael: Spaghetti Bolognese with steamed vegetables	Alice: Family-first, keen Michael: Family-first
Amanda (40s)	Husband (40s)	Ages 8 & 8	Teacher/banker	Irish, Eastern European	Chicken and dumplings	Planful
Andrea (40s)	Female partner (40s)		Librarian/librarian	Italian, White	Boneless skinless chicken thighs, well-seasoned and seared and then finished in the oven. Cauliflower puree with butter and salt and pepper. Roasted Brussel sprouts (a little crispy) with shallots	Keen, improvisational
Ann (early 30s)	Husband (30s)	Ages 2 & 8	Financial consultant/property manager	Irish, Italian	Lasagna	Family-first, planful
Ashley (50s)	Husband (50s)		Social worker/graphic designer	Jewish	Mexican lasagna	Drudge
Carolyn (late 50s)	Husband (late 50s)		Staff assistant/store manager (retired)	Italian, German, Polish	Halupkis	Traditional
Cheryl (40s)		Age 15	Print shop employee	White	Home-baked bread, spinach lasagna, salad and apple pie	Family-first

Primary cook(s)	Other adults	Children	Occupation	Self-reported ethnicities	Meal most representative of cook	Type of cook
Chloe (40s)	Husband (40s)	Ages 6, 9, 11, & 14	Nutritionist/engineer	Italian, Scottish, German	An Italian basic such as lasagna or another pasta dish, stuffed mushrooms, salad, veggies, sautéed fish	Keen, improvisational
Cynthia (50s) Christina (50s)			Senior researcher/non-profit director	PA Dutch	Cynthia: Chicken and broccoli or green bean stir fry Christina: Anything made with lemon, garlic, and olive oil	Cynthia: Keen, improvisational Christina: Improvisational
Deanna (50s)	Husband (60s)	Ages 16 & 20	Special education teacher/truck driver	Native American, German, Irish	Lasagna	Family-first
Elaine (40s)	Husband (40s)	Ages 10 & 11	Stay-at-home mom/insurance	Italian, Irish		Family-first
Elena (60s)			Substance abuse counselor	Mexican American	Everything homemade or homegrown, potatoes from the garden and veggies, etc. Homegrown meat. Homemade bread	Keen, improvisational
Emily (40s)	Husband (40s)	Ages 2 & 7	Library director/creative director	Filipino, White		Keen
Grace (20s)	Mother (40s), father (40s)	Ages 17 & 20	Waitress/salesperson/supervisor	Syrian		Family-first, traditional
Helen (40s)	Husband (40s)	Age 12	College advisor/engineer	French, Dutch, Scottish, German, Native American	Meatloaf, garlic mashed potatoes, green beans almondine	Keen, family-first, improvisational

Table 1 (Continued)

Primary cook(s)	Other adults	Children	Occupation	Self-reported ethnicities	Meal most representative of cook	Type of cook
Jack (40s) Jeremiah (40s)		Age 2	Government/non-profit director	Scandinavian, African American	Jack: Pasta carbonara Jeremiah: Tacos with all the fixings	Jack: Family-first, keen, improvisational Jeremiah: Family-first, traditional
James (30s)	Wife (30s), sister-in-law (30s), her husband (30s)	Ages 3, 8, & 10	Facilities manager/customer operations manager	African American	Bone-in ribeye steak, mashed potatoes, baby broccoli, kale Caesar salad, pound cake	Keen, traditional
Janet (40s) Kristen (40s)			College advisor/stockbroker	PA Dutch, Irish	Janet: Pizza	Janet: Improvisational Kristen: Improvisational
Joyce (30s)	Husband (30s)	Ages 2, 6 & 9	Teacher/engineer	Polish, Slovak	Turkey meatloaf, mashed potatoes, roasted Brussel sprouts	Family-first
Judith (40s)	Husband (40s)	Ages 11 & 13	Registered dietician/Unavailable	English, French Canadian, PA Dutch	Salmon with maple glaze, rice pilaf, sautéed fresh spinach, fruit salad	Family-first
Karen (50s)	Husband (50s)	Ages 7, 8, & 10	Fundraising/police officer	Irish, German	Chicken strips or fish with buttered noodles and canned vegetables	Drudge
Kaye (late 30s)	Husband (late 30s)	Ages 4 & 9	Staff Assistant/sales	Hungarian, Italian	Pork chops, mashed potatoes, broccoli, salad, biscuits and gravy	Family-first, keen
Linda (50s) Tony (40s)			Administrator/theater director	Swedish, Jewish, Italian	Linda: Pot roast with little golden roasted potatoes	Linda: Traditional, keen Tony: Traditional
Lisa (40s)	Husband (40s)	Ages 2, 6, 10, 13, & 17	Artist/biologist	Jewish, Italian		Family-first
Lois (40s)		Ages 12 & 14	Public relations	German, Norwegian	Not available	Keen
Lorraine (early 40s)	Husband (early 40s)	Age 3	College instructor/unemployed	Irish, Italian, Yugoslavian	Spaghetti and meatballs	Family-first, improvisational

Primary cook(s)	Other adults	Children	Occupation	Self-reported ethnicities	Meal most representative of cook	Type of cook
Margaret (50s)	Husband (50s)		Staff assistant/draftsman	PA Dutch	Roast beef, mashed potatoes, gravy, peas, corn, rolls, pie, homemade ice cream	Traditional, Family-first, planful
Melissa (30s) Brandon (30s)		Ages 8 & 10	Art teacher/chiropractor	White	Melissa: Salad Brandon: Roasted chicken with mashed potatoes, grilled vegetables	Melissa: Drudge Brandon: Family-first
Mira (40s)	Female partner (40s)	Age 5	Psychologist/psychologist	Malaysian, Latina	Homemade pizzas. Any kind of ethnic cuisine: Malaysian, Indian, Korean, Moroccan	Keen, planful
Monique (40s) Joseph (40s)			Instructor/teacher	Afro-Caribbean/Afro-Caribbean	Monique: Baked macaroni and cheese Joseph: Haitian rice and beans	Monique: Improvisational Joseph: Traditional, keen
Paige (30s)	Husband (30s)	Ages 10, 13, & 16	Teacher/attorney	Scots-Irish, White	Mexican chicken casserole	Family-first
Pamela (60s)			Staff assistant	Irish	Lasagna	Traditional, keen
Patricia (late 40s) Emma (20s)	Husband (late 40s)	Ages 17, 20, & 22	Teacher/TV postproduction	Italian	Patricia: Torta, stuffed mushrooms, roasted peppers Emma: Seafood risotto, asparagus and salad	Patricia: Family-first, traditional, planful Emma: Keen
Pauline (40s)	Husband (40s)	Age 15	Project manager/media staff	Irish, Polish	Roast turkey, Duchess potatoes, orange-cranberry sauce, gravy, green beans almondine, spinach salad with poppy seed dressing, hazelnut torte	Family-first

Table 1 (*Continued*)

Primary cook(s)	Other adults	Children	Occupation	Self-reported ethnicities	Meal most representative of cook	Type of cook
Peter (40s)	Wife (40s)	Age 8	Sales/consultant	White	Pan roasted salmon with mushroom risotto and pinot noir reduction, grilled asparagus	Keen, family-first, planful
Rebecca (50s)	Husband (50s)	Age 16	Homemaker/technology firm owner	Italian	Pan seared fish over mashed purple potatoes and sautéed Swiss chard	Keen
Ruth (40s)		Age 16	Professor	Jewish	Summer salad of melon, cucumber, and avocado; another salad of grilled corn and feta; and another salad with a tomato base	Family-first, keen
Sara (40s) Daniel (40s)		Ages 5 & 7	Teacher/professor	Scottish, German	Sara: Fresh bread and homemade soup Daniel: Something delicious on the grill such as marinated chicken and veggies (e.g., zucchini, mushrooms)	Sara: Family-first, improvisational Daniel: Family-first, improvisational
Susan (20s)	Mother (40s), Father (40s)	Age 16	Sales/mechanic	Irish, Italian		Family-first
Teresa (40s)	Husband (40s)	Age 5	Consultant/social worker	White	Asparagus soup, roasted chicken with carrots, brownies for dessert (no frosting)	Family-first
Victoria (40s)	Husband (40s)	Ages 8 & 11	Spec. ed. teacher/sales	PA Dutch	Ham, mashed potatoes, and broccoli	Family-first, planful
Virginia (40s)	Husband (40s)	Ages 2 & 7	Social worker/musician	White		Family-first

All but two primary home cooks in the study were employed outside the home, mostly in full-time jobs. Two husbands in the study did not work: one does some cooking but does not put together an entire evening meal, and the other does no cooking. Occupations of household members in the study ranged from architect to waitress. These occupations were distributed across a variety of fields including education (21 percent), media and the arts (10 percent), clerical and administration (9 percent), non-profit organizations and libraries (9 percent), social services (7 percent), construction and engineering (7 percent), healthcare (7 percent), and finance (7 percent). Over half of the adults in the study held postgraduate degrees (55 percent) and just under a third (30 percent) held at least a bachelor's degree. Another 8 percent had attended some college; 7 percent of the sample had a high school degree or less.

Respondents self-identified with a number of ethnic backgrounds; many adults identified with more than one ethnicity. Households were located in eleven different states across the United States as well as the District of Columbia. More than half (60 percent) are located in the Northeast/Middle Atlantic United States, including New Jersey, New York, and Pennsylvania. Another fifth (19 percent) are located in the Western United States, including California, Montana, and Washington. The remaining households are located in the South (16 percent), including Alabama, Florida, Georgia and the District of Columbia as well as the Midwest (5 percent), including Minnesota and Kansas.

Measures

The principal data collection procedures were the in-depth interview with the home cooks and the cooking journals that were completed by whomever cooked dinner during the study period.

Interview protocol. Interviews with home cooks were semi-structured, following an interview protocol (see Appendix A). Primarily open-ended questions focused on how the process of making dinner is typically organized in the household. A series of questions asked if the cook took into account fifteen different goals or considerations (i.e., fast or well-balanced) when deciding what to cook for dinner. There were two parts to this series of questions: respondents first indicated whether or not the consideration was taken into account when they prepared dinner, and then the interviewer asked what the consideration meant to the respondent. Another series of questions explored the cook's personal experience of making dinner: when they liked and didn't like it, when it was a chore or felt difficult, when it was a leisure activity, and when the cook had trouble deciding what to make. Questions also explored the use of recipes and grocery shopping behavior. Items regarding self-perceptions as a cook and identification with food-related identities (e.g., foodie or vegan) appeared throughout the protocol. The interviews lasted 45 minutes on average and were carried out by one of the authors. Each interview was recorded and then transcribed for analysis. Most interviews were conducted over the phone; nine were conducted face-to-face.

Cooking journal. Following the interview, the cooking journals covering a period of either ten or fourteen days were mailed or e-mailed to study participants (see Appendix B). Respondents either completed the journal in a word processing file or printed a paper version, completed it, and scanned it for return e-mail. Daily cooking journal questions included whether dinner was prepared at home that night. For each meal that was cooked at home, respondents recorded who cooked it and assisted; when it was planned, provisioned, and cooked; the menu; whether recipes were used; who ate it and how they reacted to the meal; and how the cook evaluated the meal in terms of success and enjoyment. The respondent also indicated which of the fifteen considerations (identical to those used in the interview) was important to them when making dinner that night.

Items measuring cooks' emotional experience of making dinner that night appeared several times during the journal period. These consisted of seven 7-point bipolar scales for the following affective dimensions: rushed/relaxed, anxious/clam, happy/unhappy, uncertain/confident, value/taken for granted, organized/chaotic, and creative/bored. Other questions assessed self-identity as a cook, assistance in the kitchen, what the cook would prepare if alone, food television viewership, an aspirational dinner menu, and experiences with cooking for guests. A final set of questions on the last page of the journal assessed the cook's culinary skills, a representative dinner, and how they viewed themselves as a cook.

Cooking journals were completed and returned by forty-six out of fifty-one cooks. Taken together, the completed journals represent over a year's worth of (424) evenings in which home cooking practices were recorded. A meal was cooked at home on 316 of those evening meals, roughly three-quarters of the time. On the quarter of days that dinner wasn't prepared at home, the household was out of town, visiting others, ordered food to be delivered, picked up food, or ate at a restaurant or other event.

Our cooking journals provide potentially more accurate measures of actual home cooking practice than could be obtained through face-to-face or telephone interviews. Research studies in survey methods, social psychology, and cognitive psychology have identified a number of phenomena that tend to introduce biases into the reporting of behavior (Tourangeau, Rips, and Rasinski 2000). For example, there is the widely demonstrated social demand bias associated with a respondent's motivation to be seen more positively by interviewers or observers. As a result, people tend to underreport socially undesirable behavior and overreport desirable behavior (Preisendöfer and Wolter 2014). To the extent that home cooking–related behaviors are perceived by our respondents as socially undesirable (e.g., serving convenience foods every night) or desirable (e.g., cooking a well-balanced meal with fresh vegetables), there may be a tendency for the same biases in interviews. Individuals may also unintentionally experience selective memory in which more vivid behavior is more likely to be recalled (Tourangeau, Rips, and Rasinski 2000). When behavior is recalled, individuals also tend to telescope behavior: to include behavior in a time frame (e.g., last month) that in fact occurred earlier or later than the time frame. Collection of data through cooking journals may attenuate such potential biases. The journals are completed by the home cook in the privacy of their home, not in the context of an interview or observation. The journals are designed to be easily completed each night; thus, the thoughts, feelings, and behavior reported for each dinner should be more easily and accurately recalled by the respondent. The daily cooking journal also provides a useful structure for the respondent to review and reflect upon their cooking behavior.

Analytic approaches

Analyses of the multi-method data in the study were multifaceted. Qualitative methods are particularly appropriate for research exploring social practices such as cooking and eating and how people make meaning out of those (Wills 2012). The study's interviews and responses to open-ended questions provide data regarding practices within the social context of the household. We learned about not just what was prepared for dinner but who ate it; how they reacted to it; what was the cook's concern before, during, and after; and what kind of week it had been for the household. Both spoken (the interviews) and written (cooking journals) methods provide a way for the respondent to use their own language, grounded in their own social reality (Highet 2003; Wills 2012). Our approach to analyzing the data follows upon feminist methodological and epistemological approaches such as those put forward by Dorothy Smith (1987) in her classic *The Everyday World as Problematic: A Feminist Sociology*. We reject *a priori* conceptual practices that would "transpose knowing into the objective forms in which the situated subject and her actual experience and location are discarded" (Smith 1987: 153) but rather work toward understanding and representing the subjective knowledge and experience of our participants.

The authors read the interview transcripts and journals to devise coding to describe participants' perceptions, practices, emotions, and beliefs about food and cooking. Guided by the research questions, the first round of coding focused on the following constructs: enjoyment, success, planning, perceived challenges, and motivations for cooking. Using the constant comparative method (Lincoln and Guba 1985), repeated readings and analysis of excerpts generated by the initial broad coding categories led us to further elaborating on and breaking these categories into subcategories facilitating conceptual interpretation. Eventually, as the participants' thoughts, feelings, and practices related to making dinner became better understood, we developed the ideal types of cooks. To increase reliability, the data were first coded individually and later compared between coders. All disagreements were resolved through discussion.

For each category, we noted both frequency/importance and type of the construct under study; for example, when coding whether the dinners were considered successful, we noted all reasons meals were considered successful and which explanations occurred most frequently and which were most important to the participants. After collecting these descriptive accounts within coding categories, we compared the cooks, noting similarities and differences. This type of analysis is suitable for description across cases (individual participants), categories (different types of families), and themes (time, success, etc.), with the aim of conceptualizing data and building a theory that offers an integrated framework of the phenomenon (Merriam 2009).

Analysis of the study's quantitative data consisted of t-tests, ANOVAs, and chi-square tests for single-level data (e.g., comparing competencies between cooking types). A series of statistical procedures known as hierarchical linear models (HLM) were used to test the statistical relationships between type of cook and data reported for meals reported in the cooking journals (e.g., whether emotional experiences of cooking dinner differed by types of home cook). Meal data were modeled at level one, which was nested within each cook at level two. HLM analyses used a series of multilevel generalized linear models (for emotion items) or logistic regressions (for consideration and planning) with the meal at level one and the cook at level two.

Types of cooks

The cooks we discuss here were the main cooks for their household, with primary responsibility for planning, provisioning, and preparing the evening meal. In eight households, the responsibility of doing these cooking-related tasks was shared equally between a pair of spouses or partners. Our home cooks shared beliefs about the importance of preparing healthy and economical meals that were well liked by their families. As working adults, they faced similar time constraints that dampened their enjoyment of cooking and often prompted them to choose meals that might be less healthy or economical but could be prepared quickly and easily while still being liked by their families. Almost all of them struggled at times to decide what to make for dinner. Yet within these commonalities, we found much diversity in the general orientation of the home cooks to cooking; their typical approaches to the task of making dinner; and how they thought and felt about food, cooking, family, and self.

Inductive analysis of the primary motivations and practices of domestic cooks—what is important to them and how they enact their usual practices in planning, shopping for, and cooking dinner—enabled us to construct four analytical categories of home cooks: *family-first cooks, traditional cooks, keen cooks*, and *drudges*. In addition, analysis of how cooks vary in their approach to the time dimension of making dinner led us to identify *planful* versus *improvisational* cooks. These are Weberian ideal types of home cooks. Family-first cooks are motivated primarily by their families' likes and needs; traditional cooks prepare a limited repertoire of dishes they perceived as traditional; keen cooks enjoy challenging themselves to learn more about food and cooking; and drudges do not enjoy cooking.

When we say that family-first, traditional and keen cook are ideal types, we acknowledge that individual cooks will seldom conform to a type in all respects. Some will cook in a manner that places them in multiple types and some will not fall into any type. In other words, our contention is not that the attributes of a type of cook are exactly correlated, but that each approach to cooking has internal coherence. So, for example, keen cooks tend to value challenges in cooking, judge success based on the quality of the food produced, and seek out knowledge about food and cooking. We also note that cooks may not only embody more than one type but also move into and out of types over the course of their home cooking careers: a keen cook who has a child may now become a family-first cook, and a family-first cook whose children have grown and moved away may become keen.

We find that these distinct approaches and orientations to home cooking order and shape how cooks negotiate the cultural, material, and social factors that make up each evening's cooking event and impact how they think and feel about cooking for their families. For all but the drudges, being a good home cook is a key mode of self-identification that gives meaning to their lives. What being a good home cook means, however, differs for family-first, traditional and keen cooks.

Thinking about cooking

All human history attests
That happiness for man,—the hungry sinner!—
Since Eve ate apples, much depends on dinner.
—Lord Byron, Don Juan, Canto XIII, stanza 99

Heal the World: Cook Dinner Tonight.
(Screen printed on a tie dyed dish towel from Penzeys Spices, a gift to the authors.)
—Penzeys Spices 2017

Cooking Solves Everything: How Time in the Kitchen Can Save Your Health, Your Budget, and even the Planet.
—Title of Mark Bittman's (American food journalist) Kindle single (Bittman 2017)

Everything rests, therefore, on the shoulders of the cook.
—Kaufmann 2010: 241

As Lord Byron noted, we can go back to Eve's original choice of fresh fruit as an example of how choices regarding the dinner menu may hold fairly significant implications for humanity (Lord Byron, Don Juan, Canto XIII, stanza 99). More typically, however, writers have alluded to the potential for our dinner choices to make things better, including improving our health and helping our budget (Bittman 2017) and even healing the world (Bittman 2017; Penzeys Spices 2017). Given these sentiments, Jean-Claude Kaufman's quote regarding the awesome burden of the cook seems less hyperbolic (Kaufman 2010).

Food itself has long been accorded great value and weight. In her 2013 book *Eating Together*, Alice Julier notes that in the past fifteen years or so, the body of social scientific scholarship on food and social life has grown to the extent that her book did "not need to begin with disclaimers or long explanations of why it's so important for social scientists to study food" (p. 2). Scholarship on food has advanced from the formative contributions of anthropologists Claude Levi-Strauss (1970) and Mary Douglas (1966) to the institutionalization of food studies as an academic area of specialization, complete with journals, books, and academic programs at all levels (Belasco 2008). As Avakian and Haber (2005) point out in their invaluable review of the history of feminist food studies, "One of the most basic assumptions of scholarship in both food studies and women's studies is that the daily life of ordinary people is not only worthy of study but necessary to any understanding of past and present worlds" (p. 16). Food has been firmly established as a worthwhile object of theoretical and empirical investigation.

But what of cooking? As food scholars, we have not been entirely successful in resisting what Marjorie DeVault in her groundbreaking work *Feeding the Family* termed the "pervasive trivialization" of domestic cooking (1991: 56). The home cook's mental load of planning, coordinating, negotiating, strategizing, and juggling needed to feed a family, in addition to the simpler tasks of chopping an onion or pushing a cart through a grocery store aisle, remains largely unseen and unacknowledged in much popular and academic discourse about the nature and state of home cooking. Given how important home cooking is presumed to be, there has been surprisingly little social scientific research on the practice and meaning of home cooking in people's everyday lives.

Social scientific analyses of food have mostly focused on the consumption and symbolic meanings of food rather than on the production of food and meals through home cooking. In their call for papers on studies of food in everyday life for the Eleventh Annual New Zealand Symposium of Gastronomy held in 2017, anthropologists Sam Hassibi and Amir Sayadabdi note that "the biological imperative that makes eating a necessity often makes us look at it as a mundane practice. Cooking, too, especially in its 'domestic' context, may seem insignificant and uninteresting." It is an indicator of the persistent and pervasive trivialization of domestic cooking that the organizers of such a conference felt it necessary to acknowledge that while home cooking might seem unworthy of study, it is important to study as it is through cooking that "food-related practices, habits, and values ... are constantly being passed in ordinary kitchens from one generation to the next" (FoodAnthropology 2017).

In *The Raw and the Cooked*, famed anthropologist Claude Levi-Strauss (1970) placed cooking at the center of the human experience with his claim that, symbolically, cooking marks the human transition from "raw" nature to "cooked" culture. A half-century later, biological anthropologist Richard Wrangham took up this claim of the centrality of cooking in *Catching Fire* (2010), arguing that since its inception cooking has been the main driver of human evolution. In *Purity and Danger* (1966), anthropologist Mary Douglas showed how social groups maintain their separateness and build their sense of group identity through using food rules as boundary markers. In *Cooking, Cuisine and Class* (1982), Jack Goody argued for the importance of social structure in shaping cooking, including such environmental and technological factors as the role of writing and cookbooks as well as changes in agricultural and preservation processes. Goody also highlights the importance of class inequalities in allowing the development of elite cuisines through which cooking reflects other divisions in society into "the high and the low" (Goody 1982: 97).

Much of the burgeoning research in food studies in recent years has utilized cooking as a nexus to examine relationships between important social, cultural, and political matters and food, such as food and the body (e.g., Probyn 2000), politics (e.g., Nestle 2013), and race (e.g., Williams-Forson 2006), rather than as a subject interesting and important as an object of analysis in its own right. Dorothy Smith in writing about feminist sociology noted that documentation of women's lives had largely been left to the novelists and poets and that women's everyday lives had been thus rendered invisible in academic knowledge (1987). David Sutton (2014) points out that "one can find no ethnographies with cooking as their central subject in the anthropological literature up to the turn of the twenty-first century" (p. 18) and suggests that this paucity of interest can be chalked up to male anthropologists' trivialization and lack of interest in women's activities. Arlene Voski Avakian and Barbara Haber (2005) note that early feminist scholarship on housework tended to ignore cooking "as if it were merely a marker of patriarchal oppression and, therefore, not worthy of attention" (p. 2).

Beginning in the 1970s, feminist social scientists began to break down the divide between the public and the private spheres that had kept hidden domestic work and the home kitchen. The key question for feminist scholars was the role that cooking could play in both women's oppression and in their empowerment. Scholarly work began to emerge demonstrating that cooking could serve not only as a means of women's oppression but also of their empowerment by providing a "vehicle for women's creative expression" (Avakian and Haber 2005: 2) and serving as a "recipe for agency" (Counihan 2010: 128). For example, in "Female Identity, Food, and Power in Contemporary Florence," Carole M. Counihan shows that many contemporary women occupy a contradictory position: they want and need to work outside the home yet still believe that a "good" woman is defined by her clean house and her good home-cooked meals. When women lack access to public power, they may gain private influence through giving in the form of cooking and cleaning. The women Counihan studied give to others through their cooking while receiving in return "love, favors, good behavior and the power that comes from being needed" (1988: 53). Meredith Abarca demonstrates how working-class women who own small food stands in Texas and Mexico transform their home cooking abilities into economic resources, empowering themselves and becoming agents of social and cultural change through their cooking (2006).

Home cooking has been and remains a deeply gendered practice (Cairns and Johnston 2015). In her essay on American cookbooks from the 1950s, Erika Endrijonas (2001) argues that postwar prosperity and promotion of cooking elaborate dishes as a way to get women back in the kitchen, along with aggressive marketing of processed foods, produced enormous contradictions for women's roles as home cooks. "Buy processed foods but cook from scratch; be creative but follow directions precisely; accommodate all family members' preferences but streamline the food purchase and preparation process; work part-time but be a full-time homemaker; and do it all with little or no training" (Endrijonas 2001: 157). These contradictions still hold today, although the expectation that they can afford to work only part-time is no longer true for the majority of American women.

Part of what makes studying cooking interesting is that it is both about consumption and production. Much of the process of home cooking depends on consumption through planning and provisioning. Home cooks choose and buy their ingredients in the marketplace, influenced by culinary experts, by advertising, by other cooks, by considerations of healthiness and what is "good" food, and by their tastes and those for whom they cook. But for these consumer goods to then become a home-cooked meal, the home cook must put them together into recognizable dishes appropriate for the particular meal according to cultural norms, sometimes apply heat, manipulate or cut them, etc. There is always an element of production in making dinner, even if it is only choosing and heating frozen vegetables, dried pasta shapes, and jarred sauces. For many in the contemporary world, cooking is the sole form of production in which they engage in everyday life.

Cooking is also understood as a practice through which people can create and communicate their identity, status, or lifestyle (e.g., Cairns and Johnston 2015; de

Solier 2013; Kaufmann 2010; Short 2006). Frances Short identifies beliefs and values prevalent among her sample of British home cooks such as the creative ideal, concepts of success and failure, and the endless search for the interesting and different dish. Jean-Claude Kaufmann's study of twenty-two home cooks in France (2010) examines the meaning of food, cooking and eating in family life, and how cooks think about food and cooking. Kaufmann argues that home cooks create and shape social relationships through the act of making meals. David Sutton's (2014) ethnographic study of households' cooking practices on the Greek island of Kalymnos demonstrates how gender and generation shapes cooking and highlights themes of continuity and change in cooking, which is situated in a specific milieu with associated technologies. Kaufman's and Sutton's works in particular highlight the complex social relationships involved in home cooking.

Mills and colleagues' systematic review of research on home cooking (2017) demonstrates the importance of multiple factors and contexts as determinants of home cooking practices and outcomes. They analyzed thirty-eight qualitative and quantitative empirical studies from a wide range of disciplines and concluded that home cooking is influenced by age, household composition, socioeconomic status, time scarcity, social relationships in the household, skills, cultural and ethnic background, and aspirations for the meal. Gender roles, time, employment status, the social context of the household, and cultural background were the most powerful determinants of variations in home cooking skills and practices in those studies. This work underscores the range of interacting influences on home cooking, consistent with our approach to the factors shaping the practice and meaning of making dinner.

Cooking and culture

Cooking, food, and culture exist in a reciprocal relationship. As Avakian and Haber note, "Necessary for physical survival, daily meals are no less crucial to the construction of cultures and the people within them" (2005: 16). It is widely acknowledged that food has symbolic meaning: it can be gendered, have religious significance, signal class status, invoke ideas of nationalism and ethnic pride, and more (Belasco 2008; Bourdieu 1984; Douglas 1966).

But much of what food means does not derive from the food itself but from how that food is prepared by cooks. The cultural, social, and political meanings of food may or may not have salience without the intervention of the cook, who makes that food meaningful. Take the common package of ground beef. It may have connotations of health, purity, quality, "goodness," and taste, depending upon who is contemplating it. But, in the hands of a cook, ground beef can be made into many different things with different cultural, social, and political meanings: the British mince, an American hamburger, lasagna, chili, tacos from a kit. It is the cook who makes the meaning out of the food for those who will eat it. Cooks accomplish this meaning-making through conceptualizing what they want to make out of the ground beef and then executing and serving it forth. A family-first cook might make tacos or hamburgers. A keen cook, depending on the decade, might make stroganoff or sliders or lettuce cups with hoisin and Sriracha sauces. A traditional cook might make lasagna or pelmeni or Minnesotan hot dish. In making dinner from a package of ground beef, home cooks literally make meaning.

The home cook deciding what to make from a package of ground beef is also operating within a particular cultural context, from which she will draw the meaning she attributes to her food and her cooking. From the beginnings of the social scientific study of food, scholars have demonstrated how cultures construct foods and combinations of food as good to eat. Mary Douglas, reflecting on her own household and those of working-class families in London, outlined the many rules that determined how often different foods were prepared and consumed, the types of food chosen for particular meals or snacks, the constitution of a "proper meal," and the preparation and cooking techniques employed. The rules governing each separate meal reveal its relative importance in social life and construct and maintain the social relationships among those who eat it (1972).

Anne Murcott's 1982 study of young Welsh mothers demonstrated the cultural rules that structured their food choices, serving methods, and preparation techniques. The most highly valued meal was the "proper meal" or "cooked dinner." To qualify as a proper meal, the meal had to be hot and include roast or grilled meat and at least two kinds of vegetables, one of which had to be green and boiled (Murcott 1982). Similarly, Charles and Kerr's study of mothers in the UK found that a proper meal was considered by them to include meat, potatoes, and vegetables and to be made up of fresh foods rather than processed foods (1988). A proper meal was also understood to be an event at which all family members are present and sit at the table together, taking their time over a shared meal prepared in the home and eaten together (Charles and Kerr 1988).

Murcott (1997) reviewed her earlier studies fifteen years on and suggested that within contemporary societies with greater access to industrialized, preprepared, so-called convenience foods, the rules underlying food choice and preparation practices may be in flux. Sociologist Claude Fischler suggests that concerns about the possible risks of industrialized food and rapidly changing, often contradictory, expert knowledge about what is good to eat, together with concerns about the breakdown of traditional food practices and the explosion of choices of what to eat, have resulted in an anxious state of "gastro-anomie" or normlessness about food, eating, and cooking (1979).

On the other hand, Beardsworth and Keil (1997) point to the enduring power of food rules and suggest that rather than being anxious about the multiplicity of food choices in Western food systems, people find it "quite normal and essentially unproblematic" to decide what to cook and eat (p. 168). This is possible because there is a relatively stable overall framework for meals within which the choices, fashions, and fads of a pluralistic approach to eating can be played out. An example could be kale, which has recently become quite fashionable and is constructed as a "super-food" in the United States. Because kale fits within the schema of a dinner meal with a green vegetable, cooks who see kale prominently displayed in the market may quite easily pick it up and incorporate it into their dinner menus. They "know what to do with it" because of food rules.

In contemporary liberal democracies, power functions through discourses, which produce effects by shaping what people do with their bodies, time, and lives (Foucault 1988). Dominant discourses that establish some foods as good or bad set up normalizing standards for the behavior of responsible citizens. As those standards are internalized, they become a moral compass by which people assess themselves and others. In modern postindustrial societies, force is not usually required to govern a populace; people do the job themselves through a variety of processes such as self-surveillance. These processes encourage them to discipline their own behavior and allow them to constitute themselves as good and worthy people.

"In the government of food choice, individuals *want* to be healthy, experts instruct them how to be so, and entrepreneurs will exploit and enhance a market for health" (Coveney 2006: 121). As a discourse of power, nutrition situates individuals within a field of knowledge and surveillance about health and food. The modern household and the modern home cook are shaped by the knowledges and practices derived from expert knowledges about families through discourses of parenthood and family life and expert knowledges about food and cooking produced primarily through discourses of nutrition and food risk.

Cooking and the family: Feeding work

Making dinner is a site within which home cooks enact, create, and sustain particular constructions of family and self. Lupton (1996) posits that the dinner table is symbolic of ideal family life. Sociologist Marjorie DeVault (1991) argues that food preparation, which she terms "feeding work," is a social practice that is central to the construction of the family: through the act of care involved in feeding a family, home cooks achieve the symbolic representation of a family and its reproduction over time. The practical and emotional responsibilities of caring for families through feeding are disproportionately met by women (DeVault 1991; Finch and Groves 1983; Hochschild 2012). Through this work, DeVault argues, "Women quite literally produce family life from day to day" (1991: 13). Feeding work, as noted previously, includes both physical and mental labor. It is also work that remains invisible as work, often even to the women who do it.

Paradoxically, although feeding work that is done well remains unacknowledged and often invisible, public discourse about the state of home cooking in the twenty-first century tends to posit a decline in the practice of home cooking and the loss of the family meal, with dire results often predicted for the health and well-being of the American populace. Twenty years ago, Anne Murcott's critical inquiry into the supposed decline of the family meal began with the observation that "family meals, it is said, are on the wane, rapidly and worryingly becoming a thing of the past" (1997: 33). She demonstrated that the frequent complaints about the demise of the family meal in Britain were based on a misreading of the history of the family meal, noting that, for example, upper-class children in the nineteenth and first part of the twentieth centuries ate their meals in the nursery, apart from the adults in the household. Furthermore, concern with the decline of the family meal can be identified in both Britain and the

United States since before the Second World War (Murcott 1997). As early as 1882, social critics decried the loss of traditional cooking skills among housewives (Short 2006: 51). Murcott thus suggests that the home-cooked family meal functions as a very powerful metaphor for "the family" and concerns for its decline are to be understood as a "standing item on the agenda of twentieth century public commentary on the nature of family life" (1997: 46).

Joining the concern with the decline of the family meal is a growing concern with the supposed loss of cooking skills. Given the huge market for industrialized "convenience," ready-made, takeout, microwaveable, etc., food in the United States, social critics warn that a process of deskilling of home cooks has begun that could ultimately lead to a loss of cooking skills among the general population, further increasing Americans' dependence on industrialized convenience and ready-made food (Bittman 2014; Pollan 2006; 2009a; 2013). At issue here is who gets to define the family meal and who gets to define cooking skills. Irrespective of how much "cooking" or deskilled preparation may be involved and whether the family eats the meal in shifts or on the couch while watching television instead of together around a traditional table, home cooks and those they feed perceive the evening meal as "Mom's cooking" or "Jack's cooking" and as "eating dinner." And although they may fail to acknowledge the care and complexity of the work that got the dinner to their plate—they may not like the food, and they may even find family dinner a traumatic experience—the family meal is an irrefutable fact of daily life for those who eat it.

Cooking as caring: Why cooks cook

Lorraine is a New Yorker who works full-time and cooks dinner for herself, her husband, and her young daughter almost every night. The family very rarely order out or eat out, and Lorraine has no help in the kitchen. Why does she make dinner every night?

> First of all, it's economical. But second of all, because I feel like it's pretty important to everybody to just kind of sit down and eat and to eat something that's, I guess something that's made fresh. I just, it's kind of hard to explain, and I feel sometimes like ordering out, and I am by no means a health nut at all, I could eat garbage, but I feel like there's something to it, for people to sit down and eat something that one of them made. So to me stopping at the Chinese place and picking up something, it's a little less personal. (Lorraine)

A number of studies have suggested that home cooking may be becoming less prevalent in the United States over the past half century. Americans are eating out more: the proportion of total calories consumed by Americans that are produced at home has declined by about a quarter from the 1960s through the early 2000s (Smith, Ng, and Popkin 2013). (This could, of course, mean that restaurant meals have increased in calories and/or that home cooking is less calorific than before.) Time use studies show declines in the amount of time spent cooking at home. Analyzing changes in six national surveys, Smith and colleagues (2013) found that while almost all US women (92 percent) spent some time cooking each day in the 1960s, in the 2000s, only roughly two-thirds (68 percent) did so. When they cooked, the amount of time women spent doing so each day also decreased from an average of 113 minutes a day to 66 minutes. Over the same period, however, the proportion of men who cooked at home increased from less than a third (29 percent) to over four out of ten (42 percent). When they cooked, the amount of time men spent cooking showed a modest increase—from thirty-seven minutes to forty-five minutes.

A number of explanations for the decline in prevalence of home cooking have been put forward. One explanation is time scarcity: with declining real wages and women, especially mothers of young children, working more hours outside the home for pay, Americans have less time available for home cooking (Smith et al. 2013). When Americans do cook at home, convenience foods can reduce the time required to make dinner, as we discuss below. Some have also argued that the decline in home cooking may be attributed to a decline in cooking confidence and skills among home cooks (Short 2006).

What are the implications of less home cooking? Because home cooking is a complex process difficult to define and operationalize and to untangle from other variations in individual and household practices, there is little evidence linking home cooking directly to health or social outcomes. Home-cooked meals (as opposed to meals that are consumed outside of the home or are prepared outside of the home) lower the risk of obesity (Berge et al 2015; Chan and Sobel 2011; Fulkerson et al. 2014; Tumin and Anderson 2017) and are considered by nutritionists to be a major strategy in reducing obesity (Kopelman, Caterson, and Dietz 2010; Nestle 2010). In addition to the nutritional advantages, eating a meal cooked at home provides opportunities for commensality that creates and cements social relationships (Kerner, Chou, and Warmind 2015). Eating home-cooked meals together with family socializes children into normative food practices, social behaviors, and identities (Charles and Kerr 1988). Home cooking provides a setting in which a positive self-identity may be enacted (Wright-St. Clair et al. 2005) and furnishes a means to link household members to their families of origin and ancestors (Avakian 1997).

The persistence of the ideal of the home-cooked dinner was established by food scholars in the 1980s and 1990s (e.g., Charles and Kerr 1988; DeVault 1991; Murcott 1997). And indeed, despite the changes noted above, the practice of home-cooked dinner has persisted as well. Meals cooked at home remain the primary source of calories for Americans, and most US households regularly cook dinner at home (Smith et al. 2013). In their analysis of NHANES (National Health and Nutritional Examination Survey) data from 10,149 households in 2007 and 2009, Virudachalam and colleagues (2013) found that roughly half of US households cook dinner at home six or seven days a week and roughly four-fifths of the rest cook dinner at home two to five days during the week. In addition, most Americans (57 percent) say they enjoy cooking; a quarter (27 percent) particularly enjoy the activity (TheHarrisPoll.com 2017).

So most US households regularly cook dinner at home, although "it is increasingly feasible to choose not to cook and still be fed" (Trubek et al. 2017: 298). As a result of our purposive sampling, the home cooks in our study have enough economic resources to feed their families while doing very little, if any, cooking themselves. Holm (2001) in her study of the family meal in Nordic countries notes that people will go to great lengths and effort to plan, create, and conduct occasions to eat a meal together: our findings confirm this observation. Why do home cooks who can afford alternative means of getting the evening meal continue to make dinner at home, even on those days when they don't really feel like it?

One approach to understanding why cooks choose to cook suggests that cooks will make the effort if they believe the reward will be sufficient, in a kind of kitchen calculus. For example, Short claims that ideas or guidelines about when to cook and when to use preprepared foods are "underpinned by a belief that the effort put into cooking should equal the reward received" (2006: 87). In her interviews with British cooks of all sorts, Short found that many aspects of cooking were thought to be an effort: cleaning up afterward, finding and using recipes, making a special shopping trip, preparing messy foods, preparing everyday food and meals "just for us," making food for special occasions, serving more than one course, and cooking with fresh rather than preprepared foods. She asserts that "being prepared to make an effort involves being confident that sufficient, compensatory reward for doing so will be received" (2006: 33). Reward for cooks' efforts can take different forms. These include seeing others' enjoyment of eating the food they have prepared, satisfaction with the standard or appearance of the food in question, and receiving others' compliments on one's abilities as a cook or host.

When cooks do not receive the expected reward for their efforts, Short claims, they feel disappointed, unsatisfied, or frustrated. For example, one of Short's respondents spoke about her feelings after having prepared a casserole that was quite a lot of effort but didn't taste very good: "It can be so annoying when you spend time on something" (2006: 34). Similarly, one of the cooks in Luce Giard's study of cooks in France recalled getting "so upset" when she "made so much effort without results" as she tried to vary the meals she cooked for her young son who "didn't want anything!" (1998: 190). But as Michael Symons points out in *A History of Cooks and Cooking* (2000), "Technically, cooks practise a basic form of economic exchange known as reciprocity. Even if payment is not immediate, things will work out over the long run. This is because pivotal social relationships are sustained" (2000: 173). Generosity is the ideal we set for home cooks and is an integral part of the social construction of femininity, which, given the historical and cultural association of women with the home kitchen (Cairns and Johnston 2015), is inextricably bound up with how we think about home cooking.

While home cooks do measure the effort they should put into a particular meal based on social factors—considering what is the occasion and who are the diners—their continuing commitment to cooking for their families is not based on expectations of tangible rewards or acclaim from the diners. If it were, we would expect fewer home-cooked meals to be produced. Despite frustration with dishes that failed or family members who didn't like the meal, making dinner is a meaningful part of our home cook's daily lives. Indeed, they sometimes go to great lengths to preserve the practice of sharing a home-cooked meal, preparing multiple dishes to suit family member's divergent preferences and needs or eating in parent-child shifts to accommodate the children's schedule of activities. Providing a home-cooked meal for their families is of great importance to our respondents who struggle against significant temporal and logistical challenges to successfully put dinner on the table.

Home cooks persevere in making dinner because it is a way that they express love and care for their families. Cooking proper meals is something that women are expected to do to care for their families (Bugge and Almäs 2006; Charles and Kerr 1988; DeVault 1991; Murcott 1983). For example, when asked how she decides what she will make for dinner, Christina said, "I think about what can I cook that expresses my love for Cynthia [her wife]. I want something to make her feel nurtured and warm." Caring, like cooking, is a complex practice that includes both labor and love and can be both oppressive and empowering (Supski 2006). The caring unpaid work of kin in the home is organized by gender and "caring touches simultaneously on who you are and what you do" (Graham 1983: 13).

Fisher and Tronto's (1990) widely referenced feminist theory of caring maps onto the process of feeding work for the family. In this framework, caring includes four dimensions or components: caring about, taking care of, caregiving, and care-receiving.

> Caring about involves paying attention to our world in such a way that we focus on continuity, maintenance and repair. Taking care of involves responding to these aspects—taking responsibility for activities that keep our world going. Caregiving involves the concrete tasks, the hands-on work of maintenance and repair. Care-receiving involves the responses to the caring process of those toward whom care is directed. (1990: 40)

For home cooks, *caring about* means caring about the continuity, maintenance, and repair of the family and the internal and external relationships that constitute it. Doing feeding work is *taking care of* the family, the mode of action that home cooks take responsibility for in order to keep their families going. Preparing and cooking, making the dinner, is how home cooks *give care* to their families. And when families eat their dinners, their responses constitute *care-receiving*.

The *taking care of* dimension of feeding the family implies that the primary cook is responsible for initiating and maintaining caring activities, in this case for planning and making decisions about the family's food and meals. Aspirations for their family that they care about and are important to the cook drive the ways in which cooks organize the feeding of their families. If cooks care that their families eat healthily or carry on family traditions or support community farming, then cooks will try to provision and produce meals which are consonant with these ways of thinking about food and family. Direct caregiving—actually making dinner—involves more continuous and dense time commitments than *taking care of* and therefore requires a greater level of responsiveness to the unfolding exigencies of everyday life. Consequently, in the daily expression of their care for their family, making dinner for home cooks often becomes more about the direct caregiving of feeding their family a home-cooked dinner and less connected to other goals they also care about. Thinking about the practice of home cooking through the lens of feminist theories of caring helps us understand why home cooking is so meaningful to those who cook and how it remains so even when cooks must compromise.

Kaufmann concludes his brilliant book about French home cooks by suggesting that cooks cook because the concrete act of cooking fulfills relational and emotional needs.

> The decision to cook a meal is prompted by emotional impulses and multiple and ill-defined desires. The new passion for cooking is a combination of a desire to be creative in aesthetic terms, gastronomic hedonism and a longing for greater conjugal and familial intensity. We want to feel emotions we cannot really express and we use food as a language of love because we have no other. Love is not just an abstract feeling that exists apart from the ordinary world. It is also something we construct day by day, sometimes with our hands. (2010: 242)

Cooking and the self

Like caregiving and being a caregiver, home cooking may be both something you do and something you are. What role does home cooking play in self-identity in the early twenty-first century? Through our analyses of the interview and cooking journal data, we identified four types of home cooks: family-first cooks, traditional cooks, keen cooks, and drudges. Family-first cooks are motivated primarily by their families' preferences and needs. Traditional cooks prefer to cook a limited repertoire of dishes they perceive as traditional. Keen cooks enjoy challenging themselves to improve their knowledge and skills regarding food and cooking. Drudges do not enjoy cooking and the task is not very meaningful to them.

For family-first, traditional, and keen cooks, being a good home cook is also a key mode of self-identification. Our concept of the types as modes of self-identification follows Jeremy MacClancy's (2004) argument for the use of "modes of identification" rather than "identities" as modes are more indicative of the fluidity, multiplicity, and relational aspects of identities. "Modes of identification" is a dynamic concept inclusive of the roles, motivations, and actions of agents in the process of developing, maintaining, and enacting a sense of self (MacClancy 2004). Individuals initiate and perform actions in particular contexts for the purposes of self-identification: family-first cooks, traditional cooks and keen cooks plan and cook in distinctive manners that produce and affirm their sense of themselves as good home cooks.

Modernity, writes Anthony Giddens (1991), "is a post-traditional order in which the question, 'How shall I live?' has to be answered in day-to-day decisions about how to behave, what to wear and what to eat—and many other things—as well as interpreted within the temporal unfolding of self-identity" (p. 14). This post-traditional order of modernity is marked by individualism, mediated experience, fluidity, ambiguity, and reflexivity (Beck 1992). Our identities no longer defined for us by tradition or our place in the system of production, we must create identity and meaning in life for ourselves (Beck and Beck-Gernsheim 2001; Giddens 1991). Self-identities become a matter of sustaining coherent yet continuously revised biographical narratives and come as much from "lifestyles" as they do from the classic sociological concepts of gender, class, and race/ethnicity (Beck 1992; Giddens 1991).

Lifestyles here are understood as more or less integrated sets of routinized practices, attitudes, and beliefs, which individuals adopt, not only to live in the world, but because they "give material form to a particular narrative of self-identity" (Giddens 1991: 81). In the post-traditional era, since social roles are no longer automatically conferred upon us by society, we have to choose a lifestyle and adopt modes of identification within the particular social structural constraints and opportunities available to us. Individuals who engage with more post-traditional settings will be more likely to make and remake self-identity through lifestyle (Giddens 1991). For everyone, from this perspective, our everyday choices about what to eat and what to cook are decisions which position ourselves as one kind of person and not another. Thus, cooking practices make and perform a particular cooking self.

Cooking, as noted earlier, is about both consumption and production. It is through consumption, many argue, that we make our selves in the post-traditional world (Baudrillard 1998; Bourdieu 1984; Featherstone 1991). A substantial body of empirical research demonstrates that individuals use consumption of food to construct and express self-identity (Bartels and Reinders 2010; Berger and Heath 2007; Dean, Raats, and Shepherd 2012; Escalas and Bettman 2005). As Isabelle de Solier succinctly writes, "We make our selections from the array of goods on offer and combine them to shape who we are or who we want to be: selves, then, are made through things" (2013).

Food and eating are "intensely emotional experiences that are intertwined with embodied sensations and strong feelings" (Lupton 1996: 36). Discourses of food, especially nutrition and health, and the power relations inherent in them, together with these embodied experiences of eating, render food, according to Deborah Lupton, "central to individual's subjectivity and their sense of distinction from others" (1996: 36). Annie Hauck-Lawson's (1998) concept of food voice as a methodological tool for understanding how foodways inscribe aspects of individual and group identity suggests that what a person chooses to cook and eat can make powerful statements about who they are and wish to be. Food and cooking as part of a lifestyle is a practice through which people can create and demonstrate their identity and status (e.g., de Solier 2013; Kaufmann 2010; Short 2006). For example, based on her study of French women's cooking practice, Luce Giard argues that cooking can be a means whereby individuals claim autonomy and individuality within consumerist society (Giard 1998). Annechen Bahr Bugge and Reidar Almås (2006) demonstrate how young Norwegian mothers "actively construct social identity through their dinner practice" (p. 204).

Like any other mode of self-identification, it is important to home cooks to succeed, based upon their own criteria, at making dinner, to be a "good" home cook. For those whose self-identity is based in part on being a home cook, their cooking is imbued with moral value. Identifying as a "good home cook" may be a form of Naccarato and Lebesco's notion of "culinary capital" (2012), a way of creating and sustaining an identity marked by status, power, and culinary knowledge. Cooks' overall approach to cooking—whether the ultimate goal of their cooking practice is to nourish and sustain their family, to continue their family traditions, or to challenge themselves to produce the highest quality food they can—shapes their beliefs, feelings, thoughts, and practices related to cooking. In the following chapters, we explore in depth how family-first, traditional, and keen cooks think and feel about cooking, how they typically approach the task of making dinner, and how cooking functions as self-making for them.

Each dinner they make provides home cooks with evidence regarding their performance as a cook, which may or may not align with their beliefs regarding what kind of cook they should be. Consistent with the self-discrepancy theory of E. Tory Higgins (Higgins 1987; Higgins et al. 1994), cooks may experience a variety of emotions as a result of a match or mismatch between their perceptions of what kind of job they did cooking dinner and how they think of themselves as a cook. According to the theory, our actual self-concept (based on current self-perceptions) may diverge from our ideal self (attributes that we would like to possess); falling short of the person we would like to be may lead to feelings of frustration, depression, and sadness. A home cook who aspires to be a great traditional Italian American cook and cannot make a good meatball may experience frustration or sadness. Current self-concepts may also diverge from our beliefs about the person we believe we ought to be (based on the attributes that we think other people believe we should possess); failing to be the person we ought to be may lead to experiences of guilt, shame, or anxiety. A person who believes that a home cook should be able to make dinners that everyone eats and enjoys that are healthy—and perceives themselves as failing to do so—may experience anxiety as a result. Consistent with a self-discrepancy approach, home cooks could make the same dinner and have varying emotions when reflecting upon the meal, as a result of different beliefs about what kind of cook they are, what kind of cook they should be, and what kind of cook they want to be.

Theoretical perspectives and research from the fields of anthropology, sociology, food studies, and women's studies inform our analysis of the practice, meaning, and social dynamics of home cooking. A social-psychological perspective on cooking dinner also informs our work. Consistent with a person-environment or interactionist approach (Funder and Ozer 1983; Ross and Nisbett 1991), we see the cognition, affect, motivations, and behavior of the home cook in preparing dinner as functions not only of the individual but also of the physical and social environment, which is made up of situational factors including the material, temporal, cultural, and social. Simply put, cooking in the home kitchen is mediated by the wider contexts in which it takes place.

The process of making dinner as a set of behaviors includes the actions, thoughts, beliefs, and emotions of the individuals who do the task of home cooking: the home cooks. Our findings suggest that to understand how people think and feel about doing domestic cooking and how they decide what and how to cook for the evening meal, it is necessary to consider the overlap and intersection of five dimensions of the process that is making dinner. In the pages that follow, we suggest how personal, cultural, material, temporal, and social factors combine to shape the practice and meaning of cooking the evening meal for the household among home cooks. Through examination of this process, we seek to uncover the complex relationships between the material and the symbolic dimensions of our everyday lives. When home cooks undertake the daily task of making dinner for their families, they make much more than a meal. They also make meaning out of their daily lives as they construct and reconstruct their sense of self and their relationships with others through their cooking practices.

2

The Basics of Making Dinner

In this chapter, we look at the basics of how our respondents organize the everyday task of doing the cooking in their households, including the division of labor, routines, shopping and planning habits, recipe use, and cooking skills and abilities. The work of feeding a family includes planning, provisioning, cooking, serving, and cleaning up. Who plans and makes dinner? Who does the shopping? And who helps? Who does what is part of the social dimension of making dinner—practices that are negotiated within households—that in turn are shaped by cultural norms, beliefs, values, and ideologies, especially those related to gender.

Who makes dinner? The division of labor in the home kitchen

During our interviews, participants reported who typically cooked dinner in their household and who provided assistance. Among the forty-two households in the study, two consisted of women living by themselves and three were single-mother households with children. Of the remaining households with at least two adults, one adult assumed the role of primary cook for three-quarters of the households, bearing sole responsibility for the planning and preparation of the evening meal. In 93 percent of two-adult households with solo primary cooks, the cook was a woman, consonant with larger national studies of the gendered division of labor (Flagg et al. 2014). In the remaining one-quarter of households with two adults, both adults shared cooking responsibilities in a more equitable division of labor. Five households included same-sex couples: three of these shared dinner responsibilities. Several of the forty-two households in the sample included adult children still living at home. While daughters sometimes helped with cooking dinner, only one (Grace) had complete responsibility for planning or preparing the evening meals for the household.

The use of daily journals provided a revealing source of data that allows us to understand cooking practices much more clearly than interviews alone. This was particularly striking in terms of the household division of labor regarding home cooking, where reliance on the interview data alone would have skewed our understanding in favor of a more equitable division of labor. This may be due to a greater likelihood of social demand bias in the interview situation, or it may be due to the opportunity that the journals afforded for cooks to reflect on their taken-for-granted everyday lives. For example, Emily said in her telephone interview that she split cooking with her husband;

however, during the course of the journaling, he helped with only two dinners. Emily reflected upon her household's division of labor at the end of her journal:

> It was a pleasure to participate in this project. Actually documenting our meals gave me some insight into how our family's day to day life runs. Most importantly, I discovered that the division of (cooking) labor is not equal and I am the primary chef in the family.

An evening meal was prepared at home on three-quarters (316 of the 424) of the days reported in the journals. Applying this proportion to a week, a home-cooked dinner occurred in the average household five out of seven nights. Dinner was cooked six or seven nights a week in 42 percent of households. This figure is slightly lower than prevalence estimates of dinners cooked in an average US household. Using the NHANES national survey, Virudachalam and colleagues (2013) found that 49 percent of households cooked dinner six or seven nights a week. All but two of the primary home cooks in our sample worked outside the home for pay, most full-time, which may account for fewer home-cooked meals. The remaining 58 percent of households in our study cooked three to five times a week, on average. Almost 90 percent of the 316 evening meals reported in the journals were prepared by the primary cook of the household.

In almost half of the households that completed the cooking journals, a single home cook prepared without any assistance *every* dinner their households ate at home during the ten days or two weeks of journaling. Some of these cooks reported that they did not want any help. For example, Lorraine prepared a home-cooked dinner every night for the two weeks of the study for herself, her three-year-old child, and her husband who was unemployed at the time.

> Maybe once or twice in about ten years, my husband has cooked something. However, I am generally the type of person who's not big on getting help, especially when it involves food. I get a little grossed out at the idea of someone else cooking food that I would eat. (I know that sounds weird.) (Lorraine)

Roughly one-quarter of households in the study reported an equitable distribution of the work of planning and cooking the meal, with couples sharing cooking responsibility for their households. In most households with more than one cook, one of the partners will take responsibility for planning and preparing dinner on a given evening. For example, in Linda's house, husband Tony is a freelancer and is often at home in the afternoon. He takes on a roughly equal share of the cooking and planned and prepared five meals during the study period. Sara and Daniel cooked about a third of their evening meals together and each did another third of the meals solo. Daniel explained, "Sometimes we both try to cook something and that doesn't work. Usually she starts dinner, and I come in and interrupt … We kind of have different styles, so we get in each other's way."

Although we had only five gay or lesbian households in our sample, it is notable that same-sex couples were much more likely to be egalitarian, with 80 percent sharing cooking responsibilities. Given that four of the five same-sex couples were women, it may be that gender roles prescribing that women take on responsibility for home cooking supported the lesbian couples in sharing the home cooking role. For example, Cynthia and Christina share cooking responsibility. They have different work schedules and eat together about two or three times during the week and on the weekends. When they are both at home at dinnertime, "it goes either way. It depends on who wants to make the main dish and the other person will make the side or one person will make it all. Whoever cooks doesn't have to clean, but it doesn't always work that way." Jack and Jeremiah take turns planning and preparing the dinner: "It is almost always one person. We have done it [both cooking], but usually it's one person making dinner and the other providing for our [two-year-old] son." Janet and Kristen's household was unique in our sample: both adults cooked and they cooked each dinner together. Cooking dinner serves an important role in their relationship. "We both cook. We cook together. It's how we go over our day." Cooking is "a joint adventure" for Janet and Kristen.

Men as home cooks

Almost 20 percent of the home cooks in our study are men. Men and women shared cooking duties in roughly a quarter of the study's households. In two households, men assumed the role of solo primary cook (Peter and James). The disproportional division of labor in our sample mirrors findings of numerous studies of food and gender and gendered domestic work in the United States (DeVault 1991; Warde et al. 2007), the UK (Charles and Kerr 1988; Murcott 1995), and Australia (Lupton 1996). For example, O'Connell and Brannen's (2016) mixed-methods study of forty-seven UK households found that roughly a third of men shared the home cook role. Despite changes in the number of women in the workplace and expectations regarding male domestic roles, significant gendered asymmetries in home cooking persist (Segal 2007). We discuss gender ideologies and cooking in more detail in Chapter 6.

In our study and others (Sobal 2005; Szabo 2012), men are more likely to assume the role of cooking the evening meal in more leisurely contexts than the weekday grind. Other men cook for the family only when the primary cook is absolutely unavailable. When cooking for the household only occasionally, men tend to take on a "sous chef" or assistant role to the women (Metcalfe et al. 2009). Men are more likely to prepare snacks or weekend breakfasts (Williams and Germov 2017) or cook when outdoor grilling or barbecuing is involved. Giard found that among younger French couples in the 1970s, men enjoyed cooking more than the prior generation but they cooked only "from *time to time*, for a festive meal more elaborate and costly than an ordinary everyday one" (Giard 1998: 218). Several families in our study like to cook outdoors on the grill when they entertain—this means that men are more likely to get the glory when the family has dinner guests.

In 2009, Poortman and Van Der Lippe used data from the Dutch Time Competition Survey on men's and women's attitudes toward household labor to explore the gendered meaning of domestic work. They found that women held more favorable attitudes toward cooking than men. Women enjoyed cooking more, set higher standards for it, and felt more responsible for it. On the other hand, trends over the past several decades would seem to suggest changes in the gendered nature of home cooking and home cooks. Women's participation in the paid workforce has been increasing (Stats. oecd.org 2016): all but two of the women participating in our study work for pay. This increases the likelihood that men do at least some of the cooking for the family. In Western societies in general, more men are showing interest in and spending more time cooking (Ekstrom and d'Orange Furst 2001). There are increasing numbers of families headed by single fathers or by gay men who are the primary cooks for their households (Szabo and Koch 2017). Our study included seven men who share the responsibility of cooking with their partner: Jack and Jeremiah, Alice and Michael, Linda and Tony, Daniel and Sara, Brandon and Melissa, and Joseph and Monique.

For most families, men can and often do "opt in" to doing the cooking. Women, however, do not "opt in" to being the primary family cook: gender ideologies presume that this is part of women's role (Cairns and Johnson 2015). Women can, however, occasionally opt out, if there is another household member willing and able to do the work. In their introduction to *Food, Masculinities, and Home* (2017), Joyce Szabo and Shelley Koch note that "recent research is showing that some men with domestic care responsibilities are using food to nurture loved ones and create feelings of care, comfort, and 'home'" (p. 3). About 20 percent of the home cooks in our sample are men who cook in this way. They are all married or in long-term relationships. Jack and Jeremiah are both family-first cooks with a young son. Jack is a keen cook and Jeremiah is a traditional cook. Peter, who cooks for his wife and daughter, is a family-first cook and a keen cook: he is the primary cook in his household. James, who cooks for his wife, daughters and extended family, is a traditional and keen cook who is the primary cook in his household. Daniel, Brandon, and Michael are all family-first cooks with children at home who share cooking responsibilities with their female partners but tend to take turns doing the cooking rather than sharing the kitchen.

While the number of men in our study who have primary cooking responsibility for their families is too small to make any definitive conclusions, we did observe a gender-based difference that is interesting to speculate about. Perhaps because it is not part of their traditional gender role, men who take on the cooking responsibility in heterosexual households with small children seem to have more space to focus on the cooking while someone else (we assume the mother) looks after the children. While we heard several stories from women of making dinner while watching small children that conjured up the image of a harried woman moving from fridge to sink to stove with a toddler clinging to her leg while pots boil over and dinner burns on the stovetop, we just did not hear about this type of experience from the men with female partners in our study. One male primary cook with young children did burn the broccoli one evening and had to start over, not because he was juggling watching the kids and cooking but because he was cooking while simultaneously cleaning out the attic. Of course, our numbers are small and individual cooks do vary in regard to the equanimity with which they accommodate children in the kitchen.

Secondary evening meal cooks in the household

In most two-adult households with only one primary cook (about three-quarters of our sample), the other adult and/or children may very occasionally assume responsibility for cooking the evening meal. Often this "backup" cook is not responsible for all the planning and provisioning tasks provided by the primary cook. For example, Margaret's husband grilled hamburgers and prepared corn on the cob one evening for himself and his adult son while Margaret worked late. However, Margaret had planned the dinner and purchased the ingredients earlier in the week.

When men cook on occasion, women may remain in charge of planning and provisioning for the meal that the men will cook. When cooking the evening meal, men often still rely on women for instructions and other aspects of the invisible work of making dinner (DeVault 1991). Some men in our study cooked occasionally when their wives were unavailable or specialized in more stereotypically masculine activities such as grilling and chili-making. One evening, Pauline's husband made his specialty, "Dad's spicy chicken," while Pauline prepared spaghetti squash and salad. She wrote, "We don't often have the opportunity to cook together. That's the most enjoyable part of it." The primary cooks generally expressed gratitude when men would cook their specialties (especially family-first cooks). For example, Helen's and Teresa's husbands assisted in the preparation of at least one evening meal during the study period. Helen's husband is currently unemployed and specializes in grilling or making chili. He assisted in grilling one meal and prepared the sauce for frozen chicken wings for another meal. Carolyn's husband "is not a cook," although he does carry out the grocery shopping every week. He specializes in grilling and grilled pork chops for one dinner while Carolyn prepared the balance of the meal.

Generally, though, the male partners of female solo primary cooks are not seen as proficient in the kitchen. This may be a means whereby women transform the responsibility of cooking for the family into a position of power. Although their husbands took responsibility for cooking at least one meal during the study period in Joyce, Kaye, and Karen's households, the meal was prepared for the children in the household and involved a limited amount of preparation. Joyce's husband prepared dinner for the children one night when she was not available, although she had earlier planned the meal. Cooking was limited as the menu included vegetarian corn dogs and green beans. Likewise, Kaye's husband cooked one meal for the children, consisting of items she had purchased and planned:

[I decided what he would cook for dinner on] my way to the store. I ended up teaching tonight when I didn't realize I would be, so I had to go for quick and something that my husband wouldn't mind dealing with. It needed to be husband-friendly. (Kaye)

Pauline's husband has a long commute. Although she says that he will occasionally help out by making dinner for their daughter when Pauline is bogged down with schoolwork for her master's degree, he did not do so during the study period. Even when he does, Pauline is not really happy with the results:

He just doesn't take to the details in the same way as I ... not too adventurous and will stick to making the same things. I do have to say that he does tend to take the easy way out and order out! When my husband is left in charge of the kitchen, I notice that the finishing of the task isn't always complete. There's always something left undone in the sink and the stove is usually not wiped down—that does drive me crazy! (Pauline)

Men's rare appearances in the kitchen are sometimes welcomed by the primary cook. For example, Teresa's husband cooked along with her to prepare a special meal of fish tacos (fried cod, slaw, corn tortillas) and black bean salad that they shared with her mother-in-law and brother-in-law. Teresa said, "It was really fun! My husband rarely cooks with me, but he did tonight and it was great." The meal was "a big fun success" according to Teresa.

Lisa does almost all of the cooking in her household, but her husband will cook once a week. "He likes to cook. We took a twelve week cooking class together. He thinks he is an expert. Makes a big pot of minestrone soup." Ann cooks all the weekday dinners in her household and her husband specializes in cooking dinner on Saturday nights. Ann wrote, "Cooking at home for a 'date night' is always our favorite on a Saturday night." During the study period, he cooked a steak, garlic mashed potatoes, and asparagus for the two of them, accompanied by a red wine reduction. He also prepared a meal of grilled cheese sandwiches, which the children ate earlier in the evening. Ann considers her husband the "creative" cook in the household and he usually plans and shops for the meal.

Some households have more unusual means of dividing the labor of planning and preparing the evening meal. For example, in Melissa and Brandon's household, Brandon often plans and partially prepares the evening's dishes in the morning or the night before, and at night Melissa will reheat or finish them up and serve them to the children. In Cheryl's household, her fifteen-year-old daughter recently decided to become vegan, prompting a renegotiation of the division of labor. According to Cheryl in her interview, her daughter now cooks for herself after school: "She does her own thing, she recently became vegan and we have an agreement that she would cook her own food." In practice, Cheryl's cooking journal indicated that Cheryl was seeking out and trying new vegan recipes to prepare dinners that she and her daughter could share. She was pleased when the vegan falafel that she prepared was well liked by her daughter. Even more unusual was the parallel dinner-making that occurs in Ashley's household. She and her husband are empty nesters with grown children not living at home and usually eat dinner together. However, they do not cook for each other. Instead they plan, shop for, and cook their own meals, finally sitting down together to eat them.

Kitchen helpers

As noted above, in many households, the primary cook occasionally has help from an adult partner, from children, or from other friends and family members in preparing the evening meal. We asked the home cooks whether any members of their household helped in the kitchen and how they felt about helpers. Some home cooks do not like help in cooking dinner, although many state they like and wish they had more help in related tasks such as cleaning up, setting the table, etc. Others in the kitchen can sometimes threaten the cook's space: Helen expressed a common sentiment among those home cooks who were less open to helpers: "They usually act as my sous chef. I am a bit territorial in my kitchen but if someone is willing to just follow instructions, then I have no issue." Although they like helpers, the small size of their kitchens precludes much helping activity for several of our home cooks.

Margaret is the most enthusiastic about helpers: her husbands and kids all help her in the kitchen. Said Margaret,

> Chopping, husking, peeling, grilling, stirring … anything I ask them to basically. I love helpers in the kitchen! Love the interaction and the different cooking styles we can learn from each other—at any age. (Margaret)

Children often do help in the kitchen, with the difficulty of the task generally increasing with age. In O'Connell's and Brannen's study of UK households (2017), children helped with some production and baking, serving dinner, and cleaning up thereafter. In most households, however, they did not carry out a significant amount of the foodwork. Several cooks in our study have children who help in the kitchen, and this activity is generally viewed positively. Joyce's oldest daughter likes to help mix and pour, and Joyce reports that she "likes her help." Chloe's kids help occasionally, and she has taught her older children to make a few dishes. One evening, Chloe and her family, including kids, made fireplace-grilled cheese sandwiches, popcorn, edamame, and pickles for dinner using a campfire cooking Christmas gift on their indoor fireplace. Lois and her two children cook together often, and this is very important to her, as discussed in Chapter 8. Alice and Michael's young daughters often help prepare meals. Alice's assessment of helpers is that "[I] love 'em, though it can slow things down to instruct." Sometimes Sara and Daniel's daughters help in the kitchen: "We have to give the kids different jobs—so they are doing things they can manage (or it doesn't matter if they can't), they don't burn themselves, and they don't fight."

Some home cooks, particularly mothers, who did not enjoy or encourage kitchen helpers nevertheless felt rather ambivalent about this. Part of the gendered role of home cook is the expectation that mothers are responsible for teaching children, especially girls, to cook (Cairns and Johnston 2015). For example, Kaye does virtually all of the cooking in her household. While her children assisted once in microwaving macaroni and cheese, she indicated, "I don't usually get them involved with the cooking of dinner, because by the time I get home, I don't have the time to let them help, you know." But Kaye wonders if she is neglecting the cultural expectation for mothers to teach children how to cook: "My thought on helpers is that I wish I was the kind of mom who could do that, but I'm usually either short on time or patience, neither condition being conducive to helpers."

Several mothers in our study expressed regret about failing to teach their children to cook. Ruth's sixteen-year-old son Harry goes to pick up a pizza every Wednesday night: "It is his weekly contribution to our meals." He doesn't help her in the kitchen: "I can't really get Harry to work with me in the kitchen, although he will cook meals occasionally on his own." Still, she dreams of taking an expensive cooking class with her son before he leaves home. Pauline notes that she used to ask her adult sons to help more than she has been asking their younger sister. She mused, "I guess with her being the last one home, I don't require my daughter to do as many kitchen jobs as I made and needed the boys to do when they were living home. This is making me think that I need to involve her in dinner making more."

Shopping for dinner

Where and how do home cooks obtain the foods they make into dinner? Most food shopping in the contemporary United States occurs at grocery stores, with roughly $670 billion spent annually at 38,000 locations (Fmi.org 2017; Ruhlman 2017). This is true for the cooks in our study as well, who purchase most food for their households through shopping at grocery stores, other large retailers, food specialty stores, and neighborhood markets. Some of our respondents also get food from their own gardens, famers' markets, and CSA sharing arrangements.

When shopping for food, home cooks must choose from a seemingly endless array of selections to fill their shopping basket. There are roughly 350,000 food and beverage products available in the United States (Nestle 2007) with 25,000 new products entering the retail market every year (Fmi.org 2017); the average supermarket carries about 40,000 of them. From this dizzying number of choices, cooks are challenged to select food that they can afford and that is "good" for their families. Deciding just what is good is not always easy: shopping is a highly mediated activity. In the twenty-first century, old and new media about food, nutritionists, social movement activists, specialty markets, food producers, and others are involved in the construction of new categories of "good" food. As they go about their daily business of choosing and cooking food for themselves and their families, home cooks negotiate these extra-local expert discourses on food, including those related to health and nutrition, sustainability, and foodism/gourmet foods.

The task of shopping for food includes deciding where and when to shop as well as what to buy. Although most of our home cooks shop at national and regional grocery chains almost exclusively, shopping for dinner in the contemporary United States can take many different forms and our cooks reflect this. Elena lives on a farm outside a medium-sized city in the Northwest United States. She cooks a large Sunday dinner for her grown children and eats the leftovers as a solo diner during the week. She "does a big shop" once a month at a discount store like Costco or Walmart. Most of her vegetables and meats are grown and raised at home (she freezes surplus for year-round use). Living in the much more urban District of Columbia, Jack and Jeremiah order their groceries online: their selections are delivered weekly to the home they share with their two-year-old son. A few times a month, Mira and her wife order in a home-delivered meal kit that contains premeasured ingredients and recipes. Taking advantage of living in one of the finest food markets in the world, Ruth shops nearly every other day at various markets and specialty food shops for herself and her teenage son in the San Francisco Bay area.

The frequency with which our cooks shopped for food ranged from two to three times a week to twice a month: twenty-five households shop once a week, sixteen shop more than once a week, and one household shops once every two weeks. Those who shop for food less frequently tend to go on the same day of the week in a routine fashion. For those who shop more than once during the week, the second shopping trip is usually a fill-in with a smaller order or at a smaller store. A few cooks always go to the same large chain grocery stores regardless of how much they are buying in a given trip. Several households do one big trip to a chain grocery store (such as Giant, Costco, Wegman's, Whole Foods, Winn Dixie, Publix, or Trader Joe's) and then fill in with smaller stores, specialty stores such as health food stores, bakeries and cheese stores, and farmer's markets. Eight households regularly shop at farmers' markets or receive vegetables and fruits through sharing arrangements at CSA farms. One couple who share cooking responsibilities typically shop at four different stores over the course of the week. Several of our cooks frequently stop by the store on the way home from work if they have not planned what to cook for dinner that evening.

In over half of our households, grocery shopping is carried out exclusively by the primary home cook. In most others, shopping duties may be carried out alternatively by the cook or his/her partner, depending on their schedules. In three households, the husband or partner was primarily responsible for carrying out the grocery shopping rather than the cook. In Carolyn's household for example, her husband, a retired grocery store manager, shops from a list she provides.

Most cooks take a list when they go food shopping, although a few of our respondents do not ever use a list. Some buy a standard roster of foods and generally adhere to that list. Some use lists only when shopping for holidays or special occasions or when trying a new recipe. Some make lists only for the proteins for the evening meal and choose vegetables and fruits based on what they find appealing in the store or market. When they didn't shop themselves, most cooks were still responsible for providing a list for the person doing the shopping to follow, even if the cook would not ordinarily use one when doing the shopping him/herself. One exception was Janet and Kristen, who cook together every night that they eat at home: Kristen does all the food shopping and Janet is not even sure if she uses a list or not. This works out well for them, as Janet prides herself on being an adventurous and creative cook who improvises with what ingredients are available.

Fidelity to the shopping list is varied, and buying things not on the list can be seen as negative or positive, depending on the cook. Our cooks are roughly split in regard to how strictly they follow their list. Some buy only what is on the list; often this is seen as a money-saving measure. Others bought things not on their list if they were on sale or were perceived to be a good bargain. Foods purchased that are not on the list include those that are routinely purchased each week (e.g., milk and bread), are on sale, are impulse buys, or that capture the shopper's attention. The purchasing decisions of cooks who do not use lists are sometimes driven by bargains and sometimes by perceived quality of an item.

What cooks buy is related to the cook's knowledge of and confidence in their ability to prepare that item, the time available for making dinner, the tastes of family members, and the desire of cooks to prepare economical and healthy meals. Shopping is important in regard to nutritional gatekeeping: it is the channel by which food comes into the house. It is also a very important facet of making dinner, because as we shall see later, one popular strategy for solving the dilemma of what to make for the evening meal is to "ask the fridge": to make decisions about what to cook based on what is available in the refrigerator or pantry.

Economizing

Home cooks are motivated to save money and, to varying degrees, may make planning and provisioning decisions on the basis of food costs (Engler-Stringer 2010; Jones et al. 2014; Mercille, Receveur and Potvin 2012). Our cooks were mostly middle class and could generally afford to purchase most of the foods they would want to prepare dinner for their families. Nevertheless, most cooks strove to prepare economical dinners, with this consideration affecting either their purchase behavior when shopping or their preparation of ingredients once home. In their interviews, two-thirds of cooks said that choosing a dinner menu that was economical was important to them.

For some cooks, economical implied attention to the price of certain ingredients, although several cooks explained that cooking economically did not mean buying the cheapest ingredients but rather avoiding the extremes of the most expensive and the cheapest. Judith defined "economical" in this vein:

> It means that I am not going to buy an outrageous ingredient I'm only going to use for one recipe. I'm not going to have salmon every night. Not going to have steak every night. I don't really have a limit regarding how much I will spend. I will get the good chicken, even if it's going to cost more. (Judith)

For Lois, being economical means minimizing her purchasing of steak: "Steak only once a week because it is more expensive. Economical usually always because I am a single mom. I always have to think of something that isn't super expensive." Pauline seeks the middle, rather than the cheapest: "I don't go for the cheapest. I buy uncured hotdogs and they're not cheap. But economical means not buying everything at Wegman's [an upscale grocery chain]. Keep things at a medium range." In another household, the cooks try to save money by shopping as much as possible at Aldi (a discount grocery store).

A common strategy that cooks use to economize while shopping is to buy the meats that are on sale and plan their menus around them. For example, Kaye says, "I just go through the store and if it's on sale or if it's cheap, then I guess I'll buy it. And I guess that's where my inventiveness comes into play at home." Elaine also lets the protein take the lead when shopping: "I try to get what might be on sale, meat wise. I try to focus on the meat stuff first and the other will follow."

Other strategies that cooks used to economize while shopping included buying the store brands, not buying specialty ingredients that wouldn't be used often, using coupons, and shopping less often. Several cooks lamented that shopping for groceries more than once a week was more expensive than doing a big shop. One of our cooks was trying to shop for groceries only twice a month to economize.

For some cooks, economy was realized when preparing a meal. For example, preparing a dish that would be eaten on more than one occasion was viewed as economical. Leftovers are economical and may allow the cook to purchase more expensive ingredients with the assurance that the ingredients would be used for more than one meal. Janet described how the promise of leftovers rendered expensive ingredients economical:

> Economical doesn't mean the cheapest. It means that we will eat organic, but will freeze portions for lunches or things like that. If we are going to use more expensive ingredients, we will try very hard to get several meals (frozen) out of it. Not cheapest. Best use of ingredients. (Janet)

Likewise, Andrea reports, "I don't like to save money on meat and I try not to buy any special ingredients, but I will buy ground beef and make chili that can last for a couple of days so that is economical to me."

Several cooks felt strongly that avoiding wasting food was very important. This was partly due to the need to economize and partly based on ethical or moral considerations. Chloe claims to cook with "zero waste" and proudly states that her kids never know what they are going to get for dinner. Janet most enjoys cooking on Sundays when she "opens the fridge and makes soup from whatever's left from the week." Ruth said, "I don't really run my menu based on if something is on sale. I do use up all the food in the house since I don't like it when it goes to waste."

Daniel and Sara prioritize healthiness in their home cooking. Daniel explained, "We have found out that the cheaper you eat, the less healthy you eat. So we spend more money than we should on our perceived idea of healthy food." They pick up a share of seasonal vegetables at a local CSA farm and shop in several different organic or specialty groceries. At the same time, they report that they are also trying to shop more at a large chain grocery store on the way home from work to save money.

Once ingredients have been purchased, the ability of a cook to render them more economical is limited to the degree to which the ingredient can be expanded to produce more than one meal or by the cook's ability to minimize wastage. In actual practice as reported in daily cooking journals, cooks said that making an economical meal was an important consideration for only about a third of the dinners they prepared. Many cooks report stopping on the way home to purchase ingredients for the evening meal, especially when they are the facing a time crunch. On these days, the cook's motivation is less on economy than on producing a well-liked dinner in a minimal amount of time.

Cooking skills

When the first author of this book was a first-year undergraduate student, she was given an assignment in composition class to write a set of instructions for a task. Choosing to write about the process of making homemade pizza, she found that it was a very complicated matter to instruct the reader in this seemingly simple task. Many multi-step conceptual, perceptual, and mechanical skills are required to transform the ingredients of the dough, sauce, and toppings into a ready-to-eat pizza. The conceptual skills needed include being able to decide what toppings go well together, how thick to make the crust, and what proportion and amounts of sauce, cheese, and toppings are wanted. Perceptual skills include knowing how to tell when the dough has been kneaded sufficiently or the crust is cooked enough. The mechanical skills needed include stretching the dough, spreading the sauce, and grating cheese and perhaps slicing vegetables for toppings. The finished assignment was pages long. And this was a set of instructions entirely without the context of everyday cooking that home cooks face.

In the context of everyday life, conceptual, perceptual, and mechanical skills are only the beginning of the skills or capabilities that a home cook needs to successfully make a pizza for family and/or friends. Home cooks have to consider the situation for which the pizza is made to decide what sort of pizza to make. Is this pizza for a child's party? For an indulgent treat for a family member who is feeling down? For a family movie-and-pizza night at home? To showcase the fresh mozzarella purchased at the gourmet cheese shop during a day trip to an Italian American neighborhood?

Home cooks setting out to make a homemade pizza have to make sure they have all of the ingredients at hand and that they have gotten the best ones, taking into account their budget and personal preferences for healthy or organic or traditional foods. Home cooks have to assess the equipment they have at their disposal. Do they have an appropriate pan? How accurately does their oven regulate temperature? Should they invest in a pizza stone? Where can they put the dough to rise and the pizza to cool?

Home cooks have to think about the tastes of the people for whom they are cooking. Do they like a crisp crust or a thicker crust? How spicy do they like their sauce? Do they hate oregano? What toppings do they like or will they tolerate? If one eater likes mushrooms and another doesn't, will the mushroom hater pick them off? Home cooks may—depending on their approach to cooking for others—consider their own taste in pizza, or they may not.

Most home cooks think about the nutritional needs of those they feed. Do they need to watch their sodium intake? Are they lactose-intolerant? Do they avoid gluten or have food allergies? Do they try to limit the amount of fat they eat or need to eat more vegetables? Lastly, home cooks have to think about how they will fit making the pizza into the rest of their day. Is there enough time to make the pizza today? When should the dough be started and the sauce made? Will there be time to run an errand or wash a load of laundry while the dough rises? Can the kids help put on the toppings? Will the eaters be assembled and ready to eat when the pizza comes out of the oven?

As Frances Short points out (2006: 63), the skills of domestic cooks versus professional cooks are distinctly different. Professional cooks' skills tend to be those conceptual, perceptual, and mechanical skills that the first author wrote of in her composition on making pizza. A successful pizza chef is one who employs these skills to conceive of and execute a flawless pizza that looks and tastes great. A successful home cook is able to employ the skills of the professional chef—albeit likely to a different standard—but they also need organizational, planning, emotional, relational, caregiving, multitasking, and time allocation knowledge and skills to get a good dinner on the table for the family. A successful home cook may produce a pizza that is blobby, soggy, uneven, or otherwise technically imperfect but nevertheless is just right for the occasion and for those who come together to happily eat it.

The home cook's skill set includes the multifaceted abilities to plan and prepare food that suits the preferences and needs of those they feed and to fit cooking around other tasks and activities. In this book, we discuss different ways in which home cooks approach these tasks and utilize these skills. Because we are interested in what food and cooking mean to home cooks and how they think and feel about cooking, our focus is not on their practical cooking skills. However, as Singleton (1978) theorizes, all practical tasks require a combination of mechanical abilities; academic knowledge; and "tacit" perceptual, conceptual, and planning skills that are used to visualize the process of a task, plan and design it, and provide the confidence to carry it out. So while our focus is on home cooks' skills beyond mechanical abilities and academic knowledge, we did want to understand how our respondents felt about their cooking competencies and what cooking tasks they felt confident in their ability to perform.

At the end of their cooking journals, we asked our respondents to indicate whether or not they felt confident in their ability to carry out twenty-six cooking tasks. These tasks were further classified into two competency domains: light and heavy cooking skills. With few exceptions, the cooks in our study indicated that they felt confident in their ability to perform a variety of cooking tasks. Confidence in *light cooking skills* consisted of twelve activities including making a homemade pizza, casserole, mashed potatoes, homemade soups, or stews; preparing fresh vegetables; sautéing or roasting meats; making homemade tomato sauce for pasta; preparing a dish using a wok or stir fry; and cooking steaks. The cooks in our study were generally confident in these light skills: cooks were confident on an average of 9.8 out of 12 light skills (see Table 2 for the percentage of cooks reporting each skill). Confidence in *heavy cooking skills* included frying chicken or French fries; cooking fresh fish; making homemade gravy or salad

Table 2 Cooking skills reported by cooks

Light cooking skills		**Heavy cooking skills**	
Mean number of skills = 9.8, SD = 2.5		*Mean number of skills = 3.0, SD = 1.6*	
Make mashed potatoes	97%	Make homemade gravy	68%
Prepare fresh vegetables	95%	Cook fresh fish	68%
Make stews	87%	Make homemade salad dressing	63%
Roast a chicken or turkey	87%	Make homemade stock	61%
Make homemade soup	84%	Fry chicken or French fries	45%
Make homemade tomato/pasta sauce	84%		
Roast meats	79%		
Make casseroles	79%		
Prepare a dish using a wok or stir fry	76%		
Cook a steak	71%		
Sauté meats	71%		
Make homemade pizza	66%		

Based upon 46 cooks

dressing; and making a homemade stock. Cooks in the study were confident in an average of 3.0 out of 5 heavy skills. There was one significant difference in confidence between the various types of cooks: keen cooks ($M = 3.75$, $SD = 1.18$) were significantly more confident than other cooks in their heavy cooking skills ($M = 2.52$, $SD = 1.66$), $F(1,39) = 6.60$, $p = .014$.

We also examined confidence among our home cooks in baking skills and planning skills. Confidence in *baking skills* included baking a cake from scratch, baking a cake from a mix, making brownies, and baking bread. Family-first cooks expressed more confidence in their baking skills ($M = 3.04$, $SD = 1.11$) than other cooks ($M = 2.22$, $SD = 1.40$), $F(1,39) = 4.42$, $p = .042$, perhaps reflecting more experience in making cookies, cupcakes, and the like for their children. Confidence in *planning skills* included planning a healthy meal, planning a meal their family will like, planning an economical meal, and following a recipe. Keen cooks were more confident in their planning skills ($M = 3.94$, $SD = 0.25$) than other cooks ($M = 3.52$, $SD = 0.71$), $F(1,39) = 5.03$, $p = .002$.

What did the cooks cook? Typical dinner menus

In our interviews, we asked the cooks what they typically prepared for the evening meal. By far the most often mentioned food in a typical evening meal was chicken: over one-third of typical evening meals as reported in the interviews included chicken, usually grilled, baked, sautéed or stir-fried, or as breaded cutlets, fingers, or strips. (No one said fried chicken was a typical evening meal for them.) The next most frequently mentioned typical dish was some sort of pasta, including macaroni and cheese, spaghetti with meat sauce or meatballs, lasagna, and other pasta dishes. Tacos, steak, homemade pizza, and meat loaf were also mentioned by several households as typical evening meals in their households. Ham, roast beef, pork chops or roasted pork were also mentioned by a few households as typical for them. Fish was the least likely dish to be mentioned, but a few households do typically prepare fish.

Using recipes for making dinner

An important component of the personal and material dimensions of making dinner is how cooks use, or do not use, recipes. We found two general patterns of recipe use when making dinner. Roughly half of cooks could be described as frequent recipe users: they consult a recipe at least twice during the week. About 8 percent of our respondents use recipes almost always when making dinner, 30 percent use recipes frequently for making dinner, and 16 percent use recipes once or twice a week when making dinner. The other half are infrequent recipe users: they rarely use recipes, use them once a week or less often, or do not currently use recipes at all.

When do home cooks turn to a recipe for making dinner? Not surprisingly, one of the most frequent reasons for using a recipe is when preparing something new. Preparing a dish for the first time requires knowledge of ingredients, sequence, measurement, timing, and how these come together in the cook's kitchen with its own equipment and spatial limitations. Kaye says, "It's kind of my rule to follow the recipe the first time and then after that I can make the adjustments as I want to." Cooks, especially keen cooks as discussed in Chapter 8, look for and use recipes when they wish to cook a new food or try a new technique as a challenge to themselves. Cooks also seek out recipes when they feel their cooking has gotten into a rut and they want to try something new. They use them when baking or making desserts as they tend to prepare baked goods more rarely and/or feel that precision of measurements, temperature, etc., are more important to a good outcome when baking. Cooks who use recipes infrequently will refer to them when cooking for holidays or special occasions—when it is important that the traditional recipe be used—or for entertaining. In Chapter 7, we discuss how and when home cooks use traditional recipes or recipes from their families.

Judith follows recipes most of the time when she cooks. What appeals to her is "knowing they have been tested and that it is going to turn out. I am a recipe addict." Every Saturday, Mira and her wife look through a folder of recipes they have collected to select meals to cook for dinner. Their recipes are mostly from *Eating Well* magazine and the Blue Apron meal-kit delivery system (these products consist of recipes along with all the ingredients, premeasured), which they use once a month. Using recipes appeals to Mira because it takes away the work of deciding what to cook and it also helps with budgeting.

Some cooks use recipes to build their repertoire of dishes and menus. Family-first cook Paige uses recipes when learning a new dish: "I do maybe the first two or three times. If we have it over and over then I don't need to look at the recipe anymore. I don't just go and come up with something [new], I need a recipe to follow." Two of our cooks explained that they previously used recipes to build their repertoire and no longer feel that they need to. Lorraine, who does all of the cooking for her family, used recipes about a year ago when she was adding some new dishes, such as chicken pot pie, to her repertoire. She no longer does: "It's got much better, you know, now I don't even have to look at a card" to be able to prepare the dishes she wants to cook. Brandon, who often prepares the dishes for the evening meal in the morning or the night before for his wife to reheat or finish at dinnertime, used to use recipes "100 percent of the time" when he first started cooking and now uses recipes "maybe 20–25 percent of the time."

Some traditional cooks (see Chapter 7), who tend to have memorized the recipes learned from their families, rarely use recipes. For example, Tony is a traditional Italian cook and says that he does not use recipes: "I cook by instinct, and I keep things in the house that I know I like to use (olive oil, garlic, fresh vegetables)." Improvisational cooks (see Chapter 4) are another type of cook who rarely use recipes, because they decide what to cook and how to cook it shortly before starting to cook. For example, Chloe is an improvisational cook who rarely uses recipes and says, "If I make something good, I'll write it down. Never make the same thing twice. Recipes come together in my head based on what I have and how much time I have."

Cooking confidence and recipe use

There is no straightforward relationship between confidence in cooking competencies and recipe use. Some cooks with higher levels of cooking confidence use recipes because they are keen cooks (see Chapter 8), who use recipes to try something new (a dish with a new flavor profile or a new cooking technique) or to expand their skills: keen cooks enjoy the challenge of something new and choose recipes accordingly.

Other cooks with high amounts of cooking confidence may not use recipes because they have memorized the recipes for all the dishes they typically cook. For example, Elena has a high level of cooking competency and has been cooking for her family for many years. She doesn't use recipes unless it's for a dessert or something "new or special." She does have what she explains are her own recipes: "They are you do a ratio—for every cup of this you add this and this, etc. It's great fun."

Some cooks who have a lot of cooking experience and competencies rarely use recipes because they have acquired sufficient knowledge and perceptual and mechanical skills in cooking food so that they do not require a recipe to tell them what to do when cooking dinner. For example, Helen reported being confident in every cooking technique in our inventory and does not use recipes during the week because she says it is faster for her if she does not. She will, however, try out new recipes when she is entertaining, which she does fairly often.

Recipe use among cooks who are less confident of their culinary abilities and knowledge takes two forms. Perhaps counterintuitively, many less confident cooks infrequently follow recipes. Their relative lack of self-confidence influences what foods and dishes they will prepare for dinner. Consequently, many of the evening meals prepared by the less-confident cooks in our study were simple and relied upon prepared foods for major components of the meal, therefore not requiring a recipe: smoked sausage with frozen vegetables and mashed potatoes or pasta with a jarred sauce and a salad, for example.

Those less-confident cooks who frequently use recipes tend to follow them very carefully. According to Ann:

> A recipe is a safety net for me. My husband never ever uses a recipe. Reads five recipes and comes up with his own take on that same dish. I can't do that, I'm too afraid that I will screw it up ... The more technical stuff (sauces, gravies) I have trouble with. I follow recipes to a T. If I skip a step in a recipe, I can't make it up. (Ann)

Cooks like Ann may lack the perceptual and cognitive knowledge to know how cooking processes and sequences are supposed to work: they cannot anticipate how the food will respond to their manipulations and are uncertain if they are doing cooking properly. A recipe can give them the confidence they need. Frances Short described one of her respondents who calls herself "Mrs. Recipe" and always used a recipe when she tried something new because then she had "something to blame if it all goes wrong" (Short 2006: 43).

In contrast, more confident cooks tend to use recipes in what Cynthia and Christina, who both cook for their household, describe as a "piece-meal approach to recipes: take a little from here, a little from there." For one evening meal prepared in their household, both Cynthia and Christina looked at recipes online and in a cooking magazine to which they subscribe to get ideas for what they might cook. Neither followed a specific recipe for the dry-rubbed chicken chop and cauliflower and turnip casserole that they prepared, but they were inspired by and got ideas from the recipes they read. Amanda uses recipes in a similar fashion:

> [I] still don't necessarily follow a recipe. I'll look at it for inspiration, but then tweak it. I might ignore the spices or vegetables. My husband jokes that a recipe never stays the same twice. If I make something with raisins, it will have something else next time. (Amanda)

Almost all of the cooks in our study made adjustments to recipes when they did use them, based on their cooking expertise and their taste. Deanna, who has a large library of cookbooks, says that once she has learned a recipe, she no longer has to follow it. She says she is an excellent cook because "I can make a new meal once and know the recipe by heart after that. I can also add to the recipe and make it better." Many competent cooks have large collections of recipes and cookbooks. They read them—often for recreation—but the recipes do not take on the same meaning as they do for the less-confident cook who may not attempt a dish without a recipe to follow. Teresa says she loves recipes but doesn't collect them: "I 'browse' them voraciously. For example, if I have a lot of sweet potatoes or cucumbers or tomatoes, etc., … I'll browse recipes to find ideas for using these ingredients. I sometimes wish I'd saved a recipe, but the Internet makes it so easy to 'Google' and find things." Jack gathers recipes but rarely uses them:

> I have a few recipes acquired at different times from family members, and some recipes that I have torn out from newspapers or magazines over the years. These loose scraps of recipes are stuffed inside the front covers of the few cookbooks that we own (*Joy of Cooking, Best 30 Minute Recipes*), and they are rarely (if ever) accessed. (Jack)

Sources of recipes

Our cooks get their recipes from a range of both traditional and contemporary sources. Given the quick availability of thousands of recipes at the click of a mouse, it is no surprise that cooks most frequently go online in search of recipes. Internet sites that our cooks used included FoodNetwork.com, Cookinglight.com, Allrecipes.com, Food.com, Ingredients.com, and, in the case of one household, websites devoted to Paleo diets and cooking. Aside from these more mainstream Internet sources, cooks also turn to blogs and other more grassroots forums; the former sources may be seen to some degree as representing a more mass-produced approach to home food preparation. One of our keen cooks, Kaye, noted:

> I've been trying lately to stay away from the main venues like Foodnetwork.com and Allrecipes and I've been trying to find more individual blogs where people post recipes. I think there are so many people out there who are so creative and I

think that the recipes that they come up with aren't just the recipes off the back of the package, you know. I'd sort of like to try that, to see what very creative people come up with. (Kaye)

Many of our home cooks have cookbooks but only some use them regularly. Many prefer to read them for leisure. A few of our households subscribe to cooking magazines and regularly get recipes from these. They include *Taste of Home, Cooking Light*, and *Eating Well*. Half a dozen households in our sample get recipes from food television. Other sources of recipes are friends, family, co-workers, newspapers, and radio shows.

Food television and the practice of home cooking in everyday life

Following up on Pollan's 2009 *New York Times Magazine* article "Out of the Kitchen, Onto the Couch," we were interested in the relationship between watching food television and home cooking. As part of their daily cooking journals, we asked cooks whether they currently watched any television programs on food or cooking, whether they had used recipes from such programs, and how successful the recipes were. Over half (54 percent) of cooks have recently watched food television. We found no statistically significant relationship between the type of home cooking that our respondents did and their likelihood of viewing food or cooking programs on television. We did find a tendency for family-first cooks to watch more food television than other cooks, but they were no more likely to use a recipe from TV than others. Several cooks in the study spoke of watching food television together with their children, so this may be for family entertainment more than instructional purposes. One family-first cook and her family, who were food TV fans, ate at a diner one night during the study period because they had attended a book signing for television celebrity chef Bobby Flay's new cookbook and as a result had no time to cook at home.

Nearly half (46 percent) of cooks had used or currently use recipes from television programs or television chefs. Most of the time (86 percent) these were judged to be successful, although not always.

> I have made a few things from TV shows and have generally been successful with them, except for one thing called drunken salsa that called for roasting dried ancho chiles. I still have a bad taste in my mouth from that one! (Kaye)

Social contexts: Cooking for guests, cooking for one's self

Dinner parties and dining alone represent the polar opposites of the social dimension of home cooking: how home cooks think about and approach the task of cooking is determined by the occasion and the diners. Ideas about what constitutes a proper dinner or one in line with culturally accepted "food rules" (Charles and Kerr 1988; Murcott 1982) are more salient when cooking for persons outside the immediate family. Home cooks on the rare occasions when they dine solo may take pleasure in throwing out the food rules and just cooking and eating what they feel like.

Making dinner for guests

Although entertaining was not a focus of our research, we did ask our home cooks about their general approach to entertaining at home. As we will see in Chapter 3, cooks are quite mixed in terms of their enjoyment and enthusiasm when cooking for guests: some cooks dislike cooking for holidays and special occasions with guests, while other cooks find these occasions truly delightful. Cooks respond to the challenge of selecting what to cook for dinner for guests in a number of ways; common to all is the goal of finding something that both the guests and household members will like. Sometimes cooks favor traditional dishes when entertaining. For example, Patricia who mostly entertains her sister and her family says, "I try to make things that my mother used to cook or that were favorites when we were growing up." Kaye tries to offer things that her guests don't ordinarily eat, "although there are some things that are tradition. Potato salad for picnics, turkey and ham for holidays. I try to get creative with sides and desserts."

Some cooks seek novelty when cooking for guests. For example, Alice explains, "When we entertain, we like to step it up." Other cooks respond to the situation of cooking for guests or for holidays differently and stick to the "tried and true" recipes that reliably work for them. Several cooks note that they avoid new recipes when entertaining, preferring to prepare already-tested recipes. Andrea does not entertain often and says, "When I have cooked for family or friends I keep it simple and definitely don't chose that occasion to try something new." Peter, who is a keen cook, steers a middle course when cooking for guests: "When I entertain I usually try to stand on proven dishes but work one new thing in."

When choosing a menu for entertaining, cooks tend to favor dishes with at least some components that can be prepared in advance. Several cooks spoke of how they like to do as much preparation for the dinner as possible in advance. For example, Mira who is a planful cook says, "I tend to plan the meal ahead of time and shop for ingredients early. I like to cook the majority of items several hours earlier and then either reheat just before mealtime or finish up cooking certain items before sitting down."

Some cooks change their ordinary strategies when entertaining. For example, Cynthia and Christina are improvisational cooks who tend to do little advance planning of what they will cook for dinner. However, when they invite people over on a weekend night, they plan several days ahead and usually get started on the prep the day before. Cynthia says, "But I find that no matter how early I get started I am still cooking up to the last minute. This is probably because we try to make at least one semi-extravagant dish when we have guests."

Some cooks said that they often use the outdoor grill to prepare food when entertaining. This is seen as more sociable. Emily explains, "When we entertain we try to use the grill and spend a lot of time outside. If it's winter, I use the oven a lot to make food that doesn't require too much hands-on-time. I'd rather spend my time talking with my friends."

Several of our home cooks with young children in the family say they do not entertain at home as often as they did before children. For example, Jack and Jeremiah haven't entertained through cooking since their son arrived. Jack, who is a keen cook, wrote in their cooking journal:

> Here in the city where apartments and kitchens are small, it generally makes better sense to meet people at restaurants. We have entertained people a handful of times in the past. I do all the cooking in the kitchen, while Jeremiah entertains the guests out in the living room. I have usually found that somewhat stressful, since you worry about everything coming out right and at the same time. Plus I wind up interacting with the guests less while on kitchen duty. (Jack)

While some home cooks with young children say they don't entertain at home as often as they did before they had children, other parents of young children do entertain at home fairly often. For example, Teresa has people over for dinner once or twice a week, sometimes extended family and sometimes friends. She likes to make meals for which lots of prep can be done in advance. Her husband is usually chatting with the guests while she does the cooking. Her kitchen is right next to her keeping room (a family room adjacent to a kitchen), "where people usually hang out," so she chats with guests while cooking, too. She wants "people to feel relaxed and welcome. I don't usually cook things that are stressful. Low key, tasty, and filling."

Dining alone

Laurie Colwin, whose brilliant and emotionally astute essays about the role of food in everyday life are missed by many, wrote:

> Dinner alone is one of life's pleasures. Certainly cooking for oneself reveals man at his weirdest. People lie when you ask them what they eat when they are alone. A salad, they tell you. But when you persist, they confess to peanut butter and bacon sandwiches deep fried and eaten with hot sauce, or spaghetti with butter and grape jam. (Colwin 1988: 27)

As we discuss in Chapter 3, the most important consideration in the daily practice of deciding what to cook for the evening meal is the taste preferences of family members. Home cooks often put their own tastes and preferences last. On one day of their cooking journals, we asked our cooks what they would have cooked for themselves for the evening meal if they were the only person eating at home. We did not receive many weird responses. About a quarter of those answering this question would have eaten the same thing that they had prepared for their families. Elaine had cooked salmon patties, green beans, salad, cantaloupe, and bread and said that she "would have cooked the same thing. I can't say that I would do that every time that I was the only one home, but it is the case tonight."

One of the drudges said she wouldn't have cooked, one family-first cook would have eaten a low-calorie frozen meal, and a couple of cooks said they would get takeout. Family-first cooks and traditional cooks were particularly likely to say that they would've eaten leftovers if they had been the only ones at home.

Other cooks' selections of home-alone dinners suggest that they are accustomed to cooking for the tastes of the others whom they feed and that they would relish eating something else. For example, Margaret is a family-first cook. On the evening she served baked haddock, green beans, salad, and mandarin oranges to her family, she would have prepared for herself alone a dish of "fresh tomatoes sliced with a little garlic, parmesan cheese, and vinaigrette (microwaved) with a small side of macaroni." Judith is a family-first cook who served roasted chicken with gravy, spaghetti squash, oven-roasted tomatoes, rolls, and salad. She would have eaten for herself pasta with the "oven-roasted tomatoes I've had in the oven for two hours."

Peter, a family-first and keen cook, served his family grilled chicken sausage and sweet potato fritters: if he were alone that night, he says he would have prepared and eaten shepherd's pie. Peter's typical cooking style features roasted, grilled, or sautéed fish or meats and grilled, roasted, or sautéed vegetables: during the study period, he did not cook any casserole-type dish such as shepherd's pie. Perhaps his family doesn't like it or perhaps he just happened to be in the mood for it or perhaps it is a comfort food for him. Jeremiah prepared penne with sausage, crescent rolls, and spinach in sauce for his family: if he were alone that night, he would have cooked and eaten turkey soft-shelled tacos with rice and beans. He wrote that he really enjoys eating this meal and that he would prepare it more often, but that his husband prefers to have more variety.

Some cooks would've cooked and eaten only one of the dishes they prepared for their family if they had been alone. For example, Patricia had cooked soup, pasta and peas, shrimp, and salad. If she were alone, she would've cooked and eaten only pasta and peas. A few cooks would prepare something simple for themselves: some chips and homemade salsa and cheese wedges; a quesadilla; buttered noodles; a grilled ham and cheese sandwich. Kaye, who cooks elaborate meals for her family almost every night, said that she would've eaten leftovers or "maybe a bowl of cereal. I enjoy that for dinner but never do it."

3

Hoping, Feeling, and the Home Cook

Every day, millions of Americans (mostly women) come home from work and head to the kitchen, where they stand looking into the refrigerator or cupboard, asking themselves, "What can I make for dinner?" The average home cook in the contemporary United States confronts a foodscape offering a wide selection of foods in various states of preparation, with thousands of recipes readily available and scores of experts proffering advice on what to cook, what not to cook, and how to cook it in order to feed their families a "good" meal. Out of the vast array of foods and potential dinner menus available to food-secure households in the United States in the early twenty-first century, home cooks must decide what to cook and how to cook it.

Their decisions about what to make for dinner are constrained by material factors such as what foods are contained in their refrigerators and cabinets, their cooking competencies, and the time they have available to cook that evening. Their decisions are also shaped by their cultural understanding of what constitutes a proper dinner and by discourses of healthy eating and "good" food. Social factors including the nature of the occasion and the tastes, preferences, and physical and emotional needs of those they feed shape the decisions that cooks make about what to cook. Personal factors such as the cook's own motivations and intentions for cooking and their own tastes, preferences, and physical and emotional needs may also shape what they choose to make for dinner. In this chapter, we discuss how home cooks who can afford most foodstuffs feel about making dinner, how they decide what they will make for dinner, and the objectives that they hope to achieve when they put dinner on the table for their families.

How home cooks feel about making dinner

> There is, it cannot be denied, unspeakable pleasure in providing sustenance for others with the labor of one's own hands. (Albala and Nafzier 2010: x)

> With their high degree of ritualization and their strong affective investment, culinary activities are for many women of all ages a place of happiness, pleasure, and discovery. (Giard 1998: 151)

I most enjoy cooking when I have some free time to do it, and have all the ingredients in hand to prepare something special. This means that it requires a little advance planning, as well as the luxury of unencumbered free time. A sweet spot is on Saturday mornings, when I can wake up early before the rest of the family does, and make a nice frittata or breakfast strata in the quiet of the kitchen while I listen to morning bird songs outside the open kitchen window. It is a treat to prepare a good meal for my family. (Jack)

Making dinner can be a source of deep satisfaction, pleasure, and meaning in daily life. It can also feel like a tedious chore and provoke boredom and anxiety. How much do home cooks enjoy making dinner? What situations increase or decrease the enjoyment cooks experience when making dinner? In exploring how cooks feel about making dinner, we draw upon a series of questions in our interviews as well as data from individual meals documented in the cooking journals.

Who doesn't enjoy making dinner: The drudges

First, we must acknowledge that not all home cooks enjoy cooking. From Peg Bracken's 1960 *The I Hate to Cook Book* cookbook to today's cooking blog Mommy Hates Cooking (Mommy Hates Cooking 2017), popular culture reflects home cooks' ambivalence and sometimes outright antipathy toward their task. We found that three of the fifty-one home cooks in the study can be classified as "drudges." According to the OED definition (OED Online 2017), a drudge is "a person made to do hard, menial, or dull work." Drudges are cooks who really do not attach much meaning to cooking. They dislike or get very little pleasure out of cooking on a day-to-day basis. Drudges do not assume the identity of a home cook, and their negative orientation to the role may represent an act of resistance to it. To them, cooking is a menial chore that they must do because of their current life situation, but they would rather not. While many home cooks occasionally feel that cooking is a chore, often when they are pressed for time, drudges feel this way almost all of the time.

One such drudge is Karen, who cooks for her husband and three children aged seven to ten years old. Karen considers herself a "boring" cook. She doesn't enjoy making dinner and dislikes "all the preparation." She reports only three skills in which she is confident: making mashed potatoes, baking a cake from a mix, and planning a meal her family will like. Karen wrote in her cooking journal, "I really do not enjoy cooking and therefore spend very little time doing it. When I do, it's something that is simple, quick, and easy—nothing fancy, pretty standard fare." She reports that she has no difficulty deciding what to cook: "Normally, whatever I buy, I buy because I know that I would cook it, not stuff that causes me to wonder what I could make." In her ten-day journal, she and her household ate a home-cooked dinner on five nights, with Karen making dinner three of those nights and her husband cooking twice. The dinners included hot dogs and applesauce, frozen chicken wings prepared by Karen's husband (she wrote that "he enjoys making wings and makes his own sauce"), ham and cheese sandwiches, and peanut butter and jelly sandwiches followed by a bowl of cereal later in the evening after the children's activities.

When do cooks most enjoy making dinner?

It is notable that while popular culture may suggest that there are many drudges among us, most cooks find cooking a meaningful activity and one that gives them pleasure and a sense of successful accomplishment, at least some of the time. Aside from the drudges, almost all of the cooks in our study enjoy cooking the evening meal, at least on some days. This is not a surprise. Psychologist Mihaly Csikszentmihalyi (1990) analyzed daily logs that more than 10,000 people kept over a twenty-year period. He found that of the sixteen most common daily activities, cooking was the seventh most enjoyable activity, outranked only by love-making, socializing, talking, eating, engaging in sports and shopping, in that order, and that it ranked above activities like watching television and reading. He argued that cooking satisfies a basic human need and therefore offers inherent pleasure to those who engage in it.

Cooking as craftsmanship, focusing on the task at hand and on improving one's skills, can also be a source of great satisfaction. For some cooks, cooking can at times represent a recreational or leisure activity. For example, Kaye finds cooking to be recreational when she makes jams, jellies, and pickles, which she will sometimes do on weekday evenings when she has a bit of time or more often does on the weekends. We discuss home cooks who typically approach cooking as a leisure activity, whom we call keen cooks, in Chapter 8.

A few cooks enjoy cooking every day, but most experience more pleasure in certain situations and less in others. We asked our respondents in what situations they most and least enjoy cooking. We also asked them if cooking ever felt like a chore—an unpleasant but necessary task—and in what situations. As noted in the next chapter, time is the crucial determinant of how much home cooks enjoy making dinner. Cooks most enjoy making dinner when they have sufficient time (Tables 3 and 4).

Table 3 Cooking is most enjoyed…

When I have plenty of time/weekend	44%
Family get-togethers or holidays/special occasions	21%
For guests	16%
When I know everyone likes what I'm preparing	9%
Other mentions:	12%
When I'm not busy with other things	
When I'm by myself and not distracted	
When I have seasonal produce from the garden	
When I'm making something easy	
In the wintertime, when I can make something hearty	

Based upon interviews with fifty-one home cooks

Table 4 Cooking is least enjoyed...

Pressed for time/in a rush	46%
Holidays	21%
Other mentions:	33%
Too busy with other things	
Negative feedback from kids	
Becomes routine	
When I'm not successful (food isn't liked)	
Have to cook in shifts	
When I don't know what to cook	
When I haven't planned anything	
Complicated recipes with lots of steps	
Mondays	
My children don't know what they want for dinner	

Based upon interviews with fifty-one home cooks

How cooks feel about cooking for special occasions exemplifies how the personal qualities of cooks shape how they respond to the social context of cooking. For some home cooks, cooking for special events is a high point and very enjoyable, while for others cooking for family get-togethers, holidays, birthdays, or other special occasions has the opposite effect. Cooking for special occasions was the second most often mentioned situation in which our cooks *most* enjoyed cooking (21 percent) and also the second most often mentioned situation in which our cooks *least* enjoyed cooking (21 percent). Deanna said, "I most enjoy cooking at the holidays. I enjoy it when everyone is thinking about the meal and pitching in." On the other hand, Lorraine reported:

> I can't stand cooking for holidays. Because it's too much pressure and even though oftentimes it's still just the three us sitting around staring at each other, I feel like a pressure to make a big turkey or a big chicken or you know something where I just agitate myself for absolutely no reason. (Lorraine)

Cooking for guests and cooking dishes that they know their family will like to eat were also mentioned by a number of cooks as times they most enjoy cooking. Linda most enjoyed making dinner for guests at a small dinner party:

> I would say I really enjoy cooking just for myself, Tony, and another couple. Four or six people sitting around the table at the house for a dinner party. I just love doing that. Doing everything right. Everything down to the silverware and the stemware and you know the wine and everything has to be ... I feel terrific preparing that sort of thing. (Linda)

Other situations when cooks especially enjoyed preparing the evening meal included when the cook was not busy with other things, when alone in the kitchen without distractions (mentioned by a cook with a toddler), when the cook had seasonal produce from the garden, when making something easy to prepare, and in the wintertime when she makes the hearty, aromatic meat dishes she most loves to cook.

Making dinner as a chore

Some of our cooks felt that cooking was never a chore to them: either they always enjoyed it or they simply didn't cook when it felt too much like a chore and ate out or ordered in instead. The latter option—not cooking when the cook doesn't feel like it—is an option more often chosen by cooks with no children (Table 5).

As discussed in Chapter 4, having too little time or being rushed was the most frequently mentioned situation in which cooking felt like a chore (45 percent). Other temporal aspects that can make cooking dinner feel like a chore involve synchronicity: the need to work around family members' busy and often conflicting schedules to plan and produce a dinner that can accommodate everyone in the household. Material factors can also make cooking dinner less enjoyable. Situations in which the household was low in groceries or they didn't have all the ingredients they needed for a particular dish or menu made cooking feel like a chore for some cooks.

Peter said that cooking was least enjoyable for him when he was "not successful." As a keen and a family-first cook, he explained that he would know whether or not he had been successful in making dinner when he and his family members took the first bite. Enjoyment in cooking here is tied to making good food that he and his family enjoy eating. Some cooks found cooking least enjoyable when they struggled to decide what to cook: as we have seen, the "dilemma of dinner" is a common problem (Rawlins and Livert 2014). Others found it least enjoyable when they hadn't planned the dinner ahead of time. Joyce said, "I enjoy cooking least when I have no idea what to make and everyone is hungry."

Table 5 Cooking feels like a chore

Too little time/I am rushed	45%
Tired/it's been a long day	31%
Other mentions:	24%
Don't know what to cook	
Too busy with other things	
Low on groceries/don't have ingredients	
Entertaining (larger amounts needed)	
Have to cook in shifts	
Raising children	
Stepchildren are at home	
End of the week	
Different likes for dinner	

Based upon interviews with fifty-one home cooks

Emotions and making dinner

Just how did our cooks feel while planning and cooking the evening meal? To get a sense of the emotions experienced by the cooks while making dinner, the cooking journal included a short inventory of how they felt when preparing the meal (this appeared on several days in the cooking journal). Seven 7-point emotion scales were completed by the cook: rushed-relaxed, anxious-calm, happy-unhappy, uncertain-certain, valued-taken for granted, organized-chaotic, and creative-bored. Thirty-four cooks completed emotional inventories for a total of seventy-one meals.

Emotions across all meals and cooks were generally positive. During most meals, respondents reported feeling confident (74 percent), organized (65 percent), happy (63 percent), and valued (46 percent). For roughly a quarter of meals, cooks felt creative (26 percent). Cooks experienced negative emotions during meals less frequently, including feeling taken for granted (13 percent), rushed (12 percent), and anxious (5 percent). These emotional experiences tended to cluster together. An examination of the correlations between emotional items indicated that cooks feeling happy during meal preparation were also likely to feel more organized ($r = .46$, $p < .001$), valued ($r = .43$, $p < .001$), and creative ($r = .39$, $p < .001$). Perhaps not surprisingly, cooks who felt rushed during a meal were also likely to feel more anxious ($r = .28$, $p = .015$), less confident ($r = -.24$, $p = .034$), and more taken for granted ($r = .34$, $p = .003$).

The degree to which cooks experienced similar emotions over different nights when preparing dinner is provided through by a statistic known as the interclass correlation: a high interclass correlation suggests that an emotion tends to be experienced consistently by individual cooks across the meals that they prepare. A low interclass correlation (ICC) suggests that the emotion tends to vary across meals within the same cook. Cooks experienced positive emotions such as feeling valued (ICC = .59), creative (ICC = .55), and confident (ICC = .37) more consistently across meals than other emotions. These positive emotions may be strongly influenced by the relatively stable social context in which they cook, such as the cook's feeling valued by household members, and by their personal qualities, such as their self-assessment of cooking skills and attributions of success. On the other hand, negative emotions such as feeling anxious (ICC = .02) and feeling rushed (ICC = .06) appear to be far more variable from day to day. These feelings may be more driven by the material constraints of making dinner that night, such as time scarcity or failure to defrost the protein.

How home cooks decide what to make for dinner

Seventy years ago, social psychologist Kurt Lewin pointed to the importance of home cook's decisions by theorizing that the home cook acts as a "nutritional gatekeeper" whose choices determine which foods end up on the family's dinner table (Lewin 1947). Food reaches the household through various channels such as the grocery store, the market, and the garden. It is the family cook, in Lewin's time almost always the wife or mother, who selects the channels and the food that passes through them. Researchers in the field of nutrition have studied home cooks in their roles as nutritional gatekeepers (e.g., Wansink 2003).

Deciding what to cook is also part of Marjorie DeVault's concept of feeding work, through which women construct and maintain family life from day to day. The work of planning meals, DeVault suggests, is like solving a puzzle. DeVault's home cooks decided what to cook by taking into account the likes and dislikes of husbands first, followed by children, all within the context of what their cultural milieu had constructed as a proper meal. "By solving this puzzle each day, the person who cooks for the family is continually creating one part of the reality of household life. At the same time, she … is constructing her own place within the family, as one who provides for the needs of others" (DeVault 1991: 48).

Most of the home cooks we spoke to experience some difficulties solving the puzzle of what to make for dinner, although the magnitude and nature of their quandaries differ. Social psychologist Barry Schwartz presented research findings in *The Paradox of Choice* (2004) that suggest that in certain situations, too much choice may reduce consumers' satisfaction with whatever choice they eventually make, create feelings of anxiety, or even render them unable to choose. This describes the experience of some home cooks but not others.

> I think that when we have a lot of choices is when we have the most difficulty. It's easier when the fridge is getting empty. (Sara)
>
> Yeah, [I have trouble deciding] every day. Sometimes it's that I haven't thought it out and I really don't have much in the fridge. I also have to figure out what the kids will eat. (Lisa)

For some home cooks, like Rebecca and Ruth, whom we describe as family-first, it can be difficult to decide what to make for dinner because of the desire to please family members' divergent tastes.

> It is hard to decide sometimes. Satisfying everybody's taste and what they want. What they will eat. (Rebecca)
>
> Right now I am in a dire period of not knowing what to cook for dinner. [Interviewer: Is that because of your work schedule?] I think it's more that I don't really care what I eat but Harry [teenage son] needs a big full meal. He doesn't want the same thing a few nights in a row. (Ruth)

A number of cooks struggle to decide what to cook because they feel they have "gotten into a rut" and need to introduce some variety into their dinner menus but also have some uncertainty about introducing something new at their dinner tables. This is especially a problem for cooks who struggle to please family members' tastes: after having success with a given dinner menu, they may be loath to stray too far from the familiar tastes and textures that have proven to be satisfactory.

> [I have trouble deciding what to cook] when we tend to get in a routine of having the same thing over and over and I start getting complaints and I try to think

of something. I'll go to Pinterest and try to come up with something new that everyone would like to add into the rotation. [Interviewer: What do the kids say in complaint?] "We're having this again?" Sometimes I'll get in a … sometimes it's not the same dish but it's the same kind of thing, like a Mexican dish. (Paige)

Some cooks experience difficulty deciding what to cook when they have to work late or have forgotten to follow their usual plan of defrosting the meat. Cooks sometimes feel that the mental load of having to decide what's for dinner day after day is a bit of a burden.

> Usually if I have forgotten to take something out of the freezer, then I have to come up with something from what's readily available as opposed to waiting for something to defrost. That's kind of it. Because I don't really have very much help from my husband. I ask him what he wants and he says I don't know and I don't even continue that conversation. I am kind of the one that decides what we're going to have. (Kaye)

Certainly the task of deciding what to make for dinner, for many cooks who do not cook a traditional repertoire of meals, is more difficult for middle-class cooks today than it may have been for their mothers or grandmothers, who had less options from which to choose. As Rachel Laudan, the food historian, writes in her blog,

> My mother's task was made easier by the scarcity that limited her choices. Rationing did not end until I was eight. Meals ran on a weekly routine: roasts on Sunday, transformed and planned leftovers for the next couple of days, fish on Fridays. Rules for those meals were laid down in stone: sage and onion stuffing and apple sauce with roast pork, marmalade not jam for breakfast. There were no incentives to experiment with money tight, no enticing supermarkets, and the danger of failing to produce something palatable to the whole family. (Laudan 2017)

As the structural constraints on cooks with adequate economic resources have changed, there is greater freedom to choose a menu for dinner. At the same time, there is greater pressure to provide a variety of meals and a set of newer discourses about food safety and health to contend with. Children's demands may have increased as well as the cooks' and others' expectations for what constitutes a good dinner (O'Connell and Brannen 2016). All these factors may make the decision of what to make for dinner a problematic one at times.

What is a "good" dinner?

The question again is, out of the enormous variety of mass-produced food available, how does the relatively affluent cook select the right foods to make a good dinner? Within the larger cultural context of home cooking, there are varying notions of what constitutes a "proper meal" and "good food." "How these different, often contradictory values play out in people's practices" (Sutton 2014: 20) is a complex process. The process of choosing what to eat and, for our purposes, what to cook, entails a combination of people's experiences with food as children and adults, the recommendations and practice of friends and family, the advice of experts including nutritionists and lifestyle advisors, official propaganda from the state, and multiple, often conflicting, messages from popular culture and commercial advertisements. With so many expectations, making a good dinner can become, as the acclaimed American food writer M.F.K. Fisher noted in 1942, a "fantastic ideal":

> In our furious efforts to prove that all men are created equal we encourage our radios, our movies, above all our weekly and monthly magazines, to set up a fantastic ideal in the minds of family cooks, so that everywhere earnest eager women are whipping themselves and their budgets to the bone to provide three "balanced" meals a day for their men and children. (p. 5)

Fisher instead argued that people ought to eat just toast for breakfast if that was all they wanted: they could always make up the nutrients at another meal (1942). Remember Kaye, who labors to cook a healthy, delicious, multi-course meal for her family almost every night, said that if she were alone at night, she would've liked to just eat "a bowl of cereal." In addition to being Lewin's nutritional gatekeepers of the family, home cooks are also eaters. In the balance between pleasure—eating only toast for breakfast or a bowl of cereal for dinner—and prudence—eating a healthy, well-balanced meal—home cooks rarely choose pleasure for themselves.

The discourse of food constructs multiple ways of understanding and valuing foods and cooking methods. A "good dinner" can variously mean "a healthy meal," "fresh food," "real food," "tasty food," "convenient food," or "traditional food." Alan Warde (1997), for example, argues that cultural imperatives about what we ought to eat and cook can be organized into four basic "culinary antimonies" that encapsulate the contradictory messages circulating in contemporary culture about what foods are "good": economy versus extravagance, care versus convenience, novelty versus tradition, and health versus indulgence. In deciding what to cook for dinner, our respondents come down firmly on the side of economy, as we see later, with indulgence saved only for special occasions. As we discuss in Chapter 4, home cooks' understanding and utilization of convenience foods to do the caregiving work of cooking dinner troubles the care vs. convenience antimony. In this chapter, we discuss how novelty versus tradition figures in our home cooks' aspirations for their cooking. Almost all cooks occasionally choose to cook something different for dinner in order to alleviate feelings of excessive routinization and lack of variety in their dinner menus. Keen cooks, as discussed in Chapter 8, regularly seek to challenge themselves by cooking a new dish or using a new technique in making dinner. Almost all cooks occasionally choose to cook something traditional for dinner in order to tap into the advantages that traditional food holds in regard to taste and emotions: traditional cooks, as discussed in Chapter 7, regularly choose traditional foods and menus in making dinner. But how do home cooks grapple with the choice between health and indulgence?

One way of framing the decision of what to make for dinner is as a choice between the principles of pleasure and prudence—prudence being defined as the ability to govern and discipline oneself by the use of reason. Is a good dinner one that tastes good or one that is good for you? Choosing between health and indulgence or prudence and pleasure is the crux of the dilemma the home cook faces in choosing what to make for dinner. Parkin (2006) demonstrates how twentieth-century American magazine advertisements construct mothers as primarily responsible for securing their families' health and happiness through food. At the same time as many home cooks have an abundance of food available for them to choose from, our culture has constructed this choice as one that risks the health and happiness of families.

Charlotte Biltekoff (2013) argues that healthy eating discourses extend far beyond nutritional science, intersecting with issues of social identity, citizenship, and morality. In his work on food and governmentality, *Food, Morals and Meaning: The Pleasure and Anxiety of Eating*, John Coveney (2006) demonstrates that notions of "good food" are increasingly derived from discourses of health and nutrition and that choices of what to cook and eat are increasingly framed as choices between pleasure and prudence. This, Coveney argues, makes the decision of what to make for dinner a source of anxiety and sometimes guilt.

> Has there ever been a time when we have been required to demonstrate such concern about our eating habits? Warnings and admonitions constantly alert us to the fact that we could be digging our own graves with our knives and forks. (Coveney 2006: xii)

Using a Foucauldian analysis, Coveney shows how "for modern subjects of the government of food choice, pleasure needs to be rationalised against the health of the body vis-à-vis nutrition" (2006: 136). Nutrition as expert knowledge provides a guide for cooks to assess their choices of what to make for dinner in terms of "what is good." For Coveney, "the term 'good food', once reserved for tables laden with tasty dishes of food, now suggests something entirely different. Today good food requires one to show less concern with the physical pleasure of eating, and more interest in the good health that results from our dietary habits" (2006: xiii). Coveney and others demonstrate that morality plays a key role in food consumption decisions for many today (Askegaard et al. 2014; Coveney 2006; de Solier 2013). Consideration of moral values around food is organized along several vectors such as fair trade (Jones, Comfort and Hillier 2003; Loureiro and Lotade 2005), organic growing practices (Arvola et al. 2008), and opposition to genetically modified foods (Comstock 2012).

In *Acquired Tastes: Why Families Eat the Way They Do*, Brenda Beagan, Gwen Chapman, and a research team (2015) explore the widespread preoccupations with food, health, and body image experienced by many in Western societies through their interviews with diverse Canadian families with teenagers. They demonstrate that the various cultural repertoires of food and eating that are available to people allow for tremendous variety in the ways they eat and the food issues they discuss. Definitions of healthy eating held by parents and teenagers vary by location, social class, age, and gender. Using a Foucauldian analysis, Beagan and her coauthors examine how individuals engage with and resist healthy eating discourses through their daily food practices, while highlighting the social consequences of doing so. Regardless of social or geographic location, they found that many mothers had internalized cultural expectations that they monitor not only their own food practices but also those of their children and their male partners by controlling what foods are eaten at home. Mothers produce themselves as good mothers, properly gendered, when they choose healthy food for their families. "Mothers who felt they were not living up to these standards often felt guilty or inadequate" (2015: 54). Similarly, Coveney argues, "The task of bringing up children is left to the cooperation of parents who seek and gain satisfaction and fulfilment through the practices of expert knowledges that construct 'proper' parenting" (2006: 126).

Food scholars have also demonstrated how values may be expressed through the choices that eaters and cooks make about food. For example, food and cooking choices can express love (Abarca 2006; Adapon 2008; Cairns and Johnston 2015). In his ethnographic account of the meaning of cooking, Jean-Claude Kaufmann finds that the practice of cooking dinner can express the overarching value of family as well as different values of autonomy and intimacy versus tradition and discipline (Kaufman 2010: 85.) Importantly, Kaufmann notes that these values are never fixed because their expression is always contingent upon the cooks' habits, desires, and traditions of food and cooking. Below we discuss how the home cooks in our study engage with the morality of food, what they consider to be "good" food, what they aspire to accomplish through making dinner, the challenges they face in achieving their objectives, and how they negotiate competing desires and needs to make the best dinner that they can on a daily basis.

How home cooks decide what to cook and how to cook it

What cooks choose to cook and how they cook it is related to their social situation, their family and community, their cultural environment, and their local milieu. The material realities of the foodscape in which cooks shop for food, that is, the availability of diverse, affordable, and high-quality foods and the economic means to purchase them, act to constrain cooks' choices. Social and cultural discourses that constitute some foods as "good" and "healthy"—virtually synonymous terms in many contemporary Western societies—further delimit what cooks will choose to prepare for themselves and their families (Beagan et al. 2015: 9).

As an organizational scheme for thinking about how people decide "what's for dinner?" Warren Belasco has proposed a culinary triangle of contradictions with the left point representing "identity," the right point "convenience," and the apex "responsibility" (Belasco 2008: 7). Identity includes factors such as taste, pleasure, creativity, family and ethnic background, and personal memories of food. Convenience to Belasco is actually more akin to access, including consideration of the resources of energy, time, money, labor, and skill needed to eat or cook a particular food. Responsibility encompasses the morality of food, the personal, social, physiological, and political implications of eating or cooking particular foods. Belasco argues that "for the most part, people decide what to eat based on a rough negotiation—a pushing and tugging—between the dictates of identity and convenience, with somewhat lesser guidance from the considerations of responsibility" (2008: 8). For home cooks, the negotiation of these culinary contradictions when deciding what to make for dinner is complicated by their need to anticipate and respond to the "identity" factors or personal preferences of those for whom they cook. In addition, society and home cooks themselves place much greater weight upon their responsibility for the health and happiness of those who eat the dinners they have cooked. While eating dinner may not always engage the morality of food, cooking dinner for loved ones almost always does. The value of Belasco's culinary triangle of contradictions, along with Warde's antimonies, is that it helps us think through the complex and competing factors that drive home cook's decisions about what to make for dinner.

Aspirations and goals for home cooking: The ideal and the quotidian

At its most basic level, the work of the home cook is to provide nourishment for their families. This means that the food must be nutritious and that sufficient quantities must be eaten by family members. Yet family dinner has considerably more meaning than simple nourishment of the body (DeVault 1991) (although those who cook for children sometimes find preparing nutritious food that will be eaten to be no simple matter in itself). We were interested in understanding the meaning of dinner by investigating what objectives our home cooks hoped to achieve when making dinner for their household. Amy Trubek's research group suggests that "to be a cook is to be *active*, with long-term, evolving goals" (2017: 303). What aspirations and goals did our home cooks have and how did these drive their daily decisions about what to cook and how to cook it?

During our interviews, we asked cooks, "How do you decide what you will prepare for dinner each night?" After they replied, we probed to determine whether any of fifteen objectives influenced their decisions, if they had not already been mentioned. We asked the cooks which of the following objectives were important to them in deciding what to make for dinner. Did they hope to make a dinner that was economical, healthy, convenient, easy to cook, fast, novel (something different), challenging (to them as a cook), in their family's traditions, comforting, trendy, authentic, showed their personal touch, indulgent or a special treat, something the family likes, gourmet, or well-balanced?

In their interviews, almost all home cooks indicated that it was important to them that the evening meals they prepare are healthy (91 percent) and, to a lesser degree, liked by their families (79 percent). Choosing a menu that would be comforting (72 percent), convenient to prepare (70 percent), well-balanced (70 percent), and economical (66 percent) was also important to a large majority of our home cooks. That the dinner embodied their families' traditions (62 percent) and was easy to cook (55 percent) were also frequently mentioned objectives. Roughly four out of ten cooks wanted their evening meal to be fast to prepare, be indulgent or to include a special treat, or to offer a novel taste or something different. Making a dinner that would be gourmet or trendy is an objective of very few cooks in our study.

Cooks' responses in the interviews regarding how they decide what to cook for dinner reflect how they think about themselves as home cooks and what general motivations or aspirations they hold for their home cooking. To what degree do these reflections during the interview—the goals that cooks say they think about when deciding what to cook for dinner—actually line up with practice? In other words, does the aspirational dinner as described in the in-depth interview actually align with the quotidian dinner as documented in the cooking journal? Or do the exigencies of daily life intervene between what is hoped for and what is accomplished? As Trubek and colleagues (2017) succinctly argue, "Home meal preparation, closely considered, is a mediation between internal desires and external realities" (p. 301).

In their cooking journals reflecting on each day's dinner, cooks responded to the prompt "I wanted to cook a meal that was …" followed by a checklist of the fifteen objectives. This methodology allows us to compare what cooks *say* is most important to them in deciding what to cook in general with what becomes important to them in the day-to-day work of planning and producing the evening meal. Analysis of the 316 dinners reported by our fifty-one cooks suggests the aspirations for dinner that home cooks reported in the interviews were not always realized in the exigencies of daily life (see Table 6). In their daily journal entries, home cooks often reported conflicts

Table 6 Objectives for the evening meal. (Interview prompt: "What is important to you in deciding what to cook?" Daily journal prompt: "I wanted to cook a meal that was …")

	Interviews with Cooks	**Daily Journal**
Healthy	91% (1)	42% (5)
Family likes	79% (2)	61% (1)
Comforting	72% (3)	31%
Convenient	70% (4)	48% (4)
Well-balanced	70% (4)	26%
Economical	66%	29%
In my family's traditions	62%	11%
Easy to cook	55%	57% (2)
Fast to prepare	43%	53% (3)
Novel/something different	40%	15%
Indulgent/a special treat	38%	14%
Challenging to the cook	34%	3%
Shows my personal touch	32%	14%
Gourmet	13%	1%
Trendy	5%	1%

Based upon interviews with 51 home cooks and 316 meals. The ranks of the top five considerations are in parenthesis.

between objectives for the evening meal, such as between the desire to provide a healthy dinner and the need to choose one that could be prepared quickly and easily because of time or other constraints.

The difference between how cooks ranked healthy, well-balanced meals in their interviews as compared to their daily cooking journals is particularly striking. In their interviews, almost all of our cooks said that cooking a healthy meal (91 percent, ranked first) and cooking one that would be liked by their family (79 percent, ranked second) were important to them. But for the dinners they actually made and reflected upon in the daily journals, a healthy meal slipped from the most important objective to the fifth and liked by my family became the objective selected most often. Clearly home cooks' hopes for what they want to accomplish through making dinner may, in the course of their daily lives, become more or less important to them as they get on with the actual work of feeding the family.

Although our cooks aspire to provide healthy dinners, their day-to-day practice reflects the competing demands of other goals as well as material constraints such as time. While almost all cooks said in their interviews that making a healthy meal was important to them, they reported taking healthiness into account in only 42 percent of the meals described in the cooking diaries. Although "healthy" was mentioned more often as an objective of their dinner-making in the interviews than family taste, cooks are less likely to report considering healthiness as a goal when deciding what to cook on a daily basis. We acknowledge that one source of this discrepancy might be the social demands of the personal interview: cooks may have said that they considered the healthiness of their cooking in order to create a positive impression. We tend to think this is not entirely the case because the cooks in our study were able to easily articulate what "healthy" cooking meant to them. It is also true that healthiness may be a more salient consideration when purchasing food than when cooking it. Cooks may have been less likely to mark "healthy" as an important objective in their decision of what to cook on a daily basis because they had already stocked their kitchens with the foods they consider healthy and didn't really have to think about it when deciding what dinner to prepare from those foods.

Similarly, although "well-balanced" was a frequently mentioned goal in the interviews, according to their daily cooking diaries, cooks marked that they considered it important that the meal was well-balanced for only approximately one in four dinners (26 percent). It appears their definition of well-balanced is part and parcel of how cooks shop for and plan their evening meals—the need to prepare a vegetable or salad or a lean protein—so perhaps it is a "taken for granted" part of how they cook the daily meals. Normative notions of what constitutes a "proper dinner" including a balance between proteins, starches, and vegetables may be so ingrained that cooks do not think about this as they prepare the evening meals: it is just simply something that they do as a matter of course.

When balancing the sometimes conflicting motivations to please family members and to cook healthy food, cooks often choose to please their families, or more accurately to not disappoint their families, when they decide what to cook for dinner. In the next chapter, we show how a lack of time is experienced as a serious constraint on the home cooks in realizing their goals and aspirations regarding dinner. Since processed food is viewed as less healthy but may be quicker to prepare, the ideal of healthy cooking is often compromised in the exigencies of daily life.

Liked by my family

Providing food that their families like is an important goal for cooks when deciding what to prepare for dinner. At minimum, food has to be liked well enough to be eaten in sufficient quantities to be nourishing. Otherwise, the cook has failed the primary goal associated with the role of family cook. Tailoring foods to accommodate individual preferences is also a way of showing love and reproducing relationships within the family (e.g., Moisio et al. 2004). In their interviews, almost all home cooks indicated that preparing a dinner that would be liked by their family was an important determinant of what they choose to cook for dinner.

> I enjoy cooking to please others. (Helen)
> I like to know what people like, and then I make it for them! (Teresa)
> [Interviewer: How do you decide what to make for dinner?] Well, I guess, mainly something that I know everyone will eat, that they like, so chicken. And I always try to have a vegetable. And most everyone in my family likes salad. That usually drives what I cook, something that will please everyone. (Karen)

The most frequently mentioned objective of cooks in deciding what to cook for dinner each day was to cook a dinner that their family would like. Daily journal data confirmed the importance of preparing food that was liked by the family in the day-to-day practice of home cooking. For almost two-thirds (61 percent) of the 316 meals prepared during the study period, cooks reported that consideration of what family members would like influenced their planning and production of the meal.

All primary home cooks have substantial knowledge about what their family members like or dislike to eat (Carrington 1999). More often than not, this was framed in terms of avoiding serving foods that members of the household disliked. Deciding what to cook for the evening meal involved evaluation of and negotiation of family members' divergent likes and dislikes, sometimes requiring the cook to keep a running total of who had and hadn't been served something they liked during the week. For example, Victoria reports, "I try to please everyone sometime within the week. Everyone has their own favorites." This is part of the "invisible" mental load required to regularly make dinner for the household.

Similar to the mental burden that mothers of young children must carry (Walzer 1996), our home cooks—predominately women—must keep in mind a broad range of other issues and statuses as well. In addition to individual preferences and whether they have been satisfied, the primary home cook must ascertain whether the needed ingredients—as well as requisite condiments (e.g., ketchup)—are in the pantry or need to be provisioned. Is the equipment necessary for making the meal clean and accessible (e.g., is the colander in the backyard in a child's construction site)? Are plates and cutlery clean and ready for serving dinner? This mental load, or cognitive burden, generally remains with the primary cook even when someone else in the household (e.g., male partner or child) assumes the duties of cooking dinner. Even if dad is cooking tonight to give mom a break, she may still have to keep in mind these invisible considerations. Deanna and Patricia describe some of the daily internal conversations required of the primary home cook.

> [The family liking it is a] big issue. I take it into consideration. Discuss what we want to eat. They don't eat it? Doesn't happen very often. I don't try anything extravagant. (Deanna)

> The two fussiest eaters in my house are my husband and son. I try to make something that I know they'll like. I try not to repeat the same thing night after night, but it's a hard thing to do. (Patricia)

If family members don't like the meal, their displeasure can make the dinner table a contentious place to be and diminish the home cook's enjoyment. Many of our home cooks, especially family-first cooks, felt hurt, frustrated, or upset when their partners or children rejected their food. Explaining what a dinner that is liked by her family means to her, Joyce, who cooks for a two-, a six-, and a nine-year old, said,

> Something that I know the kids will eat. They won't not eat it or throw it on the floor. (Joyce)

> [Liked by my family] means that we won't fight at the table about eating what I've made. I try to make things that everyone will eat. But there's always something the kids won't eat on the plate. If I can do dinner the easy, fast, traditional, etc. way, then I'm satisfied. If my husband isn't satisfied, he will modify it: put hot sauce on it or make it into a sandwich. (Ann)

Susan says that sometimes it is difficult to decide what to make for dinner "just because of the different taste buds" in her family. To avoid these kinds of problems, cooks routinely diffuse tension over the choice and content of the meal by planning and preparing meals that defer to the tastes of family members (Charles and Kerr 1988; DeVault 1991; Meah 2013).

To take the preferences of children and adults into account, cooks must know and keep up with potential changes in what each family member likes, dislikes, and will eat. Our home cooks faced the same challenge that many of Frances Short's respondents did: the necessity of being able to consistently prepare food to a standard that satisfies the taste preferences of those who eat their cooking. These preferences can be very particular in regard to specific foods, flavors, textures, colors, and meal composition. "Tomato lumps are cause for immediate rejection, though pureed tomato is fine" (Short 2006: 60). When there are children in the household, producing a dinner that is liked by those who must eat it becomes more challenging. It requires negotiating the different taste preferences of both adults and children—whose tastes may frequently change—along with trying to meet the cook's objectives of preparing a healthy, well-balanced, economical, and convenient dinner.

It makes a difference whether those who eat the dinner are children or adults. Adults are empowered to modify the food to suit their taste, as Ann's husband does, or to eat something else later if they are still hungry. Kaye knows that her husband hasn't liked the dinner she's prepared very much when he later fixes himself the "blasted ramen noodles." In Janet and Kristen's adults-only household, the risk of a disliked dinner was merely post-meal snacking:

> If we're not going to eat it, we will overeat on snacks later in the night. It's important that we can sit down and there is something there that will fill us up. If not, later in the evening, the bags [of snacks] get opened and the ice cream comes out. (Janet)

But young children are not capable of doing this, so it is more important to home cooks to make sure that there is something on the dinner table that children will eat. As a result, some cooks will prepare an alternative dish for children who don't like the dinner.

In their research on how families deal with children's food preferences in planning and preparing family meals, Thompson and colleagues (2016) suggest that home cooks may differ in their ideal of family dinner as a shared meal. Is the ideal a *shared meal* with all family members eating the same food, or is the ideal simply a *shared mealtime* with family members possibly eating different foods (Thompson et al. 2016: 329)? They identify two approaches to framing children's food preferences in making dinner. One approach, "what we fancy," is more reactive, with parents tending to consult with their children at mealtimes about what should be made for dinner and often preparing separate meals or foods to accommodate their tastes. The "regulated" approach also values children's tastes but to a lesser extent and not proximate to dinnertime. Rather, parents incorporated the families' preferences in developing a repertoire of set meals that pleased most family members' tastes but did not welcome input or negotiation at meal time (Thompson et al. 2016). We find that our home cooks cannot be so evenly divided into two types regarding accommodation of children's preferences, but many did tend to engage in one strategy more than another.

For example, Lisa, Sara, and Daniel, as well as Alice and Michael, typically choose evening meals that they perceive as "kid-friendly." Judith's strategy of leaving something plain for her young son is a common one:

> It's important [that my family likes it], but I don't necessarily not make something if one of them doesn't like it. My husband always needs to like it, but my son doesn't always need to like it. Otherwise, we would be eating chicken nuggets every night. He (husband) lets me know. I try to find, in the usual variety of foods I make, what I know he likes. If I make something new, I usually think he's going to like it. But he just might not like some combination of something. He lets me know. I will kinda work around my son, leave something plain for him. (Judith)

For some households, "kid-friendly" differs according to the kid. Lois's children have different tastes.

> [Family likes] is very important. I do have two kids who are complete opposites so I usually get one with both thumbs up and the other who is thumbs down. A lot of times they disagree, but it is important to me that at least one of them likes it. (Lois)

Jack and Jeremiah have a two-year-old son, and although they do try to incorporate kid-friendly elements into their family dinners, they have been finding this challenging. Their typical evening meal highlights how their choices are shaped by their son's tastes and their own ideas about what constitutes a good meal: "We try to make a meal where Mason can eat some or all of what we have made. We usually have to have a back-up for him. We have been trying to make it work together." Jack and Jeremiah aspire to the ideal of a shared family meal.

Another strategy employed by cooks to solve the problem of divergent tastes among family members was to prepare extra dishes to appeal to those family members they expected would dislike some component of the meal. Patricia often prepares what are essentially two entire dinner menus to accommodate the different likes and dislikes of her family members. For example, on an evening when Patricia had cooked chicken, potatoes and peas, tacos, and a salad, she rated the meal a success because "everyone had what they liked." Kaye also tended to prepare meals with many different dishes or additional components such as string cheese, granola, quick bread, or fresh fruit to ensure that her children, who could be picky eaters, would be able to find something they liked to eat on the table. Nevertheless, she sometimes made a separate entrée for the children.

> My husband and I like different foods than the kids like, so sometimes they'll get one thing and we'll get the meatloaf, which I know they won't eat, so I don't even bother trying. I'll offer it to them, but if they don't take it, I'll make them macaroni and cheese or peanut butter and jelly is always a good fall back for them. (Kaye)

In several households, arriving at a desirable dinner menu involved dialogue with those who would eat the meal, similar to Thompson et al.'s "what we fancy" approach (2016). For example, Peter prepares all of the dinners for his family (wife and eight-year-old daughter) "usually with some consultation of what people want to eat that night." Based on what he has available and planned, Peter offers options about an hour before dinnertime. Lorraine, who plans her meals by defrosting the protein, sometimes asks her young daughter what she would like to eat for dinner and chooses a menu accordingly. Lorraine was unusual among our cooks in that her own taste preferences were very important to her in deciding what to cook:

> Pretty much just kind of what I feel like. You know, I haven't had spaghetti and meatballs in a few days, maybe I should make some of that. Sometimes my daughter will say, like if I've already defrosted something, like say I have a lot of chopped meat here, let me defrost it. I'll say to her, what do you want for dinner, and she'll say hamburgers! And I'll say all right fine we'll have hamburgers. I guess, somebody's preference. (Lorraine)

Some home cooks feel that part of their role is to train their children's palates and to teach them to eat good food. For example, Amanda is persistent when a new dish is not liked by her family. She wants to teach her children to like and eat the foods she thinks are good.

> I know they don't like it when they refuse to eat it. But the rule is that they have to try it. If there is strong pushback, I won't make it again for a few months but will try it again. Husband gives feedback, but I don't take his opinion into that much consideration. [If he doesn't like it, he] will add to the meal or find a sauce. (Amanda)

"Picky" kids who refuse to eat present a dilemma for the home cook. Part of the expectations of modern parenting is to provide children with some amount of choice: by so doing, children will learn how to choose appropriately for themselves. Parents often feel, as Amanda does, that part of their task in cooking for their children is to teach children how to eat appropriately in the families' cultural context: how to choose the best foods to eat and how to eat them appropriately, in what order, and in what combinations (Charles and Kerr 1988). When applied to learning how to make appropriate food choices, though, allowing children to choose becomes problematic, as they may simply refuse to eat from what's offered. And according to the ethos of modern parenting, it is not appropriate to force children to eat. So the problem of the picky child can increase the home cook's effort in choosing what to make for dinner substantially. Herein lies the appeal of prepared foods that are marketed for children. These foods are heavily advertised, to children as well as to parents, as both delicious and healthy (O'Connell and Brannen 2016) and they may present an easy option to the problem of finding something that the children will eat. Parents in our study occasionally used boxed macaroni and cheese and frozen chicken nuggets and potato shapes in this way.

Healthy

In her journal entry for one day's dinner, Kaye wrote about her decision to make chili, which her husband likes but her children do not. She bought hot dogs on the way home for the children but was unable to find the "all-natural" hot dogs she prefers. However, Kaye felt that the banana-oatmeal chocolate chip cookies she served along with the hot dogs made the meal healthier and that made her feel better about serving a a meal that was not completely healthy. "At least I know when they eat their cookies, that they're getting a healthy, homemade item."

Kaye's desire to prepare a healthy evening meal for her family was shared by almost all of our cooks. When interviewed, 91 percent of cooks indicated that preparing a healthy meal was an important goal when deciding what to cook for dinner. For many, this is a response to the discourse of nutrition and healthy foods. For example, Carolyn reported, "I've been trying to cook more healthy, with all the information out there. I usually like to have a meat and a vegetable. We don't eat a lot of desserts. We always have a fresh salad."

For several cooks in our study, cooking healthy dinners is key to how they view themselves as cooks and as caregivers. It can also function as a mark of distinction or social comparison. Chloe, who says she is known as the "bean lady," told us, "Eating healthy has such important effects. I rarely use meat, unlike some around here." Daniel, who characterizes the cooking of himself and his wife as "more on the far end of healthy," explained, "We are part of the very few people who actually read the labels on food and since I am a chemist I can actually understand a lot of those ingredients and that makes me very selective when picking out certain types of foods."

As we see from the quotes above, a "healthy" dinner means different things to different cooks. To Kaye, foods that are homemade and "all-natural" are healthier. To Chloe, eating more legumes and less meat is healthy. To Carolyn, healthier cooking means a fresh salad at every dinner. Most often, cooks said that to cook a healthy dinner meant using fresh ingredients rather than canned or frozen. Avoiding "processed" foods was also an important component to the cooks' understanding of healthy meals. In general, homemade foods were viewed as healthier than their prepared counterparts. For Helen, unprocessed foods are healthy: "Trying to make something that's not from processed foods as much as possible. Using fresh vegetables or fresh food items." Mary defines healthy food as "real food."

For some cooks, cooking healthy means including vegetables in the dinner menu. Fresh or frozen vegetables were considered to be healthier than canned. When asked what a healthy dinner meant to her, Pauline answered: "Just something that would have a fair amount of fruit or vegetables in it. I would always throw in a vegetable. Even if it was with hamburgers or something." Virginia too says, "I like to always make sure I have some sort of vegetable" and Lois says, "We are not too hardcore about [healthy eating] but we would always have at least one vegetable."

In addition to limiting the use of processed foods, using more fresh ingredients, and including vegetables, cooks also mentioned that a healthy dinner to them meant using olive oil, a balanced representation of food groups, and limiting fat, fried food and red meat. Several households are trying to cut carbohydrates, while others are eating more whole grains. For Rebecca, healthy meant "quality of nutrients" in the food and a "nice amount of antioxidants and essential vitamins." One family with children said, "We probably try to do a Paleo Mediterranean but we are not strict." Another household consisting of a couple without children self-identifies as followers of a Paleo diet and avoids gluten and sugar. For Pauline, healthy means:

> Not overladen with starch. Not a lot of fried foods. Not a lot of fats. Always have a vegetable. Brown rice instead of white rice. Use yams rather than potatoes. Fresh or frozen rather than cans. The only canned vegetables I use are beets and string beans.

For Cynthia and Christina, making healthy dinners means "lean protein and we cook with olive oil, occasionally with butter. It means everything in moderation and we cook with lots of vegetables." According to Janet and Kristen, healthy means:

> We try to limit the amount of white. Meaning rice, flour, things like that. And definitely limit the amount of red meats. Anytime we can use fresh, the better. And

if not, use something frozen. Not into the canned or prepared. Go with fresh or frozen. (Janet)

Comforting

Paige cooked and served a comforting dinner the night before our interview:

> For the weather. We had soup last night because it's been stormy and rainy here. It is a comfort food to me. We had grilled cheese sandwiches with it. (Paige)

The goal of making a comforting dinner may arise from either the cook's own need for psychological soothing or the perception of that need among those for whom she or he cooks. Most (72 percent) of our home cooks indicated in their interviews that "comforting" was sometimes an important consideration in deciding what to cook for dinner. Some cooks reported keeping track of who has had one of their favorite dishes during the week and working to make sure that each household member feels special occasionally because they get their special food. This mental load, remembering who likes what and when they last had their favorites, is a key part of home cooking as caring about and for the family.

Part of the emotion work of cooking dinner is to prepare and serve certain meals in certain ways to suit the emotional needs of household members. Home cooks use food for emotional comfort for their families for stressors and problems as mundane as the weather and as momentous as terminal illness. When discussing how much she enjoyed cooking, Rebecca talked about cooking to comfort and heal loved ones.

> I think about making chicken soup for my dad. He was sick before he passed away. It was like a spiritual experience. You can heal people with food. (Rebecca)

A comforting dish is not only liked by those who eat it, but there is an explicit expectation that the dish will provide a positive psychological experience to the eaters. Eating foods considered to be comfort foods provides some sort of emotional comfort, consolation, or feeling of well-being when eaten: they may be used to comfort those who are troubled or used to celebrate accomplishments (Spence 2017). Comfort foods are often simple or traditional foods and may appeal to nostalgia, reminding us of home, family, and/or friends (Locher et al. 2005). The positive emotions associated with comfort foods may arise from food memories; often our comfort dishes were first consumed in childhood and may have been our favorites or may have been the foods a loved one prepared for us when we were ill. Comfort foods are often linked to a specific person, place, or time with which we have positive associations (Spence 2017).

Just what dinner foods are seen as comforting? Because many comfort foods derive from childhood eating experiences, there is a great deal of variation across both individuals and cultures in what foods people think are comforting (Brown 2017; Doré 2015; Spence 2017). For our home cooks, "comforting" did not necessarily mean the stereotypical "comfort" foods. Instead, cooks associated a wide range of foods with comfort including macaroni and cheese, French toast, brownies, rice pudding, meatloaf, ham and cheese omelet, spaghetti and meatballs, enchiladas, chili, rice, oatmeal, and corn bread. Several cooks gave homemade soup as an example of a dinner that they found comforting. For Teresa, quite a few foods were seen as comforting:

> I am big into making lots of "comfort" foods—roasted chicken, salmon with a cream sauce, mashed potatoes and I LOVE to cook vegetables—side dishes are the stars! (Teresa)

Cynthia and Christina, who both cook, also reported an array of comfort foods that they employed in their dinners:

> That would be the fried chicken (in an iron skillet) and we also think roasted potatoes in the oven are comforting. Chicken soup. Anything with a red sauce or mashed potatoes. Anything that is creamy with lots of cheese. (Cynthia)

Linda and Tony, who both cook, had differing notions of comfort food. She explained:

> Only on occasion, we have our "cheat day" for what they call the comfort foods. I myself find a good piece of rare steak very comforting and a glass of wine, that is very comforting to me. (Linda)

However, in their cooking journal, her husband Tony marked comforting as a consideration for every meal he cooked during the study period. He is a traditional Italian American cook and apparently considers the food of his childhood inherently comforting.

Karen is a drudge who doesn't enjoy cooking and who said her primary aspiration in her cooking was to make "something that will please everyone." Her definition of comfort food was food that could allay her anxiety about her cooking by representing something she could make that she knows her family likes and will eat:

> [Comfort food to me is] something we are accustomed to having. Not something new or trying something different. Something that I know they like and will eat. (Karen)

Well-balanced

There's always a vegetable on the plate. I grew up in a family where our plates always had protein, carb or starch and a vegetable. Can't get out of that. As a result, there is always a side of vegetables: green beans, broccoli, cauliflower, or peas. Or there's a salad on the side. The salad would meet that need. (Ann)

About seven in ten cooks indicated in their interviews that preparing a well-balanced meal was an important consideration in their decision about what to make for dinner. As with "healthy," "well-balanced" connotes different things to different cooks, but most cooks agree that the presence of vegetables and not just protein and starch at the dinner table is a key element of the meal being well-balanced.

Janet described well-balanced based on a proportion of vegetables to the rest of the dinner: "We try so that most of what we have is half vegetables. What makes up the rest of the plate is not all carbs or all fatty protein." Well-balanced can also mean having minimal fat and not having a disproportionate amount of protein or starch. Victoria was one of only a few of our home cooks to explicitly invoke a model from the expert knowledge of nutrition when discussing her cooking objectives: for her a well-balanced dinner means: "Not too much fat. Hitting the basic food groups."

Traditional

One evening, James cooked the following meal on the grill and in the smoker for his family and four friends. In his cooking journal, he indicated that his primary goal was to cook a meal in his family's traditions (African American from the Southeastern United States). Cooking in his family's traditions pleased both the cook and the diners. Everyone "loved the food" and James enjoyed cooking it: "It's one of my favorite things to do."

> Asparagus
> Cajun sausage, beef franks, and bratwurst sausages
> Chicken wings
> Pork ribs
> Corn on the cob and potato salad

On Christmas Eve, Chloe, who says she most enjoys cooking on holidays, prepared a traditional Italian-American Feast of the Seven Fishes for a full house including her children, grandchildren, aunts and uncles, and cousins.

> We have the Feast of the Seven Fishes on Christmas Eve. Everybody in the house participates. When we walk away from the table we can't believe we ate it. We spend hours on Christmas Eve picking, preparing, and eating.

> Shrimp, cod salad (bacalao), flounder, mussels, other fish
> Spaghetti with garlic and oil
> Roasted veggies with dip

For this occasion, Chloe followed family recipes and enjoyed cooking the meal very much. "In my family's traditions" was her only consideration when preparing the meal.

Cooking foods drawn from the traditions of their families of origin means a lot to many home cooks, especially during the holidays or for special occasions. At the same time, families can and do also create their own traditions through home cooking. The same night as Chloe's Feast of the Seven Fishes, Alice and Michael, neither of whom is of Japanese heritage, and their two daughters across the country in Washington State also prepared Christmas Eve dinner "in their family's tradition": salmon and avocado sushi with edamame. They began making sushi roll-ups for Christmas Eve dinner two years ago and have done it ever since; sushi on Christmas Eve has now become a traditional meal for their household. Someday perhaps their two daughters will prepare a traditional Christmas Eve dinner of sushi for their own families.

A bit less than two-thirds (62 percent) of home cooks in our study said in the interview that preparing a dinner "in my family's traditions" was an important consideration in their decisions about what to cook on a daily basis. We classified ten out of fifty-one home cooks as "traditional" cooks: they often or almost always cook a relatively limited repertoire of dishes in their traditional family cuisine, and cooking in their family's traditions is very important to them. In Chapter 7, we discuss how tradition shapes the practices and meanings of our home cooks in more detail.

While for some of our home cooks, "traditional" cooking meant a commonly recognized cuisine, such as Italian American, for others "in my family's tradition" simply meant the types of dinners or specific dishes that they remembered from childhood. Although ethnicity and traditional food are related for some, for others they are orthogonal. For our respondents, the meaning of traditional cooking and food extended beyond that which could be attributed to a specific ethnicity or blend of ethnicities to twentieth-century American cooking or even to traditions they began themselves in their current household. Consequently, sloppy joes or macaroni and cheese may be considered traditional foods for some home cooks. For Judith, traditional is "something that I grew up with or my husband grew up with. Spaghetti or Swedish meatballs. Something that is a meal that I've always had throughout my life." We should note that neither Judith nor her husband has Italian or Swedish family backgrounds, but these dishes have meaning as traditional for them because they are the foods of their childhoods.

In their daily journals, the home cooks indicated that for 11 percent of the dinners they cooked, preparing something "in my family's tradition" was an important consideration in choosing what to cook that night. Sometimes families cook traditional foods because they enjoy the taste of these familiar dishes. One evening, Andrea and her partner cooked a meal of roasted chicken thighs, gluten-free stuffing, pureed cauliflower, cranberry sauce, gravy, and Brussels sprouts. They did this because they wanted the taste of a traditional Thanksgiving dinner. They achieved their goal: "Everything was delicious."

> We had a nice time on Thanksgiving day at a friend's house, but the food was a little disappointing. We were both still craving a Thanksgiving-like dinner. So that was the goal of this meal. (Andrea)

Novelty/something different and challenging

In their interviews, about four in ten home cooks indicated that it was at times important to them to cook something for dinner that was novel or different from their routine. Cooks who do not aspire to trying something new when choosing what they will cook for dinner sometimes favor traditional meals, cook a standard repertoire, have picky family members, or are less confident in their cooking skills. For example, James must balance his family's preference with his desire "to try something different sometimes. My family prefers I keep to a core. I'd like to try something like lamb chops or goat chops."

In daily cooking, however, the evening meals prepared during the study period were much less likely to be shaped by considerations of novelty (about 15 percent of meals) or challenge to the cook (only about 3 percent of meals). The lesser likelihood of trying something new during the study period than we would expect given the responses on novelty in the interview is most likely an artifact of the relatively short study period: in ten days or two weeks, there simply wasn't enough time for cooks to feel the need to try something new. The very small number of challenging meals cooked during the study period is also no doubt related to time scarcity, which is discussed in Chapter 4. In order to attempt cooking something challenging, home cooks need plenty of time to focus their efforts, and our home cooks struggle to find time to cook in their busy lives.

Several home cooks noted in their cooking diaries that they occasionally struggled with feeling as if their evening meals had gotten "into a rut." Often cooks who seek to please their family members with their cooking find that their families complain of eating the same things and ask for something new. This is, as discussed previously, one of the main reasons why cooks sought out and tried new recipes.

Some cooks (40 percent) seek novelty when cooking for guests or for special occasions. For example, Alice explains, "When we entertain, we like to step it up." In the cooking journals, cooks also noted when a serendipitous shopping experience created the opportunity to try something new. In their interviews, about one-third of cooks (34 percent) said that they also occasionally seek to prepare evening meals that would be challenging to them as a cook and expand their knowledge and skills. In Chapter 8, we discuss the keen cooks, who particularly enjoy trying new foods and ways of cooking and seek to challenge themselves by trying new foods, new flavors, or new techniques.

The personal touch

In their interviews, about a third of cooks (32 percent) said that they strive when making dinner to prepare meals that show their personal touch. For example, cooking dinners for her family that show her personal touch is important to Helen. When asked what this meant to her, she said,

> My homemade meatloaf that is my husband's favorite. Or my tilapia with butter caper lemon sauce. My daughter loves it. (Helen)

For family-first, traditional, and keen cooks, cooking that shows their personal touch may be especially important, but it means different things to them. For family-first cooks like Christina and Helen, food that shows their personal touch is food that shows their love for their family and is something that they hope will make their loved ones feel cared for when they make it for them. For traditional cooks, cooking the foods of their family traditions connects their personal identity with their family of origin. Tony checked "shows my personal touch" as an objective for every dinner that he cooked during the study period. He is a traditional cook (see Chapter 7) who "cooks by instinct." For keen cooks, dishes that show their personal touch are dishes that display their culinary knowledge and skills. For example, Joseph is a traditional and keen cook (see Chapter 8) who indicated that the meals he cooked showed his personal touch, for example, through his use of spices in preparing tuna salad.

Trendy/gourmet

We asked our cooks in the interviews if they considered whether their menu was "trendy" or "gourmet" when deciding what to cook for dinner. Less than 15 percent said they considered making a gourmet meal to be important and only 5 percent considered trendiness to be important. Notably, their cooking journals indicated that home cooks considered gourmet or trendiness as objectives for less than 1 percent of the meals they prepared during the study period. Most of our cooks seemed to view trendiness in cooking negatively. Jeremiah is an exception, although his interpretation of trendiness in cooking appears to represent an increased interest in healthy cooking:

> Yes, we sometimes do trendy. Down South [where Jeremiah grew up] they would keep the grease that they cooked the meat in to cook the vegetables in and we don't do that. We use more olive oil or just butter. We used to put cheese on our broccoli and we don't do that anymore so we might be on that side of trendy a little. (Jeremiah)

Several cooks seemed to hold trendiness in cooking in disdain or to find it mildly amusing. Lois, a keen cook who watches a lot of food television, nevertheless said she didn't follow trends in cooking.

> Like quinoa or kale? I don't go out and buy that just because everyone else is. Mostly because I don't like quinoa, but no, not trendy. (Lois)

Cynthia and Christina and Jack poked fun at themselves for what they viewed as failed attempts to try cooking something trendy.

> We don't do trendy. We tried a lettuce wrap, but it became a lettuce wrap bowl. (Cynthia)

> It is very rare that I will do trendy. The other week I tried to roast a full head of cauliflower [laughs] and I only tried that because I saw it in the *New York Times*. (Jack)

4

Time and the Home Cook

[Cooking is a chore] when I'm pressed for time and I'm already tired. I leave work at varying times depending on the night of the week. Some nights when I come home I'm like oh damn I've got to make something and it's already late and the baby's gonna be, like, tired. I do it anyway, but then I'm like pretty much ticked off. (Lorraine)

We find that, across all types of cooks and all household configurations, the primary factor that takes the joy out of and attenuates the meaning-making of home cooking is a lack of time. Cooks who felt rushed and as if they didn't have enough time to cook dinner the way they would like reported feeling more anxious, less valued, less happy, and more bored while preparing dinner than cooks who felt they had adequate time. Another way time affects home cooks is as a personal factor of domestic cooking: we find that some home cooks, whom we call *planful cooks*, regularly take the time to plan out their menus in advance while others, whom we call *improvisational cooks*, make dinner à la minute or on the fly.

Time is a critical dimension of cooking. Gary Fine (1996) has characterized the restaurant kitchen as a temporal world, where time is the most important consideration and its management represents one of the biggest challenges to success. Success in the professional kitchen is inseparable from timeliness. Timeliness is no less important a consideration in the domestic kitchen when the home cook is making dinner. Most dishes require specific temporal sequencing for preparation and a discrete amount of time for completion of each step (i.e., cooking pasta, sautéing meats, stir frying). If a dish has more than one component that is time-dependent (e.g., pasta and tomato sauce), the cook must keep in mind parallel temporal processes. Moreover, one component of dinner may require the completion of other components. The home cook must know how long dishes take to cook and know how to coordinate those processes. In his ethnography of ten home cooks, de León (2003) found a range of diverse strategies to manage these temporal aspects of making dinner. Some cooks created ample time cushions to deal with any difficulties that might arise. Others noted their start time and were prepared to deal with components that may need more or less time as the cooking process unfolds.

The home cook has additional temporal constraints outside of preparation. Home cooks admittedly do not worry about losing customers if the meal is ten minutes late getting to the table. But dinner may have to be ready at a specific time so that members of the household are not late to events or can watch a favorite program on television. A child missing soccer practice or a musical performance because dinner is late may be an unacceptable consequence of mismanaging time for the home cook. Family members may become annoyed or upset if dinner is too late. Taken together, the home cook must develop an expertise at knowing when to start dinner, monitor progress of multiple processes that are time-dependent, and adjust processes if something is cooking too fast or too slow (de León 2003). Ideally, everything on the menu for the evening is ready at the same time and that time works for all members of the household who are sitting down to eat. Trubek and colleagues (2017) consider this ability—to overcome temporal sequencing challenges—as a component of cooking skills, which they term "food agency."

Beyond the need to get the temporal sequencing of food preparation right, which they share with professional cooks, home cooks face two distinct problems in the temporal organization of everyday life: time scarcity and a lack of synchronicity. Experiences of time scarcity (Warde 1999) occur when the cook has insufficient time to plan, provision, or prepare the evening meal. Time scarcity negatively impacts planning, preparation, and consumption of the evening meal (Gatley, Caraher, and Lang 2014; Jones et al. 2014; Sealy 2010; Storfer-Isser and Musher-Eizenman 2013).

Almost all of our home cooks are employed outside the home. Many of the cooks we interviewed struggle to make dinner on days when they work late or have meetings. Cooking as a form of caring for the family is unpaid work, and when this work is combined with employment, "the two are constantly in tension" as Finch and Groves point out (1983: 7). Time scarcity due to work as well as the demands of children's extracurricular activities creates formidable challenges for the home cook (Sliwa et al. 2015; Wang et al. 2014). For households with younger children, child supervision or interruptions can further steal time from preparation. For several of our home cooks, supervising children while cooking significantly impacts planning and preparation.

To get dinner on the table, the home cook needs to be in the kitchen for a long enough span of time to make dinner. Unlike professional cooks, home cooks have to carve this time out of both their working and family lives. Time scarcity thus becomes a problem for home cooks whose paid work and family members' needs make significant demands on their time (e.g., Hochschild 2012).

Not only does the home cook need to be in the kitchen for long enough to make dinner, but those for whom she is cooking need to be at the table when the food is done. This is the challenge of temporal synchronicity or temporal coordination (Brannen, O'Connell, and Mooney 2013; Southerton, Diaz-Mendez, and Warde 2012; Warde 1999). Timing the dinner to accommodate the different schedules of family members can be a complex task for some home cooks.

Alan Warde (1999) claims that the problem of timing (synchrony) supersedes the problem of shortage of time for many home cooks. Work, exercise, shopping, transporting children, leisure activities, and visiting family and friends require complex and anxiety-provoking organization (Thompson 1996). Many individuals constantly seek to optimize their schedules to do as much as possible, making organizing to meet for family dinner more difficult. "The greater difficulty of getting everyone together, of synchronizing time-space paths lies at the heart of the contemporary predicament" (Warde 1999: 527).

Achieving synchronicity is particularly challenging for households with children. Parents and children may have divergent schedules in terms of sleeping, work, school, homework, socializing, tutoring, athletics, and after-school activities. Even when there is sufficient time for making dinner, a lack of synchrony between schedules renders serving it to the family members at the same time daunting. As children age, attaining synchrony in dinner can become more difficult (O'Connell and Brannen 2016; Vincent and Ball 2007). If sitting down together for dinner is valued as a symbol of family togetherness, an inability make this happen may be interpreted as a parenting failure by the home cook.

Time and emotions when making dinner

How do time challenges impact the home cook? For home cooks, time is the crucial determinant of whether making dinner is a pleasurable experience or not. On a daily basis, our cooks, almost all of whom worked outside the home, struggled with a lack of time for cooking dinner. In his study of French domestic cooks, Kaufmann (2010) argues that cooks have a culinary schematic with two modes of cooking related to time. When there is little time, cooks approach cooking as a domestic chore. When there is more time, cooks can experience and express their pleasure in and passion for cooking (2010: 9). Our study presents converging evidence confirming Kaufmann.

Less joy of cooking

In the interviews, our respondents described the type of occasions when they most and least enjoyed making dinner. Cooks most enjoy making dinner when they are not rushed and have time to think about and focus on their activity. When asked to identify situations in which they most enjoy making dinner, the most frequently mentioned situation was having plenty of time (44 percent). As Nancy shared, "I most enjoy cooking when I have TIME to cook." Likewise Judith wrote: "[I most enjoy cooking] on the weekends or on my days off when I don't have to hurry."

Correspondingly, situations in which they have too little time and cooks felt rushed were most frequently mentioned (46 percent) as the least enjoyable times to cook. Such an occasion was reported by Ann in her journal: "No time to enjoy cooking tonight. We rushed through dinner and homework to get to soccer." Likewise, when asked in her interview for any additional things she took into account in deciding what to make for dinner, Kaye said, "Any time constraints. If I have a lot of time and can spend the whole day then I might try something more challenging. During the week, it's piecemeal. Start with something and make it my own by adding to it."

Cooking felt like a chore at times for all but a handful of our cooks. Having too little time or being rushed was the most frequently mentioned situation (45 percent) in which cooking felt like a chore. A lack of adequate time can turn cooking into a chore and create difficulties even for otherwise confident cooks. For example, Kaye said in her interview that she loves cooking. She is a cook who attributes a great deal of meaning to the role her cooking plays in her relationship with her family. In her interview, Kaye discussed situations in which cooking feels difficult for her:

> When something unexpected comes up. Like if I have plans to be home at five o'clock and be able to start cooking dinner and then one of the kids gets sick and I end up not being able to get home until seven. Then, all of a sudden, I still have to make dinner, but … you know, I'm capable of making dinner in thirty minutes if I have to, but my mind set for that day wasn't a thirty minute day. And I'm thrown off a little bit by that. I mean, I can still do it, but I don't really enjoy it as much. (Kaye)

Sometimes the lack of time caused our home cooks to give up on cooking for that particular day. Pauline recorded in her journal: "I got home from work really late (after eight pm) and actually didn't eat dinner, instead I had a bowl of oatmeal and some fruit. My husband and daughter had sandwiches."

A lack of temporal synchrony—conflicting schedules among household members and the question of when to prepare and when to serve dinner—is another situation that can take the enjoyment out of cooking. For example, Judith is a family-first cook who is a registered dietician with two young teenage children. "Something we could eat at different times when we got home from activities" was a consideration for Judith in selecting what to cook for dinner.

> I enjoy cooking least when I have got to feed everyone in shifts because someone is running out at different times or someone is getting home late. It is difficult to cook the way I would like to when four out of seven nights a week at dinnertime I have to transport the kids to sports events and other activities. (Judith)

Many cooks also felt that cooking was a chore at the end of a long day or when they were feeling tired. A working mother of children ages two and eight, Ann expressed the stress she experiences trying to fit cooking and eating dinner into her family's busy schedule:

> Cooking is a chore when I'm going from one place to another—work/school/practice/back again—trying to squeeze it in. It feels stressful, not enjoyable. "Gotta get dinner on the table, now everyone eat." I eat way too fast. I'm always feeling I need to hurry up. (Ann)

Time scarcity may also interfere with the ability of home cooks to become absorbed by and focused on the task of making dinner. It is the level of concentration that can provide a "flow" experience in the kitchen to cooks (Csikszentmihalyi 1990), the feeling of being "in the zone." During such experiences, cooks experience a clarity regarding goals, a feeling of personal control, and a sense that they are able to overcome challenges. We speculate that time scarcity—particularly among cooks who do not employ efficacious coping strategies to deal with it—will also attenuate potential experiences of flow. Such peak experiences are difficult to achieve when one is distracted by the clock on the wall.

At the end of the diaries, we invited cooks to share with us any additional information or comments they would like. Several took the opportunity to write about the constraint of time:

> Interesting project—made me realize that I would love to have more time to cook more complicated/venturesome meals. Maybe in retirement? (Margaret)

> I can't say I love to cook but I do enjoy cooking for the holidays and special occasions. I enjoy eating dinner and therefore I cook. I do find that the nights I work late (6 pm) I have less desire to cook. (Patricia)

When there is not enough time, home cooks are forced to cut corners, and that may compromise their ability to feel that they have done a "good" job. Family-first cooks have to reach for something quick and easy to cook, but it may be less healthy than they would like. Keen cooks don't have the focused time they need to cook creatively. Traditional cooks may not have enough time to make their favorites. A scarcity of time impacts all phases of the preparation process, limits options, deprives the cook of time to think, and reduces the cooking experience to that of just getting an edible dinner on the table rather than an expression of identity or creativity.

Feeling rushed

On selected days, our home cooks rated how they felt while preparing dinner on seven dimensions of affect including feeling happy, anxious, confident, and appreciated. The home cook's emotions during preparation were reported for a total of seventy-six meals. For roughly one out of four dinners (28 percent) reported in the journals, cooks felt rushed and experienced less positive emotions. Feeling rushed while making dinner was associated with feeling significantly more anxious ($r(76) = .60, p < .001$), less happy ($r(76) = -.52, p < .001$), less organized ($r(76) = -.39, p < .001$), less confident ($r(75) = .37, p = .001$), and more taken for granted ($r(75) = .24, p = .024$). These feelings interfere with the cognitive demands of planning and preparing the dinner and take the enjoyment out of making dinner. For example, family-first cook Judith did not enjoy cooking dinner very much one evening because she felt rushed. She prepared turkey stroganoff, steamed cabbage, and lima beans. She used a recipe from the back of the noodle packet and preprepared ingredients. There were no difficulties in cooking dinner, but she didn't really enjoy cooking and indicated that she didn't really care whether the meal was successful or not: "just that there is a decent meal available, that's relatively healthy."

Recapturing time through convenience

One of the ways that home cooks can deal with time scarcity is to employ foods that are convenient. Convenience food is a wide category consisting of processed and semi-processed foods that are ready to cook, ready to heat, or ready to eat (Jackson and Viehoff 2016). Using convenience food enables the home cook to reduce the amount of time required for preparing dinner and reallocate time saved by using some prepared ingredients to other cooking tasks or domestic activities, including, importantly, child care (Bava, Jaeger, and Park 2008; Carrigan and Szmigin 2006; Szabo 2011). The increased demands on the home cook's time due to the complexity of families' everyday lives, combined with persistent ideals about proper home-cooked dinners, increase the appeal of convenience food (Carrigan, Szmigin, and Leek 2006; Sliwa et al. 2015; Wang et al. 2014).

Because the category of convenience food encompasses such a wide variety of food in various states of preparation, it can be difficult to conceptualize the use of convenience foods in making dinner. For example, while there is no substantial difference in the amount of skills and time required to heat frozen, precooked chicken nuggets or to boil dried spaghetti noodles, the use of the latter does not even count as convenience food for our home cooks. The use of certain preprepared foods such as canned tomatoes has become ubiquitous. Several of the home cooks in our study explained that they only used fresh or frozen vegetables, yet their cooking journals show that they use canned tomatoes. "Cooking from scratch" and cooking with processed ingredients are therefore often conflated, both in everyday life and research.

Despite the lack of conceptual clarity, cooking with processed ingredients or convenience foods is generally looked down upon: "the idea of convenience food is tinged with moral disapprobation" (Warde 1999: 518). Cooking from scratch is constructed as inherently more caring, healthy, and sustainable than the use of convenience food (Meah and Jackson 2017). Alan Warde argues that despite feelings of ambivalence toward convenience food, "many people are constrained to eat what they call convenience foods as a provisional response to intransigent problems of scheduling everyday life" (1999: 518).

In practice, most households combine fresh and convenience foods without making a strong distinction between the two categories (Meah and Jackson 2017) and home cooks may combine convenience and fresh foods in creative ways (Carrigan and Szmigin 2006). Although Alan Warde (1997) posits care and convenience as culinary antimonies, more recent work as well as our own data suggest that they are not. Angela Meah and Peter Jackson's (2017) ethnographically informed research in households with small children and working mothers demonstrates how convenience foods are used by mothers as an expression of maternal care. They find that routines based around convenience foods such as "pizza time" provide home cooks with a way of providing a family meal while increasing interaction with their children. One of their respondents with an eight-month old demonstrated the use of convenience foods such as ready-made, pre-rolled pastry, which could be cut while carrying a child on the hip. The meaning of convenience foods for these mothers became more of an expression of nurturance and caring—giving the family more quality time together—than a reflection of the cook's lack of commitment to make a meal from scratch.

Critics have suggested that the use of preprepared foods can result in an overall loss of cooking skills among the population (Short 2006). But home cooks, we argue, use a range of conceptual, perceptual, creative, organizational, and emotional skills in addition to mechanical or culinary skills: these other skills are needed regardless of the amount of preprepared components they employ. The cook who served hot dogs one day when she was late getting home is also the same cook who can and does make chicken nuggets from scratch, when she has the time. Frances Short concurs, "Deskilled cooks and deskilled cooking tasks are two very different things" (Short 2006: 64).

A simplistic approach that critiques home cooks for their use of convenience foods without considering the context in which they use them overlooks how these ingredients may be used in creative ways that have meaning to the cook. For example, Pamela wrote about an evening meal she prepared during the study period for which she made a salad including canned chickpeas (garbanzo beans). On a Saturday after the week's work at the office, she did her housecleaning, spent time relaxing outside, and then made her dinner.

> Actually, I had a home prepared meal tonight (not cooked). I didn't plan anything. I didn't want to think of dinner after I had finished housework. I just ... went out to enjoy the beautiful day ... when I came home I made a big salad with Romaine lettuce, half of a sweet onion, dried cranberries, walnuts, fresh mushrooms, fresh red pepper, chickpeas, and some cheddar cheese in olive oil and raspberry vinegar. It was filling and healthy. I enjoyed fixing the meal. It was easy, and I was surprised that I had so much on hand to make a really good salad. (Pamela)

Almost seven out of ten of cooks in our study said that when deciding what to cook for the evening meal, convenience was very important. In almost half (48 percent) of the meals logged in their cooking diaries, convenience was noted as an important consideration. Convenience most often implies to cooks a time element: a convenient dinner can be prepared quickly. It also implies ease of cooking: that the meal is not complex and requires little forethought. Some cooks also connected convenience to ingredients: that the ingredients were on hand in the household or that the dish required just a few ingredients.

Convenience to our home cooks did not typically refer to stereotypical convenience foods or heat-and-eat meals but instead to a meal that was *convenient for them*. For example, convenient for Ann means "something I don't have to stand at the stove and watch." Ann has a two-year-old child and told us that she cannot sauté or do other types of cooking that require precise timing and attention while she is keeping an eye on her child. She prefers to cook dishes that can go in the oven or cook on the stovetop without much attention. Convenient for Deanna—who frequently uses a slow cooker appliance—means: "Can I do it ahead of time? Can I still cook dinner after coming home from work?" For our cooks, a convenient dinner menu means:

> Something that doesn't take a lot of time to make. I can buy the ingredients and we can use it for different things. Also I think about how big of a mess I am going to make. (Andrea)

> Something I had in the fridge. Didn't have to put a lot of forethought into. Chicken is always easy. If it is in the fridge, I can quickly throw something together. (Kaye)

> Convenience means basic ingredients. I have them in stock. Five ingredients or less. (Janet)

> Convenient is something you just throw in the oven like a pot pie. Get a whole chicken that isn't cooked but is preseasoned … When we say the word simple we also mean convenient. (Alice)

Cooks provided examples of dinners they considered convenient during their interview: marinated or preseasoned raw chicken, potpies, frozen chicken nuggets and a rice dish, salmon patties or a batch of chili, leftovers, or pizza. Judith said, "A convenient meal is easy to prepare and doesn't take a whole lot of preparation time. When I am rushed, that's the night I bake off some frozen chicken nuggets and make a rice dish."

Review of the cooking journals reveals that—with the exception of an occasional box of macaroni and cheese dinner, hot dogs, rice and sauce mixes, and cold cuts—most cooks in our study used very few stereotypical "convenience" foods in their dinners. Lois is a keen cook, but for her, convenience is "fairly important. By the time I get home I don't have two hours to cook from scratch. But I am concerned about sodium, so I don't use 'convenience' foods." Pamela who lives alone values convenience, especially during the summer, when she would rather be working in her garden than cooking. For her, a convenient meal is a whole cantaloupe with a chicken cutlet. Home cooks acknowledge that convenience foods may be looked down upon. For example, alongside his notation in his journal that he used canned collard greens (Glory brand) one evening, Jack wrote, "Shhh … my mother in law uses the same stuff!"

Some home cooks achieve convenience through provisioning. Online grocery delivery services are used by a few of our home cooks to shop for food. For example, for Lisa, convenience is "somewhat of a priority but I am picky with what I buy. I sometimes do Instacart where you can order groceries and someone will deliver them. I would love to try the Blue Apron [meal kit delivery service] because people really like the food." Mira uses a meal kit delivery service when she and her family are either soon to depart on a trip or just getting home and find it convenient to have premeasured ingredients delivered with no waste. So, while almost all cooks value convenience, what convenience means to individual cooks is embedded in the social context of their household, material constraints, cultural construction of convenience, and other aspirations as a home cook.

Easy and fast food

Many cooks considered easy and fast as components of convenience. In their cooking journals, "easy to cook" and "fast to prepare" were important considerations in over half of the meals documented (easy—57 percent and fast—53 percent). Choosing dishes that were easy and fast to cook came in second only to choosing dishes that the family likes in the 316 meals analyzed. A meal that was convenient, easy, and fast to cook solves the time problem and allows cooks to meet their goal of offering a home-cooked dinner. For example, Chloe explained how she decided what to cook one night in her cooking journal:

> It needed to be healthy and quick. We have a tutor coming at five, basketball practice at six. We will eat at four-thirtyish. (Chloe)

Meals and dishes that were easy and fast were defined by our cooks as something that didn't have a lot of steps, could be prepared within thirty minutes, didn't require a lot of prep work, and could be cooked in the oven. Judith explained what an easy dinner means to her:

> Something that I am cooking after work, yes, it needs to be easy. Something that doesn't take a whole lot of steps. Whatever it is, you don't have to cook it on the stove top first and then move it to the oven. You don't have to make a fancy sauce. Just something straightforward. (Judith)

James considers himself "a fast cook" and values speed of preparation during the week "because there is limited time between the time we get home from work and when we have to get ready for the next day … During weekend might prepare something that takes hours." Fast is less important when schedules are more relaxed.

What cooks find easy varies according to their cooking confidence and their social situation. Virginia considers ease of cooking when deciding what to make for dinner "because I am only an okay cook." Joyce values "dinners I can throw together when everyone is hungry within fifteen minutes. Tacos for example." Lisa finds that "Pasta is easy. You can just put it in a pot of boiling water and the kids can decide what they want on it and we can do the different sauces." Janet, who cooks together with her partner, likes easy because it is more fun:

> Easy is anything you can throw in the oven. I'm not one to make a nice fish or something. We'd have to pay way too much attention to temperature or time. Easy to cook is a few pans and not a whole lot of special technique. It's always been kind of a family fun thing to throw things together. Prep is fun, but technique is more of a concern. (Janet)

When do home cooks plan dinner?

Just when and how do home cooks in our study decide what to make for dinner? Home cooks vary in when they typically plan the dinners they prepare. In their journals, cooks indicated when each evening meal was planned. Although cooks vary widely in the degree to which they plan ahead what they will make for dinner, there was a clear trend: two-thirds of dinners were planned the same day they were cooked. In fact, roughly a fifth (21 percent) of dinners were prepared à la minute: the cook decided what to make for dinner immediately before beginning to cook. The other third of dinners cooked were planned the day before or earlier in the week.

In their interviews, home cooks described how they typically planned the evening meal. As with the division-of-labor question, we find divergences between how cooks described their typical practice in the interviews and their daily practice as reported in the cooking journals. Planning practices are most certainly subject to variations in demands of the day, the week, and the season, sometimes due to shopping in seasonal food markets, as Deanna does, or participating in a CSA share as Sara and Daniel do, or coaching during football season as James does. The modes of planning that our home cooks typically utilize include advanced planning, standing routines, shopping-inspired planning, picking the protein, feeling the mood, and asking the fridge.

Advanced planning and cooking

About one in six home cooks in the study routinely plan and shop for their evening meal menus in advance. A few of these also cook in advance, typically on the weekends for the week ahead. For example, Margaret plans for the week's dinners on the preceding weekend: "We cook four or five complete meals on the weekends. We make dishes for the in-laws and we take them over frozen. Usually do this on Saturday mornings." (We should note that although Margaret uses the word "we," she is the only one who does the cooking.) Such advanced planning is not the norm but does represent an aspirational state for some cooks, such as Sara and Daniel: they wished they were more planful and felt that they shopped too often and too "randomly" during the week. They felt that more planning would reduce the number and the cost of intermittent grocery shopping trips, which were seen as more expensive than fewer, more planful shopping trips.

Weekly routines

Planning dinner is aided by standing routines in which there is a standard menu for certain days of the week (e.g., Taco Tuesdays or fish on Fridays). The routine relieves the cook of deciding what to make for dinner that evening, regularizes the grocery list, is efficiently carried out due to practice, and sets clear expectations among members of the household for that evening. Such routines not only satisfy the primary goal of the cook—providing a dinner that the family likes—but some household members may value the regularity of routine afforded by that dinner. Despite these potential advantages, the majority of our respondents did not report standing routines for specific nights of the week. A few households routinely order pizza on Thursdays or Fridays, and another routinely eats tacos made from a purchased taco kit, also usually on Fridays. Alice's family makes pizza on Fridays, cooks vegetarian once a week, and has Taco Tuesdays. In Ann's household, Saturday's routine involves an adult meal: "Saturday is our little date night. We cook dinner after the kids go to bed. The kids eat earlier. We'll have wine and make dinner for just the two of us. We'll do a fancier meal." Grace cooks for her family throughout the week: her "only indulgence is seafood Fridays." On those nights, her fiancé joins the family for dinner: "I will make dinner for me and him and then everyone eats with us." This is the opportunity for Grace to depart from the traditional Syrian dishes she cooks for dinner during the week.

Although most cooks don't have a routine, some think it might be helpful. Lois's family "tried meatloaf Mondays for a while but it didn't stick." Similarly, Lisa's had done Taco Tuesdays, "not sure why we dropped it." Peter "tried to do Soup Sundays but that didn't really last." Similar to advanced planning, some cooks aspired to routines as one way to solve the dilemma of dinner and regretted dropping routines or wished they could develop them.

Serendipity at the market

Sometimes cooks plan dinner menus when they experience serendipity at the market. Fresh produce at the farmer's market or a nice piece of meat at the grocery may inspire a cook to create a menu around that food. For example, one evening Pauline prepared leftover grilled chicken sausage (heated up), yellow beets, mixed green salad, wheat bread, and grapes. She had bought the vegetables at Fresh Market.

> Finding the yellow beets featured in the store (and on special) was unexpected and fun. It made preparing dinner enjoyable because of the anticipation of trying something new. It was a success in terms of being balanced and healthy and somewhat economical. (Pauline)

Several of the households in our study participated in CSAs and home cooks described such serendipity as a result of discovering ingredients in their share. Similarly, Andrea does some "planning on the weekends. Here we have farmer's market all year around so we will plan out a little bit based on what looks good there."

Picking the protein

Many cooks employed a two-step process to meal planning: selecting the protein prior to dinnertime but leaving the remainder of the menu including vegetables, starches and other sides to be selected from what was available in the kitchen when they began cooking. This often meant taking the meat from the freezer to defrost in anticipation of cooking the dinner later. Sara and Daniel talked of "unfreezing the protein." Once the protein was selected in the morning, Kaye's planning was completed: "I knew I was going to make the pork earlier today when I took it out of the freezer. The rest of the meal sort of just happened while it was in the oven." Cooks who used this strategy sometimes forgot to take anything out to defrost and had to shop again that day if they wanted to cook dinner at home that night.

The journey home

A number of cooks take advantage of the transitional time between leaving work at the end of the day and arriving home to decide what they will make for dinner. Cooks may consult with family members regarding the meal—frequently by cell phone or text—and some occasionally make stops for ingredients on the way. For one meal, Lorraine reported: "[Planned] on the way home from work. After I picked up my daughter from daycare and she said that was what she wanted for dinner." Kaye stopped at the grocery store on the way home: "I had no idea what I would make, and knew I didn't have anything defrosted to make quickly. So I looked for something on sale, but didn't find any kind of meat so I headed to the fish department, which was better anyway, since fish cooks quick."

In the mood

Some cooks do not plan their menus in advance because they wait until they know what they and their family members are in the mood for at dinnertime. Lois says, "I don't know until I get home and ask the kids how hungry they are or what they are in the mood for." Others mention that they choose their menus based on what they are craving or their family members feel like eating. Cheryl says, "I just cook what I am craving." On these occasions, planning and choice is motivated by a desire to make something the family and/or the cook wants to eat.

Ask the fridge

For roughly a fifth of the evening meals reported in the cooking diaries, the cook decided the menu immediately prior to cooking it. Cooks would enter the kitchen, survey what ingredients were available, and plan the meal at that point. In such cases, the dilemma of dinner is resolved by "asking" the refrigerator and pantry what to cook. A number of cooks described this activity:

> Did not plan, made what we had in the fridge … [Planned] ten minutes before I threw it together. (Chloe)

> [Planned] when I looked in the cupboard for what I could make that would be a step above toast. (Kaye)

> We don't like to waste food in our house. We look in the fridge in the morning and figure out what we can do with it. (Cynthia and Christina)

Two approaches to a common problem: Planful versus improvisational cooks

Recall that our cooks vary widely in the degree to which they plan ahead for the evening meal. Two-thirds of the evening meals in the study were planned the same day they were cooked, 14 percent were planned the day before, and 20 percent were planned earlier in the week. We found that we could classify cooks into two distinct types based on their approach to planning their menus and preparing dinner: planful versus improvisational cooks. We consider these ideal types: these two approaches to planning do not mean that improvisational cooks never plan or that planful cooks never wing it. The use of the ideal type also means that the approach to planning of some home cooks is a mixture of improvisation and planfulness such that their cooking cannot be assigned to either type. There are seven planful cooks in the study (about 14 percent) and thirteen improvisational cooks in the study (25 percent).

Planful cooks planned more dinners earlier in the week than the day they were served (60 percent), whereas improvisational cooks planned more dinners the day they were served (71 percent). Whether cooks planned dinner at mealtime was even more striking: planful cooks were less likely to plan dinner at mealtime (4 percent versus 20 percent of all others), ($X^2(1) = 6.88, p = .009$) and improvisational cooks were more likely to plan dinner at mealtime (34 percent versus 10 percent of all others), $X^2(1) = 14.53, p < .001$.

In their study of how nine UK families thought about and responded to their children's food preferences in planning and preparing the evening meal, Thompson et al. (2016) identified two contrasting approaches to family meal routines: "what we fancy" versus "regulated" meal planning (2016: 322). Families who plan meals using the "what we fancy" approach consult and negotiate with children about what to cook for each meal. This may entail cooking separate meals or foods to appeal to each family member's tastes. It is a reactive strategy that is enacted shortly before cooking begins, similar to our improvisational cooks. The "regulated" approach to family meals involves careful preplanning of meals within established meal rituals and repertoires of a series of "set meals" that work for the family: any requests for variation are strongly resisted. The rationale for the "regulated" approach includes the pragmatic considerations of saving time and money and avoiding waste. It also demarcates an ideological difference between parents who strive to teach appropriate eating behaviors by requiring that children eat what the parents choose and parents who are more flexible in accommodating children's tastes. The parents who adopted Thompson et al.'s (2016) regulated approach are similar to our planful cooks, while the "what we fancy" approach is more like that of improvisational cooks.

The planful cook

Mira is probably the most planful cook in our sample. She and her wife plan their week's menu every Saturday. They have a folder of recipes from which they select the meals and generate the shopping list. When shopping, they do not purchase items not on the list. The result is that Mira never has a problem deciding what to cook, "thanks to the menu planning." On the seventh day (Wednesday) of her cooking journal, she prepared a Moroccan themed dinner. She had planned the meal from a recipe in *Eating Well* magazine over the weekend and purchased the ingredients during her weekend trip to the grocery store.

Wednesday: Moroccan-spiced ground lamb with pistachios
Mint and peas
Naan bread
Tzatziki sauce
Hummus and harissa

The meal is a family favorite and her "picky eater" son will eat it with little fuss. Mira enjoyed cooking it "more than average" and considered it to be a success.

Planful cooks typically plan the menus and shop for their daily evening meals earlier in the week. Some do some advanced cooking as well. For example, Patricia decides what to make and does a lot of the cooking for week on Sunday, so she is "ready for Monday to heat it." Patricia will often make a big pan of chicken cutlets, "some parmigiana and some not [parmigiana]," and will use these in her menus throughout the week.

Some cooks find that planning increases their enjoyment of cooking the evening meal. Victoria prepares the evening meals on Sunday afternoon and stores portions labeled for her children in the refrigerator (her daughter has eating restrictions due to high cholesterol). Since she has started to do this, she is "slowly starting to enjoy cooking, which I never totally enjoyed. I am now seeing the advantages of planning." Planning and preparing dinners in advance on Sunday afternoons provide Amanda with one of the most positive experiences of her week:

> I don't know what it is. I just enjoy it. I like getting prepared for the week. Prepping makes me feel accomplished, makes me sane for the week. Everyone is going to be fed. Sense of accomplishment that I didn't just make lasagna for Monday night but I made lasagna for two weeks from now. (Amanda)

How planful or improvisational a cook may be is influenced by the social context of the household. Often, cooks engage in less planning ahead for cooking dinner after having children. Joyce, who cooks for three children ages two, six, and nine, is an example of a cook who used to plan her dinner menus in advance but now no longer does.

> I used to plan more than now. It was much easier. I knew what I was cooking. Had an idea a day. Came up with five or six things to make throughout the week. Always had everything I needed. On a particular night, made what I still had ingredients for. (Joyce)

Now, Joyce says she decides what to prepare for dinner based on what she knows her children will eat and what is easy to prepare.

The improvisational cook

An improvisational cook whom we also classify as family-first and keen, Helen is confident in every technique in our cooking skills inventory. Reflecting the impact of temporal constraints on the home cook, she is an improvisational cook during the week who "might try something more challenging" during the weekend when she has a lot of time. During the week, she:

> Uses fresh things if I can, what's fresh from the garden … If I come home from work and haven't really thought about it, it is "look in the fridge." Okay I have this, this, and this. I can throw all of that together and it makes something good to eat. I pick from what I have. Things will go good with mushrooms or fish, it just comes together. (Helen)

Helen rarely has difficulty deciding what to cook and cooking is not really a chore for her. She feels that making dinner is faster when she doesn't use a recipe. During the study period, Helen planned almost all meals "on the fly" right before cooking them, except for one day when she planned in the morning to make a pot roast in the slow-cooking appliance. On Sunday, the fourth day of her cooking journal, Helen prepared the following dinner "based on items I need to use before they were no longer fresh/good." She planned the meal earlier that day.

Sunday: Penne pasta with homemade tomato sauce
Baked chicken tenderloins with fresh mozzarella and basil

Helen sourced the basil and tomatoes from her garden. She consulted a few different cookbooks "but then winged it regarding the marinara." Her family was at home and enjoyed the meal. Her daughter "doesn't normally like tomato sauce on her pasta but she enjoyed it tonight." Helen did not enjoy preparation that much, citing the tedium of preparing the tomatoes. Nonetheless, she considered the meal a success because everyone enjoyed it.

Improvisational cooks are the opposite of planful cooks on the temporal dimension. Their cooking is extemporaneous: they make up dishes and menus out of the foods they have at hand in their refrigerators and pantries. They rarely plan in advance, and they do not tend to follow recipes. About a quarter of our sample can be classified as improvisational cooks. Improvisational cooks tend to enjoy cooking on a day-to-day basis more than family-first cooks and traditional cooks do, largely because they attach less importance to the necessity or desirability of preparing a home-cooked dinner on days when cooking feels like a chore. Improvisational cooks also suffer less anxiety and take more pleasure in cooking in the face of time constraints than other types of cooks. They rate their cooking competencies relatively high. Arguably improvisational cooks must possess a good deal of confidence, cooking competencies, and knowledge of cooking (and/or perhaps less demanding eaters) in order to successfully employ the improvisational cooks' strategies of making dinner on the fly.

We find that improvisational cooks' self-assessments and cooking confidence are less contingent on the social context of the family dinner than that of other cooks: they (and those they feed) tend to accept a certain element of risk of failure in their cooking practices. For example, Janet and Kristen decide what to cook based on what they find in the fridge and are open to the possibility of failure, as indicated by the need to order in a pizza. Describing planning dinner, Janet answered: "Open the fridge; what can we make from these ingredients." Reflecting on her cooking practice, Janet wrote, "I will try anything ... even if it turns into an 'oh no, perhaps we should go get a pizza' result."

Improvisational cooks may experience the greatest joy in cooking. Lois is an improvisational cook who cooks for herself and her two children. She was the only cook in our study who said that there were no situations in which she liked cooking any less: "I think I actually like cooking all of the time. It is super nice looking into the fridge and the cabinets and seeing what I have and trying to see what I can make with a limited amount of items." Lois's and other improvisational cooks' approach to cooking is in line with the philosophy of literary food pioneer M.F.K. Fisher as exemplified in her wartime book *How to Cook a Wolf* (1942) in which she sought to inspire home cooks to cook creatively with a limited amount of ingredients and a sense of experimentation and adventurousness.

Our cooking journal data suggest that improvisational cooks affectively experience cooking dinner in a way that is distinctive from other home cooks. On the emotion items in their journals, improvisational cooks were much more likely to report feeling creative than others ($b = -1.18$, $X^2(1) = 5.15$, $p = .023$). They were also more likely to feel confident when making dinner ($b = .093$, $X^2(1) = 6.33$, $p = .012$), and more organized

($b = -.90$, $X^2(1) = 4.20$, $p = .040$). Certainly the nature of improvisational cooking is by definition creative. Improvisational cooks have in general high levels of confidence in their cooking abilities. Given that they decide what to cook based upon what they have ready in hand, improvisational cooks seldom experience the disorganization that can result when a cook suddenly discovers they are out of an ingredient needed for a dish they are in the midst of cooking.

One of the strengths of employing the cooking journals is that we were able to identify cooks whose skills—improvisational skills—would have not been evident with other means of non-direct observation such as interviews or surveys. Improvisational skills include the ability to negotiate emerging issues and problems that arise in every home kitchen. These skills include cooks' ability to strategize how to make a home-cooked dinner when scheduling is disrupted, the kids have lots of activities, they haven't defrosted anything, they don't have the parmesan cheese or other ingredient, something burns, or the pan isn't working right. Trubek and colleagues (2017) in their conceptual paper on food agency point to adaptability and flexibility in coping with kitchen challenges as a key determinant of food agency. Although the popular conceptions of cooking skills might include the ability to dice an onion, the improvisational cook also brings to bear an equally important set of skills: the ability to adapt to the inevitable culinary setbacks that occur in the home kitchen (such as the absence of a key ingredient) while perceiving such a situation as a positive challenge.

We argue that improvisational cooks engage in culinary bricolage. Claude Levi-Strauss (1962) used the term "bricolage" (derived from the French verb meaning "to putter about" or "to tinker" and noun referring to a jack-of-all-trades) to distinguish between two ways of investigating and understanding the world, that of the bricoleur and that of the scientist. The scientist uses a set method to move abstractly and hierarchically from axioms to theorems to corollaries, whereas the bricoleur constructs theories by arranging and rearranging a set of well-known materials. Perhaps the more appropriate metaphor for understanding cooks as bricoleurs than the contrast category of scientist is to think of the planful cook as an engineer. Engineers rationally select means to achieve a given project (Turkle and Papert 1990): planful cooks decide their menus in advance and have everything on hand when they begin to prepare the meal. They do not include in their menus foods that they cannot obtain or dishes that call for skills they do not have.

Bricoleurs on the other hand collect skills, means, and materials according to the principle that "they may always come in handy" (Levi-Strauss 1962: 18). Improvisational cooks often like to read cookbooks, not necessarily to follow recipes, but to gather ideas on the principle that they may come to be of some use. They are more likely to pick up random items at the grocery store on the off chance that the fig jam, nutmeg, or smoked paprika will come in handy some evening. Engineers try to work outside of a given context in line with abstract principles and standards, whereas bricoleurs always work within context.

For bricoleurs, the meal arises from the context, what skills and foods are at hand. Bricoleur cooks prefer negotiation and rearrangement of their materials, "playing around" to see what goes with what and what works. "The bricoleur resembles the painter who stands back between brushstrokes, looks at the canvas, and only after this contemplation, decides what to do next" (Turkle and Papert 1990: 136). Improvisational cooks may taste more often and adjust their ideas about what exactly they are cooking as they go along.

Examples of improvisational cooks. Improvisational cooks are not born overnight; instead we find that they have amassed considerable experience and some have developed scripts within which they innovate. As with planful cooks, cooks may become improvisational on the basis of their experiences over time and changes in the social context. Some have memorized recipes and can improvise at the last minute. Others have developed a level of expert knowledge that enables them quickly to recall a meal they were served and recreate it in the kitchen, with some modification. We see too that an improvisational orientation permits cooks to respond deftly to family taste preferences as well as temporal constraints that emerge over the week.

Lorraine is an improvisational and family cook of Irish and Italian background with a husband and a three-year-old daughter. In the past, she used recipes and shopped specifically for the ingredients with a list. She no longer does this because she says she now has "a good variety of spices and that sort of thing." She no longer needs to use recipes because "now I know how to make things." One night Lorraine made cheeseburgers on toast, which she planned "about two seconds before I started cooking it. I had no hamburger rolls and didn't feel like going to the store and I remembered once I went to Friendly's where they serve hamburgers on toast." Lorraine reports that she never has any difficulty deciding what to cook. Lorraine says she is a good cook, "I cook every night whether I want to or not, I never under/overcook anything, I always try to add a vegetable to make something healthier, and whatever I make always tastes good." Although she is average in terms of competence in cooking skills, she feels that she is good at cooking what she wants to cook. Because they don't use recipes, improvisational cooks' personal taste preferences may figure more largely in their cooking practices than the taste preferences of other cooks.

Improvisational cooks Janet and Kristen have no kids and share the planning and cooking for the evening meal. Cooking together plays a role in the emotional life of their relationship: "It's how we go over our days." They do absolutely no planning. They, like other improvisational cooks, value the ability to "use up" ingredients and to produce and consume leftovers. Janet calls herself an "adventurous" cook and loves cooking. She most enjoys cooking on a Sunday when she opens the fridge and makes soup from whatever is left from the week. Cooking never feels like a chore. Janet considers her spontaneity in preparing the evening meal essential to her identity as a cook: "If we're at home, we open the fridge and start throwing stuff into a pot. Only two meals we've actually repeated." Janet and Kristen have developed several scripts to facilitate their flexibility and creativity. In one script, if neither feels like cooking, they look in the fridge and cabinet and one partner selects three possible menus, then the other one chooses: "If neither one of us wants to make dinner, we open the cabinet and find three choices. One of us throws the choices out, and the other one picks." Another script involves choosing a "base" upon which to build dinner using the ingredients available in their kitchen: "There are three families of evening meal: salad base, pizza base, sandwich base."

Chloe is an improvisational and keen cook and has a household with four children between six and fourteen years old and a husband. She rarely uses recipes, usually decides what to make right before she cooks it, and says she is a "creative" cook who strives for "zero waste." Being an improvisational cook enables Chloe to minimize waste. She decides what to cook for dinner based on what the family hasn't eaten lately, what is available, and what needs to be used: she gives the example of having a lot of broccoli in the fridge that needs to be used up and deciding to make broccoli soup for dinner. "If I make something really good, I'll write it down. Never make the same thing twice. Recipes come together in my head based on what I have and how much time I have, rarely make anything the same way twice." As noted earlier for improvisational cooks, Chloe enjoys cooking in "any situation—whether it is cooking or throwing something together."

The temporal dimension of home cooking

Applying an interactionist perspective, we note that there may be significant person-to-person differences in how home cooks respond to temporal challenges (Kaufman-Scarborough and Lindquist 2003). Differences in personal qualities affect how home cooks typically approach the dimension of time in their cooking lives. Researchers have found that individuals vary in the degree to which they respond to the passage of time and deadlines. Time-urgent individuals tend to be sensitive to external deadlines, often set their own internal deadlines and timelines to guide their activity, and are sensitive to the passage of time, often feeling rushed (Landy et al. 1991; Waller et al. 2001). We speculate that planful cooks are more likely to be time urgent. The advanced planning that planful cooks undertake provides a way of avoiding the negative experiences of feeling rushed they would experience if they were planning dinner at mealtime. Likewise, we might expect improvisational cooks to be less time urgent.

A qualitative study employing grounded theory underscores the importance of considering individual differences among home cooks in dealing with time challenges. In interviews with thirty-five women, Jabs and colleagues (2007) identified three coping strategies used by mothers facing time scarcity when making dinner: proactive planning, reactivity or a sense of lack of control, and spontaneous or going with the flow. Similarly, we found differences in how our home cooks approached the temporal dimension of making dinner. Planful cooks engaged in proactive planning, while improvisational cooks were spontaneous.

Time shortages and a lack of synchrony in schedules represent significant challenges for the home cooks' everyday practice. Time, or the temporal dimension of home cooking, presents an interesting place to examine how the interaction of personal, social, cultural, and material contexts shapes how home cooks approach and experience their task. In the following chapters, we turn from considering our home cooks as a group to examining the kitchen lives of family-first, traditional, and keen cooks.

5

Cooking and the Self

I think it's fun to consider how we develop our relationship and identity with cooking. I am the oldest daughter in a large family and my mom did not like to cook. I was a failure in the housecleaning department, but earned my keep [smiley face emoticon] by cooking for everyone. For this reason, I'm really comfortable cooking for groups (eight to twelve people) and I cook to please. I like to know what people like and then I make it for them! As a mom, I am really focused on health and whole ingredients (foods that are not processed). Cooking is one of my favorite things and it was fun to keep this journal. (Teresa)

We share Teresa's interest in how home cooks think and feel about themselves as cooks and in the relationships between food, cooking, family, and self. When we began our research, our primary interest was in how home cooks decided what to cook and how to cook it. In the process, however, we found that home cooks' overall approach—whether the ultimate goal of their cooking practice was to nourish and sustain their family, to continue their family traditions, or to challenge themselves to produce the highest-quality food possible—shaped their beliefs, feelings, thoughts, and practices related to cooking. Furthermore, for most home cooks, cooking was a meaning-making practice that they used to construct and maintain their families as well as their sense of self. The home cook mediates the influence of social, material, temporal, and cultural considerations on the prepared meal; this mediational process is shaped by the cook's own meaning-making, sense of self as a cook, and self-perceptions of competencies.

As Scholliers notes, "Identity contributes to how individuals and groups perceive and construct society, how they give meaning and how they (re)act, think, vote, socialize, buy, rejoice, perceive, work, eat, judge or relax" (2015: 5). Identity and feelings of belonging do not only come from food choices and preferences but also from how we organize, serve, prepare, and cook food. As Annechen Bahr Bugge and Reidar Almås write in their study based on in-depth interviews with twenty-five Norwegian mothers of young children, "women's dinner practice should be understood not only as an act of caring for others (care work), but also something they do for themselves, a kind of identity work" (2006: 204). In the following chapters, we demonstrate how for family-first, traditional, and keen cooks, being a good home cook as defined through their primary motivations and practices is a key mode of self-identification through which they develop, maintain and enact a sense of self. We argue that self-identity involves a continually dynamic process, including the home cook's assessment of their performance, what kind of cook they want to be, and what kind of cook they should be (Higgins 1987; Higgins et al. 1994).

"I am a [blank] cook": How home cooks think about themselves

To uncover just how study participants thought of themselves as household cooks, we asked them during our interviews to complete the sentence, "I am a _____ cook." (See Appendix A for the interview schedule.) The question was modeled on the Twenty Statements Task used by social psychologists investigating self-concept for over fifty years (Kuhn and McPartland 1954). Our expectation was that this question would collect data on the social, personal, and relational self-identity of cooks, that is, how they saw themselves as cooks, perhaps as vegan cooks, Italian cooks, or gourmet cooks. However, almost all respondents answered this question with an evaluative statement on the quality of their cooking: "I am a good cook, a pretty good cook, an OK cook." This suggests that to home cooks, their performance—whether or not they are a *good cook*—is the most salient aspect of themselves as cooks.

Participants' responses to the "blank" cook question yielded a range of evaluative statements revealing their self-assessments as cooks embedded in the social relations of their households. Nearly three-quarters of cooks filled in the blank with a positive adjective such as "good," "pretty good," "pretty competent," or "very good." While regarding themselves positively, their evaluations of their cooking were not exemplary: only one person in our study regarded herself as an "excellent cook." The remaining one-quarter of the cooks considered themselves to be less than good cooks, describing themselves as "ok," "plain," "boring," "no-nonsense," or "not very creative."

We recognize that our sample is not representative of all US home cooks. As a purposive sample, our goal was to examine how a structurally similar set of households reacted to similar challenges associated with the evening meal. In recruiting participants, we were careful to emphasize that we were looking for all types of home cooks, not just those who were particularly skilled, but it is possible that those who felt their cooking skills were below average were less likely to participate and that more confident cooks are overrepresented in our sample.

Self-assessment of cooking skills and culinary confidence is not a straightforward matter. What we have identified as the personal dimension of domestic cooking includes the cooks' skills, confidences, motivations, and cooking modes of identification. In turn, home cooks' understanding of their capabilities and identities as cooks is shaped by the social, cultural, temporal, and material dimensions of making dinner: cooks also have a sense of what they should be doing as a home cook. The social dimension of making dinner includes what occasions and what persons they cook for and the responses of those who eat their food. The cultural dimension includes normative definitions of a "proper dinner" and discourses related to food and cooking such as discourses of gender, health, parenting, and tradition and authenticity. The impact of temporal factors such as time scarcity may induce positive challenge or anxiety, depending upon the cook's self-appraisals. The material dimension of making dinner includes the resources available to the cook (economic and technological) and the material properties of the food itself: did it turn out as it should? Modes of self-identification and other aspects of the personal dimension of home cooking shape how home cooks respond to, engage with, and make meaning of the social, cultural, temporal, and material dimensions of their experiences making dinner. Discrepancies between a cook's self-appraisals and their beliefs regarding what a home cook should be may lead to experiences of negative emotions, depending upon the degree of incongruity. Furthermore, a sense of oneself as a cook develops and changes over the life course: it is fluid, flexible, and situational.

How Patricia and her 32-year-old daughter Emma evaluate themselves as cooks illustrates this complexity. Their household is typical of the twenty-first-century trend toward adult children continuing to live with their parents throughout college or the early years of their careers. Patricia's three children live with her and her husband—the oldest son is in his early twenties as is Emma, and the youngest daughter is seventeen. Patricia and Emma both participated in the study. Patricia does most of the cooking for the household, although Emma will cook for the family when her mother is delayed at work. Emma is learning to cook and likes to try out new recipes. Patricia is a traditional Italian American cook who has cooked for her family for many years and makes relatively technically difficult dishes: torta, roast beef, Italian cookies. She expresses confidence in her ability to carry out a wide range of cooking tasks. Yet Patricia rated herself in the interview as just an "average" cook or an "okay" cook, while Emma said she was a "good" cook.

Emma is unusual among our cooks, because she does not particularly care whether the family likes what she makes or not. She is a keen cook who "will try anything once." Her mother does most of the preparation of the evening meal for the household, perhaps freeing Emma from the concern with preparing food that the family will like.

When asked to reflect upon their self-appraisals after completing the cooking journal, Patricia said, "Yes, I still feel that I am an average cook. I don't have the knack to know what herbs and seasonings go good with other foods. I can't make a good meatball no matter how I try. After doing the food journal I realized what a lack of variety I had with the meals." Emma said, "I still feel I'm a good cook. I like to challenge myself when I cook and when I seek out recipes I never think about a level of difficulty. I'm willing to try anything once."

Based on our limited data, we don't know the real explanation for the more experienced, more competent cook rating herself as only "okay," while the neophyte who cooked only one meal during the study period says she's a good cook. Patricia explains her self-assessment by pointing to a few things she doesn't know or dishes she cannot make, like the meatball. Perhaps being a traditional cook sharing her kitchen with a learning cook who is trying out unfamiliar foods and dishes has caused her to question her knowledge of food and led to her belief that she doesn't know what herbs and seasonings go with other foods and that her cooking lacks variety.

The meatball is a dish that a good Italian American cook would be expected to know how to make well. As a traditional cook, Patricia judges her meatballs to an exacting standard and finds them lacking. On the other hand, Emma's justification of why she's a good cook seems to hinge on her boldness, her willingness to challenge herself and to "try anything once." It seems that her definition of a good cook is developed with her mother's cooking as a contrast category (although she would never say this and loves her mother's cooking). The lack of variety Patricia condemns herself for could be due to her daughter's bringing in new recipes and new ideas about foods, or it could just be the familiar lament that we heard from many home cooks in the study, especially family cooks like Patricia who have "picky" people to cook for. While Emma doesn't care about whether the family likes what she cooks, Patricia has "picky" people (her husband and her son) who she tries to please at dinner. She often makes a dish of macaroni for her husband and son when the dinner menu deviates from the household's relatively limited set of traditional Italian American foods.

Although it is not possible to definitively elucidate the complex process whereby cooks assess their competence and gain their confidence as cooks, we did find some emergent themes in our analyses. At the end of the cooking journal, we reminded our respondents of how they had answered the "fill in the blank" cook question in the interview and asked them if, upon reflection at the end of keeping their cooking journal, they still felt they were a "blank" cook, and why or why not. This generated responses further articulating just what our respondents meant by a "good" cook. Cooks' self-perceptions as cooks are jointly shaped by their own self-efficacy—their confidence in their cooking skills—and the context in which they practice those skills, namely the social environment of their household. We find that such self-evaluations are most often shaped by the reception that their cooking elicits from others in their household or the extent to which their cooking is liked by those they feed. For some cooks, their self-assessment of their cooking was also driven by their own judgment of the quality of the food they produce. Our respondents based their self-assessment as a cook on a number of rationales.

Skills and experience

A large proportion of home cooks base their self-evaluation on skills and knowledge developed over their career of home cooking. A few cooks based their notion of themselves as cooks on years of cooking dinner night after night, without referencing specific skills or knowledge they may have gained through their experience.

Deanna, a family-first cook, described herself as an excellent cook and was confident in her skills on most cooking tasks: "I can make a new meal once and know the recipe by heart after that. I can also add to it and make it better."

Elena is a keen and improvisational cook who makes everything from scratch and identifies as a "homemade cook … I don't use any mixes ever." As an empty nester, "I don't cook as much as I'd like."

Sara is a family-first and improvisational cook who considers herself "a farmhouse" cook. Her husband **Daniel** is also family-first and improvisational and considers himself an "efficient cook," referring to his ability to utilize leftovers.

Jeremiah is a family-first and traditional cook who has an average set of cooking skills and identifies as a "practical cook. I am the person who is more likely to read the back of the rice box. I think I am pretty good at looking at what's in the fridge to see if I can make something better." He prefers tried and true strategies for making dinner and is "really into standard so I make a lot of the same things."

Linda describes herself as a "very traditional" cook and was quite confident in her cooking skills; we likewise type her as a traditional and keen cook. Her husband **Tony** was equally confident in cooking; he specializes in making homemade Italian American food and makes and cans his own tomato sauce; he is typed as a traditional cook as well.

Helen is a keen, family-first, and improvisational cook. She reported a high level of cooking skills, which was reflected in her identity: "I'm a pretty competent cook." In addition, she admits to being a "Food Network Junkie."

Margaret is a traditional, family-first, and planful cook who considers herself a "good" cook and is confident in most culinary skills. When asked if she enjoys cooking, she replied, "I have cooked all my life, for my brothers and sisters, my fiancé and then my husband. And for my children. My mother died young. Cooking is like second nature to me."

Creativity and challenge

Another group of cooks considered themselves to be creative and innovative cooks.

Kaye is a family-first and keen cook who is confident on all light and heavy cooking skills. Her self-assessment echoes this confidence: "I think I'm a good cook. An 'inventive' cook. I like to try new things. I like to read food blogs and I like to see recipes that other people have done and I like to try to incorporate them into what I do for my family."

Janet, who is an improvisational cook, in a child-free household, is both a confident cook and an "adventurous" cook: "I will try anything."

Chloe is a keen and improvisational cook who feels confident on an average number of skills and considers herself a "creative" cook. She cooks a lot of "one-pot" dishes and uses up what "needs to be used."

Emily, a keen cook, was confident in nearly all cooking skills: "I would say that I am a good cook and I do not rely on recipes." After keeping a cooking journal for two weeks, she reflected that "it was nice to actually observe my own habits and I discovered that I am comfortable improvising with ingredients and measurements, confident that the food I make will turn out well."

Several cooks based their self-evaluations on their eagerness to engage with challenging dishes and situations; they perceive making dinner as an opportunity to extend their skills and expand their knowledge. The challenge of making dinner is perceived positively; the home cook motivated to persevere in the face of adversity (akin to the challenge component of the hardy personality, see Kobasa 1979).

Peter is a family-first and keen cook who often integrates new challenges into cooking the evening meals for his family. Rather than rating himself on a good–bad dimension, he instead explained that he is a "messy" cook. "I tend to use a lot of dishes and make a bit of a mess."

Lois is a keen cook who calls herself a "curious home cook." She keenly enjoys cooking as do her children. She reports enjoying challenges and will pick out something that is rated at a more difficult level to learn a new technique and try something new.

Affective experience of cooking

Some of our cooks connected their cooking identity to a positive enthusiasm for the activity. As they discuss their self-perceptions as a cook, they appear confident and committed to the activity in a way that evokes the positive engagement reminiscent of "flow" (Csikszentmihalyi 1990).

Cynthia and **Christina** trade off the task of cooking the evening meal. Cynthia is a keen cook. Both are improvisational cooks and have considerable skills. Cynthia considers herself an "optimistic and very good" cook while Christina thinks herself a "pretty good" cook. They both spoke of truly enjoying the experience of cooking.

Jack is a keen cook who says, "I am a good cook. I know there are people way better than me, but I like to do it and I think I do it well." After keeping the daily journal for two weeks, Jack's perception of himself as a cook did not change: "Yes, I still think I'm a good cook. Others may have much more advanced skills, but I can follow a recipe and prepare something delicious (and unburnt) for my family and myself to enjoy."

A few cooks had negative affect associated with cooking the evening meal, and this affected their assessment of themselves as cooks.

Karen is a drudge who does the majority of cooking for her three children, ten years old and younger, and considers herself a "boring" cook. She doesn't enjoy cooking food and dislikes "all the preparation." She reports only three skills in which she is confident: making mashed potatoes, baking a cake from a mix, and planning a meal her family will like. Her post-journal reflection did not change: "I really don't enjoy cooking and therefore spend very little time doing it. When I do, it's something that is simple, quick and easy."

Overcoming adversity and getting it done

Several cooks based their self-assessment as cooks on their ability to overcome the challenges of the evening meal despite constraints of time, dietary requirements, or logistical requirements of the family.

Lorraine is a family-first cook who reports an average level of confidence in her skills but considers herself a "good cook," due in part to a repertoire of dinner menus she has mastered: "Absolutely—I cook every night whether I want to or not, I never under/overcook anything, I always try to add a vegetable to make something healthier, and whatever I make always tastes good."

Cheryl is a family-first cook with relatively few cooking skills in which she feels confident but nonetheless considers herself "an imaginative cook." This reflects, in part, Cheryl's daily task of planning and cooking evening meals that fit her newly vegan daughter's and her own preferences.

Modest claims

Another group of our home cooks made relatively modest identity claims as cooks. Cooking the evening meal is a task for which they have responsibility, but from which they do not gain a sense of self or personal achievement.

Family-first cook **Brandon** preps the majority of meals for drudge cook **Melissa** to cook in the evening. "I will try to prep in the morning for her and then she has just to throw it together." He is confident in all of the cooking skills, while Melissa was confident in very few. Although he preps most of the evening meals in the household, Brandon modestly identifies himself as a "decent" cook.

Andrea is a keen and improvisational cook who cooks for herself and her partner and has a number of confident skills. Although a keen food enthusiast, she identifies as a "no-nonsense cook. I don't like recipes that take a long time and I like to keep it very simple."

Monique is an improvisational cook who identifies as a "lazy cook" who "prefers dishes that deliver big payouts with minimal effort."

Paige is a family-first cook who must juggle different food preferences of her three children as well as practice schedules when planning dinner. She considers herself a "good cook. Not great but not bad. Maybe boring."

Although traditional cook **Carolyn** has been cooking since she was thirteen, enjoys cooking, and reports a number of cooking skills, she was unable to report how she viewed herself as a cook: "Oh boy, can I come back to that?"

Contingent on the family

Rather than basing their self-evaluation as cooks on their perceived skills and competence or on their affective experience of cooking, many of our cooks expressed a contingent identity. That is, the evaluations by members of the household who ate the food they cooked influenced how the cook viewed his- or herself. These include the family-first cooks whom we discuss in Chapter 6. The ways cooks evaluated themselves based upon family feedback provided by household members ranged from highly positive to fairly negative. Household members could be quite harsh in their criticisms, and cooks often expressed frustration with selective palates and even fear or anxiety that a meal would be rejected. Making a dinner that was liked and eaten by their family shaped how cooks viewed themselves. For families that had selective and nonoverlapping tastes, the cook's self-appraisal tended to be muted. Those contingent self-assessments are subject to change as a result of modifications of family structure, maturation of children, and changing tastes and dietary needs of family members.

Pauline is a family-first cook who reported a high level of cooking proficiency and expressed confidence in nearly every skill. She is a bit more restrained in her identity, considering herself "pretty good" cook owing to her role as household cook. "[I'm] all right, according to my kids."

Joyce is a family-first cook who has children in first grade and third grade as well as a toddler. She reports most light skills but few heavy cooking skills. She considers herself a "satisfactory" cook: "I don't think I'm great. I try. But more times, convenience and ease win out over other factors." Like many home cooks, Joyce's self-perception of herself as a cook is contingent on her family's current composition: "I'm somebody who would like to cook. Like to be better at it. Aspiring. Someday when my kids aren't little, I'd like to get better at it."

Victoria is a family-first and planful cook who reports few cooking skills and says that she is an "OK, plain cook." She shared that her family feels that "cooking's not my forte. You can see that in our meals."

An empty nester who lives alone, traditional and keen cook **Pamela** has transitioned from being the family cook to cooking for herself. Her abilities include most light cooking skills and several heavy skills. Despite living alone, Pamela's identity as a cook is still based on her family's perceptions: "My kids think I'm a good cook."

Lisa is a family-first cook whose mixed self-evaluation reflects the preferences of her household's members: "Half the time I'm adventurous and great and half the time I am not." Her cooking is shaped by the need to satisfy the various preferences of her household members: "I would make a really good meal but then I would make a Rice-A-Roni. I think I am all over the spectrum from fancy to not fancy … I really do like to cook but there is so much stress when making dinner since everyone is so picky."

"Many thoughts rushed into [**Ann's**] head" when asked to describe herself as a cook. When the family-first and planful cook was told she could share all of her thoughts, she shared that she was an "awful, healthy, rushed, juggling, and not very creative" cook. Her confidence in cooking was relatively low, but she does report a number of cooking skills. Ann enjoys cooking and wishes she had more time to spend on it. Although her husband rarely prepares the family meal (only once during the study period), his cooking style in comparison to her own may be what drives Ann to describe herself as an "awful" cook. As a family-first cook, Ann's fear of preparing a meal that her family does not like leads her to stick with dinners that are "safe" for her, causing her to be "not very creative."

What does success mean to home cooks?

Like any other mode of self-identification, it is important for most home cooks to succeed at making dinner based upon their own criteria. Home cooks develop their own goals and criteria on which they are able to assess their performance as a cook; sources may include personal experience observing other cooks (e.g., mom, grandmother, or friends), cultural influences (e.g., print media or the Food Network), or other social contexts. Perceived success on these dimensions can be a source for a growing sense of identity as well as self-efficacy: that the cook can succeed in preparing a "good" meal in a variety of situations (Bandura 1986). Family-first cooks judge themselves based on their ability to nurture and nourish their families with dinners that are well liked and relatively healthy. Traditional cooks judge themselves on their ability to prepare specific dishes that taste and look as they should according to traditional standards. Keen cooks judge themselves on their ability to make food that tastes and looks as it should according to the standards they have adopted based on their knowledge of food and cooking. In the following chapters, we explore in depth how family-first, traditional, and keen cooks think and feel about cooking, how they typically approach the task of making dinner, and how cooking functions as self-making for them. Here we look at how all the cooks judge their success in making dinner.

Family dinner is a complex social interaction. To be successful, family dinner requires the alignment of the goals, feelings, skills, and knowledge of those who cook with the goals, feelings, and tastes of those who eat. These alignments and negotiations take place within the context of structural constraints such as time available to cook, family schedules, and what foods are available in the kitchen at the time that cooking begins. To investigate what success means to home cooks, we included a question in the cooking journals for each dinner they prepared: "Considering what was important to you in preparing tonight's meal, do you feel the meal was a success? Why or why not?"

Consider one of Pauline's dinners as a window into the complicated ways by which successful home dinners are constructed by home cooks. She prepared a meal of shrimp Alfredo with spaghetti squash, fresh broccoli and fresh corn on the cob. Her daughter had requested that she cook the main dish, which the family hadn't had for a while. Pauline could not find the recipe she'd used before, so "a simple Google search brought up several options, from which I chose one. But, I varied the recipe based on others that I saw." Pauline experienced some difficulties cooking the meal including:

> the recipe snafu and I discovered that we are out of one important ingredient—parmesan cheese (the last person to finish the bottle did not put it on the grocery list—yes, that was the husband!) (Pauline)

But despite the difficulties and the missing cheese, Pauline judged the meal to be a success and was pleased that there would be leftovers for the next day's meal:

> My daughter was thrilled—the house smelled good. I knew it was a healthy meal. I'm not sure that my husband was too thrilled that the cheese was missing, but he didn't complain (the way that I know is that he is not taking the leftovers to work tomorrow—and he loves shrimp! That's okay, the leftovers will make it to dinner tomorrow). (Pauline)

Remarkably, only seven (3 percent) of the 256 dinners rated by cooks in their journals were considered to be failures. Attributions for why dinner failed were quite varied. For some keen cooks, failure derived from their own assessment of the quality of the dish they prepared. Elena considered her beef tacos a failure because they "didn't taste right. Needed seasoning." Likewise, Alice considered one dinner unsuccessful due to a "spaetzle failure" rate of 75 percent. In another case, Kaye's husband cooked a meal for her children when she was unable to cook; according to Kaye, "it was a disaster!" because it consisted of processed foods. For other family-first cooks, an attribution of failure was based on feedback—either explicit or implicit—of household members who ultimately ate the dinner. Joyce reported failure based upon leftovers, "which weren't much of a hit" with household eaters.

On the positive side, almost all of the (97 percent) dinners logged in the journals were considered successful by the cooks who prepared them. Our home cooks attributed their success to factors including acceptance/rejection of the meal by others in the household, speed and efficiency of the meal preparation, and their own evaluation of the meal's quality in terms of taste and nutrition. These attributions for success are discussed in detail below. Before doing so, we may wish to reflect upon the overall magnitude of success: just why are our dinner cooks so successful?

There may be very little failure in making dinner because almost all of the home cooks in the sample—family cooks, drudges, or enthusiasts—have substantial experience in what they do. Most of our cooks have been preparing the evening meal multiple nights a week for a combination of adults and growing children from several years to several decades; the cooks possess thousands of days of experience dealing with variation in dishes, circumstances, diners, schedule, etc. They have learned to adjust their own expectations and to align their dishes with the preferences of those around their table. They have developed a toolbox of culinary tricks for dealing with time crunches, unexpected company, sick children, and soccer practice. A parsimonious explanation for why so many dinners were viewed as successes by their cooks is provided by food historian Rachel Laudan's (2017) mother's definition of a good cook: "the cook who has a hot meal on the table at the appointed time." Feeding their families a home-cooked meal has great value for home cooks. Just getting a meal on the table—just doing the home cooking—may be enough to render the outcome of the cooking a success in the eyes of home cooks.

In his study of the meaning of cooking for French home cooks, Kaufmann suggests that successful meals are a way of promoting the value of family (2010: 85). When asked why they considered the dinners they cooked to be successful, our home cooks provided several rationales. What did success mean to cooks as they reflected on the dinners they had made?

The family liked it

The most frequently reported measure of success was that the family liked and ate the meal that was prepared for them; this was mentioned for 36 percent of dinners cooked at home. Indicators to a home cook that the family liked their dinner were often obvious and sometimes subtle. In many situations, the home cook observed the quantity of the meal that was consumed by those around the table: if the family ate a lot, they liked it and therefore the meal was a success.

> If there are no leftovers, I consider it a success. (Carolyn)
>
> Meal was a success—everyone had seconds! [Drew a smiley face] (Helen)
>
> Everyone ate it and had seconds. My wife is taking leftovers for lunch. (Mira)
>
> Yes, because my sister ate the whole plate (and asked for more mashed potatoes). And she made a point of saying that she never ate mashed potatoes before I started making them. (Lorraine)

One example of consumption-as-liking is provided by Ruth, who lives in a California city renowned for its restaurants and cooks for her fifteen-year-old son, whose feedback was the key determinant of her perception of her success. For example, one night when Harry returned home from a trip, she cooked a menu that she had planned the previous week. She shopped for bread and cheese at separate stores, while also planning to use up some high-quality ricotta cheese she had at home. Ruth made baked ziti using a recipe she learned while studying in the Northeast and served it with broccoli, green beans, and bread. "Harry loved it so much that he ate too much and then felt sick!"

When cooking previously successful menus, cooks are confident that their success will be repeated and often favor the "tried and true." Emily anticipated her black bean and corn soup would be a success based on its track record in the household.

> [It's a] pretty forgiving dish .... Everybody loves this soup ... It's on our regular rotation and I always enjoy preparing it because I know it will go over well. (Emily)

In many households, whether or not the children liked the meal was a key indicator of success. For example, Sara and Daniel reported many meals that were moderately successful but "not a raging success because the kids didn't love it." Every attribution of success in their cooking journal was linked to whether or not the children liked the meal. For others, success can be measured by family members' satisfaction. If family members are satisfied with a meal, they won't go looking for something else to eat after dinner. For example, one night Kaye wrote, "My family ate, and my husband didn't go scrounging in the fridge for extra stuff. That sums up success in my house!"

It was fast and easy

Nearly a third (32 percent) of dinners were considered successful because the home cook was able to quickly prepare them or because they were easily prepared. Most often, the context of this particular evening meal made a fast and easy meal desirable for the home cook. For example, after arriving home exhausted from a long trip, Monique and Joseph made peanut butter and jelly sandwiches that "fed me in a hurry: our objectives were met ... No joy, just thankful there was something in the house." Emily attributed success for one meal to her selection of a fast and easily prepared dish that was a tried and true success with the children: "I like to make the greatest hits when I have to work late." Teresa's son was sick several days during her cooking journal, so when he was able to eat, she needed something fast and easy to prepare that was also a comfort food for him. These meals were considered successes because they suited the particular context of the family's day.

A quality meal

Just over a quarter (29 percent) of successful meals were considered as such due to the home cook's appraisal of their quality. For our cooks, a quality meal was defined based upon the food's taste or how well it was cooked and the perceived nutritional value or healthiness of the menu.

> Yes, because I cooked the chicken perfectly and just about had everything ready at the same time. (Judith)

> Yes, it was a success! Usual reason—easy and delicious! (Ann)

Aside from taste, home cooks also considered meals that were perceived as particularly healthy to be a success, sometimes even in the absence of being liked by everyone who ate it. Although Melissa and Brandon considered everyone liking it as one sign of success, they also reported meals that were considered successful because the adults ate something healthy, although the children did not like the healthy ingredients. For example, one successful dinner consisted of beef stew, which included vegetables sourced from their CSA share and a stop at a grocery store earlier in day: "The kids did not care for it all that much since there were a lot of root vegetables in it. It was [a success because it was an] easy to cook, nutritious meal despite the fact that not everyone liked it."

Leftovers as success

Leftovers—both their consumption and their creation—were cited as a source of evening meal success by one out of ten (9 percent) of our cooks. For example, Deanna said, "I successfully used leftovers and made it not feel like we were eating leftovers." With his husband and son at home, Jack cooked chicken curry, rice, roast cauliflower, and a separate dish for the child. He enjoyed the cooking process and claimed success due to the meal's taste, the expression of his skills, and the generation of new leftovers for the household:

> I cooked something delicious from scratch, thanks to having more time on a Saturday. I was glad to use some food that we needed to cook before it lost its freshness (the chicken). The recipe also yields a lot of leftovers to enjoy later this week. (Jack)

Thoughts on success

A handful of failures aside, it is striking that fully 97 percent of dinners were judged by those who cooked them to be successful. Home cooks face numerous challenges in deciding what to cook for dinner. They must juggle temporal constraints and family schedules, they must negotiate the tension between their motivation to feed their family healthy meals and their family members' differing likes and dislikes, they must create a meal out of what food is available in their kitchens, and they must maximize economy. When the family finally sits down at the table (even if they do so in shifts), the home cook wants above all for them to eat their dinners. Even home cooks whom we label drudges are good at getting the meal out and can make something that people will eat. They don't like the process, but they carry it out. It appears that by overcoming the challenges they face when they confront the dilemma of dinner and put an edible dinner on their family's table, home cooks feel they have succeeded in their task.

After cooking a meal one evening that could be eaten in three different locations (including the car on the way to an extracurricular event), Judith reported a success: "Relatively, we ate a healthy meal, it wasn't take-out." She added, "I don't always care whether the meal was a success, just that there is a decent meal available that's relatively healthy."

Modes of identification as home cooks

What role does home cooking play in self-making in the early twenty-first century? For family-first, traditional, and keen cooks, being a home cook is a key mode of self-identification. Our concept of the types as modes of self-identification follows Jeremy MacClancy's (2004) thinking that the use of "modes of identification" rather than "identities" is preferable as modes are more indicative of the fluidity, multiplicity, and relational aspects of identities.

Analysis of the motivations and practices of domestic cooks—what is important to them about their cooking and their usual practices in planning, shopping for, and cooking dinner—enabled us to construct four categories of home cooks: family-first cooks, traditional cooks, keen cooks, and drudges. Family-first cooks are motivated primarily by their families' preferences and needs. Traditional cooks prefer to cook a limited repertoire of dishes they perceive as traditional. Keen cooks enjoy challenging themselves to improve their knowledge and skills regarding food and cooking. We find that these distinct approaches or orientations to home cooking order and shape how cooks negotiate the cultural, material, and social factors that make up each evening's cooking event and impact how they think and feel about cooking for their families. Being a family-first, a traditional, or a keen cook informs how a home cook evaluates the discourses of health and food, tradition and authenticity, and good cooking. These modes of identification represent distinct ways of engaging the social, cultural, and material dimensions of making dinner.

As different approaches to making dinner, the types of home cooks can also be seen as social psychological orientations to making dinner. As such, different types of home cooks will tend to utilize different cognitive schemas for thinking about dinner; exhibit different behavioral tendencies in planning, provisioning, and preparation; have different goals or objectives for their cooking and different levels of confidence in their ability to achieve these; and experience different affective reactions during the production and consumption of dinner. Different orientations toward making dinner provide distinctive schemas or cognitive frameworks that organize how home cooks think about making and eating dinner and render certain aspects of the situations of cooking and dining more salient to them.

Cooks can and do have multiple modes of identification: we have traditional cooks who are also keen, keen cooks who are also family-first cooks, and every other combination. Some cooks are drudges and their cooking is just another household task for them, unimportant in their self-making. Some cooks move back and forth between modes depending on the occasion and the amount of time they have to devote to cooking. And some cooks do not have a coherent mode of identification in regard to cooking. We find that over the life course, cooks may adopt different orientations to cooking. A family-first cook's last child leaves the house and she has the time to return to her formerly keen interest in food and cooking. After the loss of a grandmother, a home cook is motivated to recreate her traditional cooking for his own dinner table. A keen cook marries, adds stepchildren to her dinner table, and sets about binding the new family together by caring for them through her cooking.

Given that interpretations of dinner vary by orientation, different cooks will have divergent affective reactions to the same situation. Picture a family sitting around the table just finishing up dinner. The home cook looks around at the family dinner that she or he has created through planning, provisioning, and preparation. What home cooks perceive and how they think and feel about the situation they have made and are a part of is shaped by their cooking orientation. The drudge pushes back from the table and thinks, "Another dinner done. Is there time for a walk?" The traditional [Polish American] cook looks around and thinks, "Look at those beautiful halupkies [cabbage rolls]. Almost as good as grandma's." The keen cook takes a final taste of the entrée and thinks, "Hmm, that was good. Think I'll try a dry rub instead of a marinade next time." The family-first cook looks around the table and thinks, "Oh, look at us. I love us."

6

The Family-first Cook: "The Point of My Cooking Is to Nourish My Family and Make Others Happy"

On a Thursday night, Jeremiah cooked dinner for himself, his husband Jack, and their preschool son Mason. Jack and Jeremiah share the cooking responsibilities in their household, cooking solo on different days according to whose work schedule can best accommodate making dinner. They both dislike making dinner most when they are getting a late start and both cite a crying or fussing child as a factor that decreases their enjoyment of cooking. Jeremiah described a successful dinner in this way: "We all got to eat together at a reasonable time. We were able to have a good conversation with no melt down during the meal."

If Jeremiah had only himself to cook for on that Thursday night, he would have eaten turkey soft-shelled tacos with rice and beans, a standard meal in their household that Jeremiah really enjoys. In their joint interview, we found that their tastes diverge. When Jeremiah explained, "I am really into standard. So I make a lot of the same things," Jack quickly followed with "I hate to eat the same thing all of the time. I like to have variety." Because Jack had "been asking for food a little out of the ordinary," the menu that Jeremiah chose to prepare included:

Thursday:	Skillet parmesan penne pasta w/sausage, baby spinach, sun-dried tomato and yellow pepper cooked in chicken broth (one dish)
	Pillsbury crescent rolls
	Perdue chicken nuggets (for Mason)
	Chobani strawberry yogurt (Mason dessert)
	Cara cara oranges (Mason dessert)

The food was delivered via a major grocery chain's home delivery service, which they use weekly. Jeremiah planned the meal that same night. He wanted to make a meal that was easy to cook, fast, healthy, well-balanced, comforting, liked by his family, and was something different. He followed a recipe from the cook book *The Best 30 Minute Recipes* and used canned chicken broth and bagged baby spinach in the pasta dish. That evening, Jeremiah "did not dislike cooking, but did not necessarily enjoy it." This is because he experienced some time scarcity and some parenting challenges while making dinner:

> I picked up Mason after work later than planned and stopped at the playground and got home later than planned. Mason had a temper tantrum once we got home, potentially because he was hungry, and emptied a box of teddy grahams all over the kitchen. Jack was also annoyed to be eating so late. All of this distracted me and stressed me while I was cooking. (Jeremiah)

Although he didn't really enjoy cooking the meal and it wasn't what he would have eaten if he hadn't been taking his family's tastes into account, Jeremiah nevertheless judged the meal to be a success: "I think everyone enjoyed it. Mason ate a lot of it and the main dish contained important healthy elements."

Jeremiah's Thursday-night dinner illustrates several of the typical concerns and motivations that shape how family-first cooks think and feel about food, cooking, family, and self. He needed to create a meal that would satisfy the tastes and preferences of his family members—including a young child—while also being what he considers to be healthy or nutritious. He faced temporal and logistical challenges related to work and childcare that caused him to experience stress as he struggled and failed to get the dinner on the table at the expected time. He paid attention to the emotional needs of his child and husband. He had to clean up the teddy grahams. Despite all this, he put a good dinner on the table and judged the meal to be a success because his family ate it, they enjoyed eating it, and it was relatively healthy.

Family-first cooks: It's about family

Kaye is a family-first cook who judges herself on her ability to provide well-liked, healthy meals. She associates home cooking with serving the emotional as well as the nutritional needs of her family:

> The point of my cooking is to nourish my family and to make others happy. I love when my kids have a meal where they look at me and say, "This is the BEST pork chop I've ever had!" and then they proceed to finish all their food. If it makes others happy and keeps them healthy, then I've done a good job. (Kaye)

Family-first cooks use food to nurture their family members and to create feelings of care, comfort, and "home." As Coveney writes, "The modern family is realized in family mealtimes" (2006: 139). The meaning-making and practice of family-first cooks are shaped primarily by the social factors of family composition and by how family members react to their cooking. How they think and feel about cooking is also influenced by cultural factors including discourses and ideologies about family, gender, parenthood, and health. These social and cultural factors intersect to make possible the construction of a sense of self in which nurturing and caring for the family through cooking is an important source of meaning in their lives: these are the cooks whom we have classified as "family-first."

We classified twenty-eight out of the fifty-one home cooks in our study as "family-first cooks." The ideal type of family-first cooks hinges on their motivations and practices. The cooking practices of family-first cooks are primarily motivated by their desire to provide healthful, delicious meals for their families. They derive great pleasure from seeing their families enjoy their cooking. Family-first cooks place much emphasis on providing home-cooked dinners for their families. Their cooking journals demonstrate that many of them will go to great lengths to achieve this goal, despite the challenges that everyday life with a family inevitably poses. Home cooking is central to their self-identities and to their conceptualizations of their family life.

Family-first cooks are especially motivated to be a home cook who consistently prepares delicious (and possibly healthy) evening meals that are eagerly consumed by everyone at the table. The family is nourished on a daily basis through dinner, strengthened through commensality, and comforted by the family table. The family cook that one should be is difficult to attain on a consistent basis given the factors (e.g., social, temporal, material) that impact what the home cook prepares each evening. When the family doesn't like what was prepared for dinner, this discrepancy may lead the family-first cook to be particularly upset and anxious: they have failed at being a family cook (Higgins 1987).

The key feature driving the family-first cooks' choices of what and how to cook is whether family members like and will eat the food they prepare. For example, we asked the home cooks to tell us what menu would best represent who they are as a cook. Family-first cooks referenced family preferences in their answers. Deanna said that lasagna would be the meal that would best represent her as a cook: "You can add to it and change it a little bit and people will still enjoy it, maybe even more than they did before." Lorraine's representative meal was "definitely spaghetti and meatballs—my favorite—and also it's quick and easy and my daughter and I both love it." When asked what meal she would prepare given unlimited amounts of time, money, and talent, Melissa's reply was "whatever each of the kids would have eaten." Asked for her representative meal, Kaye wrote:

> We do all love pork chops (my kids LOVE their pork products!), with some mashed potatoes (with a bit of cauliflower snuck in for good measure) and broccoli and salad and biscuits and homemade gravy. And a GIANT homemade chocolate cake. (Kaye)

Lisa is a family-first cook who struggles with juggling her family's taste preferences. A creative professional who works from home, she faces less time scarcity than most of the other cooks in the study. She is the primary cook for her blended family, including her husband and five children and stepchildren ranging from age two to seventeen. Her typical evening meal is very "kid friendly, pasta, chicken nuggets from scratch, salad, grilled hamburgers and hot dogs." Deciding what to cook for dinner is "very stressful" for her. She plans what she will make for dinner during the day or when she is at the grocery store. "Thinking about how to please everyone" is hard for her: "Two kids don't like veggies and one kid doesn't like fish. I also try to consider what I like."

> I have trouble deciding what to cook every day. Sometimes it's that I haven't thought it out and I really don't have much in the fridge. I also have to figure out what the kids will eat. I just make a lot of pasta … I really do like to cook but there is so much stress when making dinner since everyone is so picky. (Lisa)

How family-first cooks experience cooking

At its most basic level, home cooks do feeding work to provide nourishment for their families. This means that the food must be nutritious and that sufficient quantities must be eaten by family members. In their interviews, all but two cooks indicated that preparing a dinner that would be liked by their family was important when deciding what to cook for dinner. Doing cooking for others' tastes requires knowledge of what they like and dislike (which can change over time, relatively frequently for children), knowledge and ability about shopping—where and how to purchase the foods they will like—and the knowledge and ability to prepare the food to their standards. "Coping with the emotional work of cooking requires skill" (Short 2006: 61).

Do family-first cooks have a different day-to-day experience when making dinner than other cooks? Cooks reported their emotions while making dinner for seventy-six meals. Using a statistical technique known as hierarchical linear modelling (HLM), we tested whether the emotional experience of making dinner was distinctive for family-first cooks. We found only one statistically significant difference between family-first and other cooks in terms of emotions: family-first cooks felt more rushed when making dinner ($b = -.83$, $x^2 = 4.55$, $p = .032$). Why do family-first cooks feel more rushed than others?

Most family-first cooks have children in the household and many of these households include young children. Almost all of our cooks must find time to cook after a full day of work. Synchronicity is also a greater problem for households with children. Many of our home cooks with children face scheduling challenges, the challenge of making dinner while also supervising kids, and the goal of preparing a meal that the children will like. For example, Pauline expressed feeling rushed: "I have many advanced cooking skills, but I don't always use them due to limited time."

In their interviews, home cooks said that providing a healthy meal was most important (91 percent) when choosing what to cook for dinner; providing a meal that their family likes (79 percent) was the second most important consideration. In actual practice—as revealed in the cooking journals—cooking a dinner that their family likes (61 percent) was markedly more important than healthy (42 percent). Easy to prepare was tied with fast to prepare (56 percent) in second place. Comparing the daily practice of family-first cooks to other cooks revealed that family-first respondents considered "what my family likes" for 76 percent of dinners, compared with 48 percent among other cooks ($logit = 1.28$, $X^2 = 8.83$, $p = .003$).

Teresa said, "As a mom, I am really focused on health and whole ingredients (foods that are not processed)." Managing household members' taste preferences and balancing the desire to cook healthy meals with the need to provide food the family will eat are challenges for the family-first cook. Because it can be difficult to create meals that everyone in the family will eat, family-first cooks are rather conservative in their choices and often repeat dishes that have been well received. Said Pauline: "I try to cook healthy meals, but if the family doesn't like it, I won't do it again. You know I steer within certain guidelines, finding things that the majority will like." Typical meals that family-first cooks in our study prepared include chicken, tacos, meat loaf, homemade pizza, and pasta dishes.

In comparison to the other types of cooks we identified, family-first cooks are particularly likely to view cooking as a chore versus a pleasurable activity or hobby. Sometimes this is because they persevere in preparing dinner even on those nights when the exigencies of work and family are particularly burdensome, when there is little time and they are rushed, or when there is illness or emotional upset in the family. Other times this reflects the difficulties of making a dinner that will serve the nutritional, emotional, and social needs of the family while still being well liked.

> Cooking is a chore when you just don't know what to cook. Sometimes if I've been out all day and come home late, it's either macaroni or call out. Only because my husband and son are so picky. It's not like we can say, "let's make this" and everyone will eat it. I'll make something else for the others. If I decide to make fish, I'll make macaroni for them on the side. (Patricia)

While cooking for households that include young children may sometimes be less enjoyable and more stressful, it also brings great pleasure. For Jeremiah, cooking feels like a leisure activity "when I am experiencing cooking through the eyes of my son." Jack says, "It is a treat to prepare a good meal for my family." Regardless of the age of those for whom they cook, family-first cooks report deep satisfaction when they prepare meals that are well liked by their family members.

Cooking for children: "Now … it is more about making something we can get him to eat too."

Home cooking is, as we have argued, a complex matter of individual behaviors, cognitions, and emotions that are interrelated with cultural, material, temporal, and social factors. The personal and the structural elements of home cooking change over the life course, as home cooks take on and move out of roles that have implications for their cooking practices. Transitions in household composition are a social factor that intersects with personal factors to shape how cooks make dinner and how they think and feel about cooking (Blake et al. 2011; Laska et al. 2012; Leech et al. 2014; Virudachalam et al. 2013). The changes and continuities that home cooks enact as a result of changes of household composition and life-course transitions may be considerable.

The presence or absence of children at the dinner table often changes almost everything about the practice of home cooks, at least in those families where children usually eat with the adults. The cooking lives of Jack and Jeremiah exemplify the notion that the presence and age of children in the household shape the meaning and practice of cooking the evening meal. Jeremiah said,

> It is interesting us giving this interview now with a twenty-month-old as compared to before having our son. We used to try and cook with a cookbook and now we are a little more traditional and don't try as hard. It is more about making something we can get him to eat too. (Jeremiah)

The presence of children in the household tends to change cooks' practices and motivations significantly and can transform a keen cook who relishes learning new ways to make dinner into a family-first cook whose primary goal is to produce a palatable and relatively healthy meal. For example, Pauline, who has one high school-age daughter still at home, explained, "I have many advanced cooking skills, but I don't always use them due to limited time. And, maybe I've lost interest as my family has grown." Her cooking skills and the ideal and representative meals she provided in her interview and journal would place her in the keen cook category, but her day-to-day cooking at this point in her life does not.

A number of cooks experience less enjoyment of cooking after they have children. For example, Elaine who has two children under the age of ten told us:

> I least enjoy cooking right now. I used to love cooking a lot and still enjoy it but it feels so much more like a chore. Because I'm a mom now and raising children. Before that I considered it more recreational and I loved it. (Elaine)

So cooking for children can turn what had been a pleasant, recreational leisure activity into a mundane chore. One of the ways that domestic cooking changes when there are children in the family is a heightened sense of responsibility to provide nutritious meals. This challenge is compounded by increased difficulties in cooking to suit family members' tastes when young children's tastes may be very limited—the notorious "picky eater"—or change rapidly. Most people who have cooked for young children can attest to these difficulties: a food that was happily eaten one day becomes anathema the next, a child who only eats one thing, a child who, seemingly, eats nothing. The dinner table can become an arena for power plays between parents and children who wield their refusal to eat as a strategy of resistance to parental authority (e.g., O'Connell and Brannen 2016). Family tensions over eating and not eating can make the dinner table an emotionally fraught space.

Home cooks attempt to balance their desires to provide an ideal of a healthful, delicious meal happily eaten by their families with the reality that sometimes the family just won't eat their dinners. Paige must negotiate her children's pickiness:

> Have to have some kind of starch and will mix in a vegetable with it. A lot of times there are certain vegetables that certain kids don't like. So I have to have two different kinds of vegetables. Cassie will eat broccoli and she has to have cheese on it. The boys absolutely refuse to eat broccoli. They will eat salad all the time. Cassie will not eat salad. Sometimes I have to mix it up. Broccoli for her and salad for them. (Paige)

Cooks who have to combine childcare and cooking, like Jeremiah in the vignette that opens this chapter, also have to contend with the challenges of combining toddlers, knives, and hot stoves. Several cooks we spoke with explained that they sometimes had trouble managing looking after a child and preparing dinner. For example, Ann has a two-year-old son and says she

> prefer[s] things that I don't have to stand over and watch ... like meatloaf, you can put it in the oven and wait for it to cook. Or roast potatoes in the oven. The most I

can do is sauté chicken. I'm by myself and taking care of my two-year-old son and getting my daughter's homework done. It's hard juggling it all with something [to cook] that requires a lot of attention. (Ann)

Cooking for children in the household is a task that is constantly in transition. As children mature, their food preferences change and expand. Recall Joyce, who used to be a very planful cook, but now she decides what to make for dinner based upon her children's likes and what is available. Peer influences, school transitions, and extracurricular activities create challenges to the synchrony and harmony of the meal. No longer having children at home to cook for can change home cook's feelings, thoughts, and practices in different ways, depending on the cook's general orientation to cooking, what being a home cook means to them, their cooking skills and knowledge, and their levels of confidence. For example, Pamela and Ashley responded differently to the changes in their cooking lives when their children left home. Pamela became more of a keen cook, while Ashley became a drudge.

Pamela is a cook in transition as the result of changes in her household composition. Living alone in her sixties with her grown children nearby, she no longer cooks on a daily basis the traditional meals that she had taken great pride and pleasure in providing seven days a week when her children were at home. Now that she is cooking for herself rather than her family, she is trying new ways of cooking, new ingredients, and new recipes, which places her in the keen cook category. She has become interested in healthier cooking and is reading up on foods and nutrition, mostly on the Internet. She is interested in novelty and has tried new dishes, such as butternut squash soup, a recipe she got from her daughter, and wanted to try because the precut squash newly available in her grocery store had piqued her curiosity. She "started adding dried cranberries to my salads after I had them at my daughter's house, and I really enjoyed them. They take some of the tartness from onion and vinegar, and they are healthy." Pamela has always taken a lot of pleasure in cooking and has developed over time her own recipes, such as for beef stew. "My stew gravy was never substantial and never enough. I decided to add a bottle of dark beer, and it made all the difference." Cooking, even though it is now only for herself most days, continues to be a central part of Pamela's life.

Ashley likewise is transitioning as a cook due to changes in the social context of her cooking life: she and her husband are empty nesters with grown children and the task of making dinner has changed. She considers herself a good cook, is confident in cooking most things, and used to cook more when her son was at home. Now that is just the two of them for dinner, though, Ashley and her husband separately shop for, plan, and cook their own meals. Five nights a week, they eat these separately prepared dinners together. Ashley's response to no longer cooking for children is the opposite of Pamela's. She has become a drudge who does not enjoy cooking. In her cooking journal, she only expresses enjoyment of cooking in regard to convenience. Other times, she says she finds no real enjoyment and takes little interest in cooking: "Cooking is one more thing that I have to do." If she had unlimited amounts of time, talent, and money, Ashley would cook "pasta." It is notable that in comparison to the other cooks, who wrote detailed menus of luxury foods prepared in very specific ways, Ashley's ideal meal lacks specificity and seems to reflect a lack of interest in and enjoyment of food. When asked in her cooking journal what she would have cooked that evening if she had been at home alone, Ashley responded that she would not have cooked at all. Now that she no longer cooks for her family, cooking has lost its meaning for Ashley.

Cultural factors: Discourses and ideologies of food, family, and gender

> [It's important to me to cook dinners that] show my personal touch. So someone who is typically eating my meal [husband and daughter], they could say that it is mommy's cooking or that it is my wife's cooking. That little flair. (Helen)

> I can't afford to take family vacations; I can't afford to buy brand-name clothing. Most of what I purchase, I purchase on sale. What I *can* do is put my love and creativity into something they can appreciate: food. Even if they don't realize it now, I hope that my kids can look back and say, "Mom always cooked for us." I hope they understand how very much I love them and that if nothing else, they feel that through my cooking. (Kaye)

Despite the daily challenges of feeding work, for several of the mothers in our study, cooking for their families was an important part of their self-identity as mothers and as women. Roles within the household of wife, girlfriend, and, particularly, mother are imbued with the expectation to provide household members with food that is liked (Engler-Stringer 2010). For these mothers, making dinner was a key action they used in building and maintaining their family.

Intensive motherhood and feeding the family

Why does creating memories of family dinner tables laden with "mom's cooking" mean so much to Helen and Kaye? Dinners cooked and eaten at home are complex interaction situations embedded in and constitutive of family relationships, personal identities, and ideologies of food, family, and gender. Traditionally, it is women who have had primary responsibility for the practical and emotional work needed to nurture and sustain families through food (DeVault 1991; Finch and Groves 1983; Hochschild 2012; Murcott 1982). The way the home cooks in our study think and feel about cooking does not differ significantly from the London housewives interviewed by Anne Oakley (1974) nearly fifty years ago, who tended to feel that cooking was the most enjoyable of their household tasks but also felt it could easily become dissatisfying and tiresome when busy days, others' demands, and high culinary standards meant that their food was not well received.

Most of the home cooks in our study who have primary cooking responsibilities are women, and most of our family-first cooks are mothers. Providing a home-cooked evening meal for their children is an integral component of "good motherhood" in both public discourse and for many mothers themselves. Ideologies of motherhood including scientific motherhood, intensive mothering, and mother-blaming shape the cooking experience of family-first cooks. The practice of mothering is constructed by women and men in specific historical circumstances and is consistent with prevailing cultural beliefs about gender. Since the mid-nineteenth century, a broad North American consensus has held that the care of young children is an exacting, time-consuming, and important activity that should be at the center of women's lives and that mothers are the most important caregivers of children and responsible for how those children turn out (Rawlins 2014). Sharon Hays (1996) has termed this ideology "intensive mothering."

"Good" or socially appropriate mothering as constructed by intensive mothering is child-centered, labor-intensive, and guided by professional expertise. During the late nineteenth and early twentieth centuries, physicians, academic experts, educators, philanthropists, reformers, and women's groups called for the reconstruction of traditional motherhood into what was viewed as scientific, rational, modern motherhood. This reconstruction was to be based upon expert knowledge about raising children. Expert knowledge constructs motherhood as both powerful and potentially pathological. If she engages in the correct practices, a mother can raise a child to become a successful, happy, and healthy adult; the wrong practices will lead to a sickly and nervous adult. According to the experts, mothers need education and expert guidance in order to successfully negotiate the fine line that divides good mothering from bad mothering (Rawlins 2014). Applying this to the feeding of children, mothers' choices can mean the difference between healthy and unhealthy children and productive versus unproductive citizens. Because mothers have historically been and still are often solely responsible for planning, provisioning, and preparing meals for the family, discourses of nutrition map onto discourses of motherhood such that mothers were and are constituted as the objects of what Coveney (2006) has termed the "nutritional policing of families."

Contemporary mothering ideologies include scientific motherhood and intensive mothering. These ideologies require that women put children's needs above their own, while deferring to the authority of medical and child-rearing experts. Mothers in this view are devoted to the care of others and self-sacrificing. An intensive mother is held and holds herself accountable for keeping her children fed and housed and "for shaping the kinds of adults these children will become" (Hays 1996: 108). Structured inequalities of social class, race, and ethnicity affect how mothers interpret and practice mothering and the constraints they face in adhering to the ideals of intensive mothering. Yet intensive mothering is a normative standard against which all mothering practices are evaluated. Twenty-five years ago, Marjorie DeVault (1991) published *Feeding the Family* in which she linked the production of family meals—which she called "feeding work"—to the production and reproduction of gender ideologies, class differences, and definitions of the family. She argued that women are often held to similar standards of mothering and feeding, despite the fact that social inequalities differently shape their ability to conform to these standards.

DeVault also importantly emphasized the emotional aspects of feeding work. Women, she showed, actively produce the family through the activities of shopping for, preparing, and cooking food. As they consider and respond to the personal needs and preferences of family members, mothers' feeding work demonstrates the importance of food and meals in the emotional life of the family. Building upon feminist theories of caring, DeVault documented how "feeding the family" is both rewarding and oppressive work for women. While women gain satisfaction and fulfillment through reproducing the family and their own identity, the emotional and physical labor of foodwork is disproportionately borne by women. Thus, women's feeding work reinforces hierarchical gender relations and constructs and maintains women's subordinate position in household life. Serving the family through foodwork becomes a woman's duty. Mothers make meals and thus make family. Making dinner is also a central route by which women enact gender. A dinner that is not successful thus potentially represents a failure to satisfy both gender and family expectations (DeVault 1991).

More recently, in *Food and Femininity* (2015), Kate Cairns and Josée Johnston demonstrate how women continue to face pressures to conform to idealized feminine roles as they carry out foodwork. Contemporary women use food to construct feminine selves through their practices of shopping, cooking, eating, and feeding others. Cairns and Johnston argue that to successfully perform femininity through food, contemporary women must express multiple food femininities at once: to be simultaneously the healthy eater, conscientious consumer, talented home cook, and nurturing mother. In their interviews with forty-seven mothers, Cairns and Johnston show how women express love and care for their children through providing healthy meals, socializing children's palates, and protecting children from the harmful products of the industrial food system. Even when women acknowledged how the burdens of foodwork in motherhood were unfairly gendered, most continued to carry out the work because of the emotional rewards. Performing these "food femininities" is thus experienced by contemporary women as both emotionally enjoyable and exhausting.

New discourses on cooking for children

Intensive motherhood is now joined by new discourses on feeding work. In the twenty-first century, fears of toxicity and chemical body burdens, the hopes of ethical consumption and the "organic child," a new emphasis on childhood obesity and heart disease, and moral panics over the family meal contribute to an intensification of pressures on mothers cooking for their families. Norah MacKendrick (2014) uses the concept of "precautionary consumption" to describe contemporary mothers' efforts to mediate children's exposure to harmful environmental chemicals through vigilantly monitoring their consumption patterns, including the foods and drinks they consume. Precautionary consumption appeals to mothers as it provides a sense of concrete control over the abstract threat that environmental contamination poses to children's health and well-being. Mothers who engage in this project can experience a powerful sense of accomplishment. Active management of the child's toxic body burden then becomes integral to the performance of "good motherhood." MacKendrick argues that mothers who engage in this project have actively expanded the sphere of maternal accountability to include informed and proactive mothering in regard to precautionary consumption. She interprets this as part of a negotiation with the larger cultural discourse of mother-blaming, which holds mothers accountable for their children's future.

Kate Cairns, Josée Johnston, and Norah MacKendrick (2013) interviewed female consumers and identified an emerging ideal of the "organic child" that naturalizes and reproduces the idea of care-work as "women's work" while appealing to contemporary ideas of ethical consumption and commonsense understandings of childhood purity and mothers' responsibility to protect children. The organic child ideal has profound emotional consequences and resonates with the construction of mothers as caring, protective, and self-sacrificing. In their study, mothers spoke of how they felt a new sense of accountability with regard to food, as they assumed responsibility for another person's well-being. The child's body was viewed as pure and subject to contamination by a mother's poor food choices. Respondents noted the increased time and amounts of planning it takes to provide organic food. Cairns, Johnston, and MacKendrick (2013) argue that organic food increasingly constitutes a normative obligation perceived as a mandatory part of "good" mothering. Ethical food discourse constructs consumers as agents of change and mothers have the added responsibility of consuming ethically to protect their children, preserve the environment, and socialize future ethical eaters. These narratives generate a sense of empowerment and control as well as powerful feelings of guilt and anxiety.

Another aspect of contemporary anxiety over mother's feeding of their children and also a vector of mother-blame is childhood obesity. As April Herndon (2010) notes, "Contemporary discussions about the childhood obesity epidemic showcase the still popular notion that women should be the primary caretakers of children, especially where cooking, dining, nutrition and bodies are concerned." In advice manuals about preventing or treating childhood obesity, mothers specifically are often believed to be or expected to be responsible for children's weight. Preventing obesity in children is a mother's responsibility, which has benefits for the child as well as for society at large. The childhood obesity epidemic is blamed on "bad mothers"; therefore, mothers must monitor their children's weight and intake of "fattening" foods, increasing public scrutiny of how mothers make dinner.

There is also widespread public concern over the supposed decline of the family meal. Contemporary popular writers and public intellectuals on food argue that Americans (mostly moms) must return to the kitchen and cook more often and with less processed foods (Bowen, Elliott, and Brenton 2014; Pollan 2006). The message that good parents—and in particular, good mothers—must cook for their families dovetails with increasingly intensive and unrealistic standards of "good" mothering. One could say that home-cooked meals have become the hallmark of good mothering, stable families, and the ideal of the healthy, productive citizen. These contemporary discourses on food intersect with older discourses on good motherhood in such a way as to amplify the role of Devault's unpaid, unacknowledged, and unequally resourced feeding work in mothers' lives.

Doing cooking, gender, and family

Through the overlapping discourses on motherhood and nutrition, then, women have been given the responsibility of making dinners that provide "good" food for their families. By preparing a home-cooked dinner that is considered healthy, mothers demonstrate that they care for their families. It is important to mothers to prepare dinners that are healthy, economical, and liked by their children. However, the exigencies of daily life, especially lack of time in the kitchen, mean that mothers often decide to cook what is fast, easy, and convenient while still liked by their families. Mothers must negotiate the tension between what appears as a proper home-cooked dinner in the public discourse of good motherhood, their personal aspirations for the evening meal, and their daily mothering and cooking practices. They must achieve the family dinner to avoid failing at "doing family" and "doing gender" as DeVault warns. Feeding children is indeed meaning-making labor.

Mothers must negotiate the tension between the standards and ideals of feeding the family with the practical and quotidian realities of feeding their own real-life family. These challenges mostly revolve around time, money, and tastes. As real wages have stagnated, many households depend on every adult family member working, sometimes in multiple jobs and jobs with nonstandard and unpredictable hours, to make ends meet (Sayer et al. 2009). Almost all of our home cooks are employed outside the home.

Since the 1960s, working women have cut back on the time they spend on household tasks, including cooking and cleaning. Even so, taking into account paid work and unpaid work at home, women today have less free time than they did a generation ago, and, in line with heightened expectations of motherhood, they now report spending more time engaged in childcare than did mothers in the 1960s (Bianchi et al. 2012). So it is inevitable that they struggle to find time to cook. Money is also of course always an issue in feeding the family, especially for those who are seeking to incorporate more organic or healthy foods. And, as we have seen, doing cooking is not just about the time it takes to prepare the meal. It also involves planning ahead, doing the provisioning, and especially deciding what to cook and how to cook it.

Ann and Kaye are two family-first cooks who exemplify how personal factors such as cooking identity, practice, competencies, and confidence intersect with cultural factors such as ideologies of intensive motherhood and health, material factors such as time and money, and social factors including tastes and family relationships to shape the thoughts, feelings, and practices of home cooks.

Ann is a family-first cook who is fearful of preparing a meal that her family does not like, yet she continues to do almost all of the cooking for the family, including her two- and eight-year-old children and her husband. As DeVault (1991) argues, to fail to successfully create the family meal is to fail at both family and gender expectations. Ann's fear of failure means that she takes very few risks in cooking and tends to stick to preparing the meals that she knows her family will like. This accounts for her self-assessment as a "not very creative" cook. Ann explains that the reason why she doesn't take risks is because of how much pleasure she gets out of watching her family enjoy eating the food she has prepared.

> I get a lot of enjoyment out of seeing my husband or my kids enjoy my food. It's something that's meaningful to me. Even though it sounds like I don't try very hard. I get really upset when I cook something and they don't like it. That's why I stay to the same foods. They love my chicken wraps, spaghetti, all the foods I mentioned. They eat it. They'll like it. It's safe for me. (Ann)

Nevertheless, describing herself as a "not very creative" cook indicates Ann's aspirations to rise to the expectation that a good home cook prepares a variety of foods for their family's nutritional and gastronomic needs. Ann explained that sometimes her family gets "in these funks where we feel like we eat the same foods. It's frustrating—I'm not a creative cook." Ann reflected on her cooking practice at the end of her journal question by writing, "I do try to add new foods. The soup I made last week was a good example."

Kaye is a family-first and keen cook who cooks dinner for her four- and nine-year-old children and her husband, who does very little cooking. She indicated that she was confident with all the cooking skills listed and considers herself a good cook and an inventive cook. Kaye wrote a great deal in her cooking journal: her role as the cook for her children is extremely important to her. She explained why she felt she was a good and inventive cook:

> I like to try new things, I like to read food blogs and I like to see recipes that other people have done and I like to try to incorporate them into what I do for my family. My setbacks are usually time or money related. (Kaye)

Kaye's sense of herself as a cook includes being a keen cook in addition to being a family-first cook. Unlike Ann, she seeks to challenge herself to develop as a cook and likes to try new foods and methods of preparation. She has been working to gain knowledge and skills to cook more healthy meals for her family and is engaging with some of the new discourses related to health and cooking. When asked what healthy food means to her, Kaye explained:

> Whole food. I've been trying really hard to pay attention to ingredients in the things that I buy. So I rarely buy for example packaged cookies for my kids. I make them cookies. We can have whatever we want, but it has to be something that's made from scratch or that has only a few ingredients on the list. I'm trying to keep my family away from all the things that I can't pronounce. (Kaye)

Kaye's challenges include time, money, and balancing her children's tastes with her desire to prepare healthy and creative meals. One evening she was unhappy that she had to serve her children hot dogs for dinner and this was compounded by the store being out of the all-natural ones she prefers to buy. She judged the meal to be a failure, saying, "It was premade, processed, hardly any love at all!" But she also acknowledged, "What's important is that we eat together, and secondarily, that we eat good food." Kaye sometimes offers macaroni and cheese or peanut butter and jelly if her children will not eat what she has prepared. One week night she cooked:

> Friday: Hot dogs
> Chili
> Cranberry applesauce (home canned)
> Apples
> Strawberries

> String cheese
> Banana-oatmeal chocolate chip cookies
> Orange quick-bread

She had discussed making chili earlier in the day with her husband who always likes it and which was "a meal in my family's traditions." She also purchased hot dogs for the children in case they did not eat the chili. Consistent with her expectations, the children did not eat the chili but ate the hot dogs and other "supplemental" parts of the meal such as cheese sticks and applesauce. She was concerned that the hot dogs were not all-natural:

> The chili part was a success, but I HATE serving hot dogs! And I couldn't find the all-natural ones. I'm sure having hot dogs isn't going to do any damage to my kids, but they go against my new way of thinking about food. Kids are hard to feed sometimes, especially when they're picky! (Kaye)

For Kaye as well as other family-first cooks, there is an ongoing, daily negotiation between the tastes of her household consumers and her own goals for cooking practice.

Dual family-first cooks

Based on our interviews, we found that a third of the two-adult households in the study's sample reported sharing the responsibility of cooking dinner. Our cooking journals confirmed sharing between these home cooks, though not to the extent that was reported in the interviews. We identified several pairs of family-first cooks in households where both adults in the household take on the household cook role.

One example of dual family-first home cooks is Alice and Michael, who are married with two girls aged seven and nine and live in the Northwest United States. They take turns making dinner and eat at home almost every night. The household has certain standing routines such as homemade pizza on Fridays, vegetarian once a week, and Taco Tuesdays. Alice and Michael solve the dilemma of dinner mostly based on "Simplicity. Lasagna would be an example of complicated. Rice, grilled chicken and boil some Brussels sprouts [are a typical menu]." They prepare more complicated meals on weekends when they have more time. They try to cook extra helpings for those weekend dinners so there are leftovers at least once during the week. That the family likes the dinner is important to them: "Always for the kids and we kind of step it up when we have company also." Michael describes his relationship to food as "Simplistic. I just want it to be healthy and taste good." On the other hand, Alice says she "has vegetarian tendencies." They don't cook beef due to health concerns.

They both enjoy cooking most of the time. Michael says, "I think it can be comforting." Alice enjoys cooking least "when I am just trying to get it done. I enjoy it the most when I have more time." They are confident cooks—both reporting high levels of light cooking skills and average levels of high cooking skills—and the only cooking difficulties they report are related to time or running out of ingredients they need. They are very planful and go grocery shopping once a week "so we usually have a game plan." They shop from a list that both contribute to on the fridge door. As family-first cooks, success for Michael and Alice occurs when "everyone gets a healthy, well-balanced meal and eats well," there are "clean plates," and the dinner is "eaten." Alice took the lead in preparing sushi one night, although all participated to some degree: "Sushi is mega-fun family time."

Sunday: Sushi rice
         Salmon
         Edamame
         Avocado and wasabi

On another occasion, they had neighbors over for pizza, Caesar salad, green beans, mozzarella, and ham. "Everyone loved the food, ate, talked, were merry." Another night, Michael prepared dinner for himself and his two girls. Although the girls thought the meal was too spicy, Michael declared it a success.

Monday: Pulled pork
         Basmati rice
         Brussels sprouts

The two girls help prep in kitchen: "Love 'em though it can slow things down to instruct." Michael's most representative dinner is spaghetti bolognese with steamed vegetables; for Alice, it is tofu fried rice, and roasted vegetable tart tatin. At the end of the cooking journal, their reflection was: "We learned that we might be more 'preparers' than 'cooks' but we do eat at home together as much as possible!"

Living in the Middle Atlantic region, Sara and Daniel are also married, with two girls aged five and seven. They are dual family-first cooks, valuing cooking what the family likes, but they also place a great deal of value on sourcing and cooking healthy food. Daniel reflected:

> We are more on the far end of healthy. We shop at organic food stores and try to avoid highly processed foods. Also, I think we were raised under the food groups—veggies, grains, proteins and dairy. (Daniel)

Once a week, during the season, Sara and Daniel pick up their share of fresh produce from a local CSA. Their shopping routine is variable; there is no typical shopping day: "It's always random. We go to about four different stores … We try to have a pretty healthy balance. With a vegetable and a protein. We also take into consideration what we think the kids will like. Also, one of our children has a food allergy." Added Daniel: "We try to balance cost, healthiness and time. Sometimes we don't have enough time to run to the store that has the healthier option or sometimes we don't want to spend what it takes to get the healthier option."

For Sara and Daniel as family-first cooks, the challenge is to fulfill the sometimes divergent goals of serving healthy food that the family will eat. "Everyone" in their household eats together: "We always have sit down meals … We try to make a lot of things that are kid friendly." They usually trade off cooking dinner. Daniel reports, "We usually take turns cooking" to which Sara adds, "We don't have a system, though." They don't usually cook at the same time. Daniel reports, "Sometimes we both try to cook something and that doesn't work. Usually she starts dinner and I come in and interrupt." They do not plan: "The routine is usually looking in the fridge or cabinet and see what we have." As dual family-first cooks, Sara and Daniel are closely aligned in their orientation. "We are healthy eaters. Also, do it yourself eaters." They both feel that time is their biggest challenge and they least enjoy cooking when time is scarce. Reflecting upon their household's approach to dinner, Daniel said, "I would say that we focus a lot more on healthy, fast options to feed our family. When we are relaxed we enjoy the more creative side of things, but it does not dominate our daily cooking."

Their concern with the family consuming a healthy meal was borne out in their reflection on meals recorded in the cooking journal. According to Sara, "Sometimes we make something that is pretty healthy but then the kids don't like it." For example, after picking up produce from their CSA share, Sara was inspired by a "plethora of fresh spinach" to make a recipe from the *Moosewood Cookbook*. She expected that the children would not like the homemade spinach sauce, so she added the purchased sauce to the menu: "Today, I made a spinach pasta sauce but the kids didn't like it. We really didn't like it either but one of the girls ended up just eating pasta with cheese on it."

Wednesday: Organic fusilli pasta
Bought tomato sauce
Homemade spinach sauce
Homemade applesauce
Vanilla ice cream

Reflecting upon the meal, Sara said, "It was a moderate success because they ate! Not a raging success because they didn't love it." On another night, Daniel made the following dinner.

Tuesday: Noodles
Tomato sauce
Fresh kale

He said that Tuesday's dinner "was a bit boring relative to what I prefer to make, but quick and easy on a Tuesday is important." He regarded the dinner as a success: "It was healthy, yummy and fast—it fit within the constraints of our day." This dinner that Daniel made on a Tuesday and how he thought and felt about it perfectly encapsulates what good home cooking means to family-first cooks.

7

The Traditional Cook: "Like My Mom Used to Make"

For Easter dinner, Linda prepared several dishes at the home that she and her husband Tony share and then brought them to Tony's father's house to serve. Tony claims an Italian ethnic background while Linda claims Swedish and Jewish. Evident in the food they brought to feed a total of nine family members was a confluence of both Linda's and Tony's cooking traditions. The menu was:

Sunday (Easter): Antipasto (prepared by Tony's sister)
Lasagna (prepared by Tony's sister)
Leg of lamb with mint jelly (Linda)
Roasted sweet and white potatoes with carrots (Linda)
Pies from the bakery (purchased by Tony's dad)

Linda did not use a specific recipe for the lamb, rather "I fixed the leg of lamb in the traditional way used by my mother, and fixed the veggies in Tony's mother's traditional way, too." In her cooking journal, Linda noted her aspirations for the meal: she wanted it to be traditional, indulgent, and comforting, to show her personal touch, and to be liked by her family. She considered the Easter dinner "quite successful" and was happy that she and Tony brought "a lot of the lamb" home afterward.

Pauline, who identified her ethnicity as "a boring American" in our interview, illustrates how families make meaning through traditional cooking when she recounted to us the story of her family's ritual tasting of the potica, a central European rolled pastry filled with nuts.

> We used to have the "tasting of the potica" ritual on Christmas Day when I was growing up. My great-grandmother's recipe apparently was in her head and it took many years of the ritual for my mother and grandmother to settle on a written recipe version that they felt represented the original. (Pauline)

Pauline felt a bit of regret when the tasting of the potica ritual became merely the baking and the eating of the potica. In addition to the potica, other favorite recipes Pauline the "boring American" inherited from her family traditions include Irish soda bread and Christmas fruitcake ("not the traditional fruit cake, more of a poor-man's fruitcake") from her family and Easter soup and Christmas Eve fish soup from her husband's Polish family. Pauline also notes that her aunt is "a gourmet cook, so I have gained many recipes from her (but they were not necessarily passed down the cultural generations)."

The traditional cook: It's about tradition

Our home cooks are motivated to prepare traditional dinners for several reasons: to enact their ethnic identity, to engage memories of their family of origin and recreate such memories in their own household, for the positive affect associated with making traditional dishes, and out of taste preferences. Traditional food is considered good and tasty food and it can elide cooks' concerns with newer definitions of good food as constructed by the discourses of nutrition and health. Cooking traditional foods enables cooks to reproduce the taste, appearance, and aromas of meals that connect them to their family of origin and can serve as markers of self-identity. Cooking the dishes and meals of their family of origin provides a way for home cooks to infuse their own family life with meaning and by so doing to create and sustain their own families.

Traditional cooks overlap a great deal with family-first cooks in their understandings of the role of home cooking in their self-identities and their ideas about family life. They too highly value cooking food that the family will like and eat. One of the distinctive features of traditional cooks is that they routinely plan, provision, and prepare dinner within the guidelines of a particular cuisine they consider traditional to their family or cultural heritage. Using the home cook's own description of their cooking as "traditional," we classified ten home cooks in our sample as having a traditional mode of cooking identification. The cooks' definitions of traditional foods range from canned crescent rolls to Syrian mjedara (lentils and rice) to a yellow cake "with no real name." These foods may or may not be associated with cooks' ethnicity: traditional dishes as defined by cooks themselves can encompass the broad range of mid- to late-twentieth-century American cooking. What is central is that the dishes evoke the cook's own family and associated food memories.

For 11 percent of the dinners reported in the journals, cooks indicated that "in my family's tradition" was an important consideration in choosing the dinner menu they prepared. This figure was much higher among the study's ten traditional cooks who were more likely to have cooked a dinner in their families' traditions (28 percent) compared to those not typed as traditional (9 percent) ($logit$ = 2.11, X^2 = 7.83, p = .005). Most traditional cooks do not prepare a traditional meal each and every night that they cook; however, they did so more than three times more often than other home cooks. Traditional cooks are more likely to report that they cooked a dinner that "shows my personal touch" (35 percent) than the other cooks in the sample (13 percent) ($logit$ = 1.69, X^2 = 5.87, p = .015). That a third of dinners show their personal touch is noteworthy in that indicates the extent to which traditional cooking for these cooks is an expression of self-identity.

We draw our definition of cuisine from Farb and Armelagos (1980) who delineated four components of a cuisine: a set of basic foods, which depend upon availability and culture; a distinct method of preparation, including a set of culinary techniques; a flavor profile, which they term "principles"; and normative modes of consuming the food. Those who grow up eating dinners prepared by cooks who rely upon a set of basic foods, techniques, flavor principles, and ways of organizing dinner can be said to have grown up learning to enjoy a family or household "cuisine." Invoking Hauck-Lawson's term "food voice" (Hauck-Lawson 1998), we might say that many adults' food voice bears the accent learned at their childhood dinner tables.

Household cuisines may evoke memories of specific family events, a family's collective memory and oral history, or other food memories that imbue them with deep meaning for the cook. When a traditional cook prepares a dinner that reminds him or her of their own family's cuisine, they are reproducing, albeit usually with some reinterpretation, what having dinner at home with their family meant to them. The traditional cook prepares dinners that are aligned with what their mother, father, grandmother, or other caregiver cooked for them. Often, these traditions reflect blends of ethnic cuisines.

Richard Pillsbury's reflections on his household cuisine in his 1998 history of American food habits and foodways *No Foreign Food: The American Diet in Time and Place* shows how family traditions emerge and blend:

> An agricultural cornucopia of unparalleled variety is immediately available to me, yet when I look at my weekly menu, it is little different from that steady diet my mother served when I was a child living in a small town. The variations that have crept into my home diet stem not from the vast array of fresh foods that I can purchase at any time but rather from the give-and-take of a marriage in which each of the individuals brings a different heritage to the dining table. Thus my Italian-heritage wife thinks of manicotti and spaghetti when she seeks comfort food, not baked beans. Our menu of preferred and frequently prepared foods is an amalgamation of our individual preferences, experiences, and traditions. (1998: 2)

The act of making dinner is the result of the interplay of five dimensions, which have varying and intersecting influences over time on the planning, preparation, and evaluation of the meal. Two of these dimensions—personal factors and cultural context—are particularly relevant to our discussion of traditional cooks. Personal factors include the cook's lived experience and what he or she regards as her tradition. For example, Grace, a traditional cook, has Syrian parents and thus says that Syrian cuisine represents the "traditional for her." Friends and acquaintances may further influence Grace's concept of a traditional dinner. Cultural influences on Grace's cooking of traditional meals include normative beliefs about just what constitutes Syrian cooking. Material factors also may limit or facilitate Grace's ability to recreate traditional dishes. One material influence is whether there are specialty grocery stores that cater to a Syrian clientele or larger grocery stores which stock such ingredients (Gabaccia 1998). Grace's likelihood of cooking traditional meals is also shaped by the strength of her social identity as Syrian American. Grace lives in a neighborhood that has been home to Syrian immigrants for over 100 years. Thus, her lived experience of Syrian cuisine may also be shaped by her social environment outside of her household.

There are a number of modalities through which our cooks learned the traditions that they continue or reinterpret in their household. The most direct method is through assisting and eventually cooking as a child in the household or what Sutton terms an "embodied apprenticeship" (2014). For example, traditional cook Carolyn has been cooking in her household since she was thirteen years old. Cooks have observed mothers, grandmothers, and other caregivers in action and learned techniques, flavor, principles, and recipes from them. In our study, women are much more likely to serve in this teaching capacity as they do in most societies around the globe (Beagan et al. 2008; Caraher et al. 1999).

Mom's recipes: Sustaining family, sustaining tradition

Recipes are integral to maintaining traditions for some cooks, while others are less recipe-dependent, instead cooking "in the style" of the family's tradition. This may depend on the nature of the dish: the potica reference earlier needs a recipe more than leg of lamb might. Common to all are years of food memories as well as memories of kitchen and table conversations and dynamics, which imbue the dishes with significant meaning to the cook. Almost all of our cooks have some recipes from their family, which they draw upon when preparing dinners in their family's tradition. There were a few exceptions. For example, Cheryl said she had no favorite recipes from her family because her mother "was an awful cook." Chloe, on the other hand, has too many family recipes to list. Her uncle had made a cookbook of all her grandmother's recipes when she passed away and Chloe now enjoys using these when cooking for her family.

Often these recipes are identified as belonging to the family member to whom they are attributed. Helen refers to "my grandmother's pierogies, my mom's vinaigrette dressing, my second cousin's recipe for mousse au chocolat." Tony refers to his grandmother's gravy (tomato sauce), Mother's roasted vegetables, and Aunt Nina's anisette cookies. His wife Linda refers to Aunt Sophie's cookies, Mother's cheese casserole, and Grandmother's rice pudding.

Favorite recipes inherited from their family reflected the mix of ethnic traditions in our sample, including Italian, Irish, Pennsylvania Dutch, German, Jewish, Afro-Caribbean, African-American, Hispanic, Malaysian, Filipino, Syrian, Scots-Irish, Native American, Polish, Swedish, and Norwegian. Traditional cooks' favorite recipes inherited from their families range from Italian fried salami, torta, pasta fagioli, braciole and lasagna to Central European specialties such as potica (nut roll pastry), pierogies (potato-filled dumplings), halupkis (cabbage rolls with ground beef), haluski (cabbage and noodles), pulla bread (Finnish coffee bread) and chicken paprikash to Jewish dishes such as potato latkes and noodle kugel to Haitian beans and rice, Caribbean baked macaroni and cheese and Malaysian beef rendang (stew) and Syrian mjedara (lentils and rice), to American and American Southern/Southwestern standards such as corn pie, chicken corn chowder, chili, stuffed peppers (with meat, rice, and tomato sauce), chicken and biscuits, rice pudding, leg of lamb, cranberry sauce, cornbread, cannon balls (cheese balls), green chili chicken enchiladas, wild rice soup, and chicken pot pie.

Recipes are an important part of how traditional cook Margaret makes dinner. Margaret, who identifies as Pennsylvania Dutch, is in her fifties. She now cooks for herself and her husband but has "cooked all my life, for brothers and sisters, fiancé and husband. And for children." Her mother died young and "cooking is like second nature for me." She doesn't usually have any difficulties deciding what to cook. She most enjoys cooking for large family get-togethers, special occasions, or picnics. She likes to cook main dishes and desserts from family recipes such as meat loaf, beef roast, chili, stuffed peppers, chocolate cake, fudge, and tomato sauce. She has used the same recipe for lasagna that she got from a co-worker for thirty years. "It's one of my favorite meals to prepare—it never fails to be a favorite. Everyone enjoys it and it is ready to bake when I get home."

Margaret's traditional cuisine has been learned long ago, and she is able to draw upon it with a certain degree of automaticity. On a Tuesday, she prepared a roasted chicken, salad, steamed broccoli, and frozen yogurt with sliced peaches for dinner. This dinner was is in her family's traditions because her family raised chickens as she was growing up: "I learned a lot about prepping and cooking from my mom." On a Thursday, Margaret made meat loaf, garlic mashed potatoes, baby carrots with honey glaze and dried cranberries, and mixed fresh fruit for dinner. She indicated in her journal that she was "not sure [where she got the recipe], learned it from my mother—so maybe a family recipe. Definitely a family recipe." She enjoyed preparing the meal, feeling confident and calm in doing so.

When thinking of recipes handed down in the family, the issue of "no-name" dishes arises. These are the dishes with no names that home cooks prepare and serve to families: they may have no names, but they nevertheless sustain us. An acquaintance shared with us that her husband "quips that men like to cook Thanksgiving because it's the glory meal. It's big and delicious, and the cook gets accolades. But, as he further opines, it's the everyday that sustains us. It's the one pot dinners, the leftovers, the dishes that will never have a name but feed us well." Joyce, for example, writes of the family recipe for homemade yellow cake that has "no real name." But surely that yellow cake with no name has helped the family celebrate on many special occasions. Similarly, Teresa uses no recipes, "but I often try to cook things 'in the style' of my maternal grandmother (roast chicken, roast beef, molasses cookies). I often cook things from my childhood, but no recipe is required." Andrea doesn't really use recipes from her family, but "the simplicity of the food my Italian mother cooked stays with me."

Sometimes recipes representing one's traditional cuisine aren't so easy to acquire. In her essay "Notes on an Eighteenth-century Manuscript Recipe Book," Janet Laurence (2001) recalls, "My mother was Swedish and a marvellous cook. She was born with a fantastic palate and innate sense of how to handle food. Ask her why she did something a particular way and she'd say, 'Oh, I don't know, it's just how it should be done'" (p. 145). Her mother believed that giving away her recipes would reveal the secrets of her cooking and risk diluting her status in her family, "so she guarded her dishes" (2001: 145). Cooking traditional food can be a source of power, closely held, especially for women who may lack other forms of power in the family.

Why cook traditional dishes?

What motivates traditional cooks to plan and prepare dishes that recall their family of origin? We find that cooks prepare traditional dinners for several reasons: to express their ethnic identity, for the positive affect associated with making traditional dishes, out of taste preferences and salutary beliefs, and to engage memories of their family of origin and recreate such memories in their own household.

"The food of my people"

Traditional cooks can connect to their ethnic identity through meal preparation. Eating dinner provides a vital domain in which home cooks and those they feed can express personal and group identities in a typically positive, nonjudgmental environment (Rozin 1999). Shared traditional meals can reinforce shared cultural backgrounds (Kwik 2008) and provide recurring situations through which such backgrounds can be transmitted intergenerationally (Benny 2012). Research on food and tradition suggests that people "remain attached to distinct styles of cooking and transmission of food knowledge because they regard them as providing comfort and a sense of belonging in relation to collective cooking and eating practices" (Benny 2012: 601). For example, Jack very much enjoys making cookies from his grandmother's recipes that were collected by his aunt and given to all the family members in a folio: "Baking those cookies connects me to her memory and a longstanding family tradition and they are always really tasty and nice to share."

By preparing a dinner inspired by Italian cuisine, the traditional cook raised in an Italian American family expresses his or her social identity as Italian. For some individuals, cooking their traditional cuisine may be the most frequent and influential method of identity work (Gabaccia 1998; Probyn 2000; Ray 2004; Williams-Forson 2006). When asked what "in my family's tradition" meant to her, Kaye, who is third-generation Hungarian, responded:

> You mean "the food of my people?" Ha ha! That's what my husband calls it ... as in, "Chicken paprikash *again*? Why do we always have to eat the food of your people?" Chicken paprikash and dumplings (we call them nukli [nokedli], not sure of the spelling) from my grandmother, pigs in a blanket (as we call it) or stuffed cabbages from my grandfather, Swedish pie (which is not Swedish at all, just what we call it for some reason) from my grandmother, and perhaps my favorite, chicken corn chowder from my mother. (Kaye)

As a traditional cook, Carolyn's dinners reflect her ethnic background. She is in her late fifties and cooks for herself and her husband. She did more cooking when her children were at home. Carolyn and her husband eat out less than once a month, typically for a special occasion. Carolyn identifies as having both Italian and Polish backgrounds. Her family cooking traditions tend to be more Polish, including halupki (cabbage rolls stuffed with ground meat and rice) and haluski (cabbage and noodles). She also makes pierogies (filled dumplings) when she has time. She has been cooking since she was thirteen years old and still enjoys it. Her husband is "more of a meat and potatoes guy, but he also like casseroles, so we do a lot of casseroles. Usually one or two vegetables, sometimes from the garden, and a salad." Sauerkraut chicken, mashed potatoes, buttered peas, tomato and cucumber salad, and rye bread is "one of my son's favorite meals," part of his household cuisine. Carolyn described her most representative dinner: "Being of Polish descent, I would make a large pan of halupkis. My mother and grandmother taught me how to roll these when I was a young girl. They are a special treat for my whole family and are enjoyed mostly during the holidays." Other family recipes cited by Carolyn reflected her Italian background—pasta fagioli and sausage rigatoni—and beyond: shepherd's pie (with asparagus) and chicken potpie (with homemade noodles).

Elena is a traditional cook who is Mexican American. She still cooks dishes recalled from her childhood: "yes, I try to do a lot of things my mother used to do." She is in her early sixties and lives close to her two adult children and six grandchildren. She has modified her tradition of a big midday meal to Sunday dinner to accommodate her grown children. She used to cook "the biggest dinner at noon, when we all came in from the farm." Now, she cooks a "big Sunday dinner with the kids. We alternate houses and I will cook enough to sort of last through the week." On Sundays, she cooks for ten people. She made beef tacos and beef enchiladas on one Sunday during the study period. She says she is a "homemade cook—I make everything from scratch. I don't use any mixes ever." She never uses a cookbook or a recipe unless it's something new, special, or a dessert: "Most recipes are in my head because I have done them so much."

Grace is twenty-two years old and works as a waitress. She self-identifies as Syrian Christian and says that cooking Arabic food is "just second nature" to her. For two years, she has been the primary cook for her household of two younger sisters and her mother and father. Her mother is a vegan, so when Grace cooks a meal with meat, she makes something separate for her mother. She and her sisters usually eat together, with her mother and father eating later because of their work schedules. Grace explains, "We don't really have side dishes. In Arabic cooking, it is one dish that usually involves bulgur wheat or rice." Grace often serves a salad of cucumbers, tomatoes, and garlic along with the main dish. She said that she was not interested in trying to cook anything challenging, which she defined as outside of her traditional cuisine.

> I made baked ham for the first time a couple of months ago, with pineapple and brown sugar. I had had it only once in my life. But I bought it and tried it. I didn't even know what it was supposed to taste like. (Grace)

Linda and Tony are a married couple who are both traditional cooks. Tony prepares dishes from his family's tradition of Italian American cooking: pasta with garlic and oil, spaghetti with meatballs and Italian sausage in homemade marinara. He makes and bottles his own tomato sauce, which he calls "gravy" using his grandmother's recipe. He feels these dishes show his personal touch and enjoys cooking them very much—he "could do it in my sleep." His most representative meal is lasagna "made with my own gravy" and braciole. Linda is of Swedish/Jewish heritage and cooks in her family's traditions, although this may not look like a traditional cuisine to an outsider. She describes her cooking as "very traditional, you have to have meat and potatoes. You have to have three things on the plate." Linda's representative meal would be pot roast "with little golden potatoes."

Pamela is a traditional cook who learned to cook Irish food from her mother and Italian American food from her mother-in-law. She is Irish and grew up watching her mother cook. She also learned a lot from her mother-in-law, who was a German immigrant who lived in an Italian neighborhood in the New York City area and cooked Italian-American food. When her children were at home, Pamela would cook dinners that reflected her experience including meat loaf, roasted beef, lamb or chicken, stuffed peppers, spaghetti and meatballs, and baked ziti. She likes to cook foods that show her personal touch: "When I make Italian food I make it my mother-in-law's way, has to be from scratch." When Pamela makes a dish to bring to family parties or get-togethers, she cooks this traditional food. "Did stuffed peppers at Christmas. They loved it. My grandson always asks if I will make baked ziti. It's good, with a sauce that I make myself." She cited several favorite family recipes including her German mother-in-law's traditional Italian dishes.

The emotional impact of cooking traditional dishes

The foods and dinners that traditional cooks make have emotional resonance for them and their families. The meals have meaning for them and connect them to their own family experiences. Traditional cooks also tend to make a more narrow range of dishes that are tried and true. Do traditional cooks experience different emotions in the process of preparing dinner than other home cooks?

Recall that we asked respondents to complete an inventory of the emotions they experienced while preparing certain meals in their cooking journals. Our results suggest a distinctive affective profile for the traditional cook. Traditional cooks tended to be more calm than other types when making dinner ($b = 0.86$, $X^2 = 4.98$, $p = .026$). Traditional cooks also report feeling less rushed when cooking ($b = 1.09$, $X^2 = 6.16$, $p = .013$). Why do traditional cooks feel less rushed and calmer from day to day when making dinner? Consider for a moment why food scholar Lisa Heldke (2012) likes making Thanksgiving dinner so much:

> It's because I never wonder what to fix. I prepare virtually the same meal every year. It's a ritual for me: turkey, stuffing, mashed potatoes, gravy, squash, and pumpkin and mince pie appear every year. I like it this way. It's comfortable. It's delicious. I do it only once a year. And my mom does it that way. And there, perhaps, lies the crux of the matter. I have been eating this meal one day a year for my entire life, and over the years, it has come to be virtually the only full meal that my mother and I cook in common. (p. 327)

Traditional cooks may be better able to solve the dilemma of dinner on a daily basis and therefore less anxious and rushed than other cooks. They know what dinner they are going to make and have a clear expectation of whether it will please their family.

More narrowly defined menus reduce some of the daily uncertainty of dinner. Greater amounts of experience preparing specific dishes may have led to the development of more efficient techniques. They may have committed to memory (or have accessible in easy reach) a proven set of recipes that they can draw upon. Their facility with these dishes likely renders preparation quicker and more reliable than those prepared by cooks who prepare a greater variety of dishes.

There are several reasons why traditional cooks—who tend to cook dishes long familiar to them—are better able to face dinner's temporal challenges. First, we speculate that having made the same dinner with the same dishes hundreds of times can make temporally informed dinner choices more efficient: if they find themselves short on time on a given day, they know what dishes they can make in the compressed amount of time. Once a menu has been chosen, traditional cooks may be more familiar with coordinating the sequence of the dinner's components. Traditional cooks have more elaborated schemas regarding often-served dishes, which include sequence, timing, and how to deal with the unexpected. Recall too that the factor that most reduces the enjoyment of cooking dinner is not having enough time to do so. Traditional cooks do not lose time deciding what to cook.

For these and other reasons, traditional cooks are more likely to say that they enjoyed cooking the meal (65 percent) from day to day compared to other cooks (54 percent) (*logit* = .83, X^2 = 4.08, p = .043). Katherine reports, "Cooking is a thing I do to feel better." Many of the dishes they prepare may hold strong meaning for them, which makes the preparation time more enjoyable: cooked properly, they embody the aroma, taste, and appearance of food associated with being loved and cared for by someone.

The process of learning to become a traditional cook may be a stressful one. If one is trying to directly reproduce the taste, appearance, and aromas of a dish to suit a traditional standard, those goals may be anxiety-producing; after all, there is the risk that the dish may not turn out as one desires. Perhaps this is why Monique says her mother's recipes "don't stick." As opposed to cooking something entirely new (such as Grace's ham), failure to reproduce a traditional dish may call into question the cook's skills and competencies. We imagine that our traditional cooks likely experienced this as they developed their facility with their portfolio of traditional dishes. We are reminded of Patricia's elusive meatball in Chapter 5. She bases her self-concept as a good traditional Italian American home cook, in part, on her ability to prepare meatballs to her high standards; the discrepancy holds considerable weight.

On the other hand, traditional cooks learning a traditional dish may have the experience of Joseph. He has been endeavoring for several years to perfect his rice and beans dish to achieve something comparable to what his Haitian grandmother would have prepared. Although the possibility of risk and failure is greater given a very specific goal, the challenge is imbued with strong meaning, and Joseph experiences the challenge positively. The burden of traditional cooking is that you may have to work at it. There are specific taste expectations associated with some dishes and the cook must strive to attain them. Although it can be effortful and time-consuming—as in the potica of Pauline's family and Joseph's rice and beans—once you have captured the taste of home and are able to reliably replicate it, it is an easy, relaxing, and deeply satisfying thing to do.

We should note that traditional cooks do not have to keep trying to achieve their status as good cooks through innovation. Once a traditional cook has learned how to prepare the traditional dishes well, they remain a good traditional cook for life. But because the cultural definition of healthy cooking for family-first or gourmet for keen cooks changes, they have to learn new ways of cooking to maintain their status as "good home cooks."

Traditional cooks may also experience less anxiety and more positive emotions because they are freer of the concerns associated with gastro-anomie. According to sociologist Claude Fischler's (1979) notion of "gastro-anomie," there are two trends which give rise to negative feelings when preparing meals for one's family. One trend is the intense media attention to the possible risks of industrialized and globalized food production and food additives and nutritional guidelines; this raises the anxieties of cooks and parents. A second source of anxiety is a growing concern in both media and other discourse about the breakdown of "traditional" domestic food practices: the supposed decline of domestic cooking and the evening meal that dominates food talk in the twenty-first century. Fischler argues these anxieties reflect a move from gastronomy to gastro-anomie or food disorder, which provokes fear, unease, and anxiety.

Do traditional cooks engage in practices that allay such anxieties by making dinners that are considered good and healthy, that invoke positive memories of family, and that their family will sit down and eat? Does the traditional cook's more narrow body of recipes and strategies "inoculate" them against gastro-anomie? As noted earlier, Beardsworth and Keil (1997) suggest that cooks are not troubled by the universe of food choices, given their engagement of a stable overall food framework. Traditional cooks certainly possess that stable framework, which limits the number of alternatives to choose from for dinner each night, leading to generally more satisfaction due to limited choices (Schwartz 2004).

Traditional cooking as health giving

Traditional food is considered good and tasty food, and it can elide (for many, not all, often for traditional) cooks' concerns with newer definitions of good food as constructed by the discourses of nutrition and health. This is an older, "traditional" meaning of good food. Consider two menus for a traditional meal served at a spring holiday with religious significance in the same suburb of New York City. The traditional Passover menu enjoyed by the Berkowitz's, a middle-class Ashkenazi Jewish family, includes gefilte fish (poached fish dumplings), matzo ball soup, brisket or roast chicken, potato kugel (a casserole) and tzimmes, a stew of carrots and prunes, sometimes including potatoes or sweet potatoes. The traditional Easter menu enjoyed by the McCarthy's, a middle-class Irish Catholic family in the same location at about the same time of year, includes a baked ham, scalloped potatoes, glazed carrots, asparagus and homemade rolls. As different as these menus are, the image for both families that Passover or Easter dinner invokes is the same: a table of abundance and pleasure, dressed up a bit more than usual, absolutely covered with dishes of delicious food, around which the family, also dressed up a bit, happily gathers to eat.

As Coveney points out, the term "good food" was "once reserved for tables laden with tasty dishes of food" (2006: xii) as in these special spring dinners. But "today good food requires one to show less concern with the physical pleasure of eating, and more interest in the good health that results from our dietary habits" (Coveney 2006: xii). Traditional foods offer cooks several ways to negotiate the tension between pleasure and prudence by eliding concerns with health and nutrition. Probably the most common way is when an individual gives her- or himself license to indulge in eating the good traditional food that they know is not supposed to be good for them because it is too fatty or starchy or too sugary. This dispensation that we grant ourselves can be for a special dinner, such as a holiday dinner, as exemplified in jokes about loosening one's belt or donning stretch pants before indulging in a holiday dinner. Certain dishes that are traditional can also be eaten with pleasure although they are not considered healthy, as an occasional special treat. For example, Kaye, who is otherwise quite concerned with cooking healthy food for her family, makes a traditional dish she recalls from her childhood: "chicken corn chowder from my mother. It's an old Southern recipe that I adore. It's the only thing I make where I don't bat an eye at the amounts of cream, fat and butter!"

Traditional food can also be considered healthy in its own right. Traditional, "good, old-fashioned food" is sometimes regarded as inherently healthy. For example, Michael Pollan, the acclaimed food writer and activist, made a public appeal in the health section of the *New York Times* for "food rules" that readers tried to live by: "something perhaps passed down by your parents or grandparents". His premise was that "culture has a lot to teach us about how to choose, prepare and eat food, and that this wisdom is worth collecting and preserving before it disappears" (Pollan 2009a). Some of the responses eventually appeared in *Food Rules: An Eater's Manual* (2009b), including a rule that you shouldn't eat anything your great-great-great grandmother wouldn't recognize as food. Some critics responded that most of us would be omitting a lot of healthy food from our diets if we restricted ourselves to the eating patterns of our ancestors. Members of the Association for the Study of Food and Society, an international organization of scholars, professionals, academics, and writers in food studies, posted to their listserve rules passed down from their parents, which included "Eat nothing green or fresh" and "If it's green, it's trouble. If it's fried, get double" (Rousseau 2012: xxvi). Our parents and grandparents did not necessarily cook or eat in ways that many of us would consider to be healthy, yet this perception continues. Traditional meals may be proper meals that invite minimal scrutiny because they are presupposed to be good (Charles and Kerr 1988; Murcott, 1982). Traditional meals within a culture may also represent tried and true sources of strength and comfort. For example, in the culture of many of our Dominican students, traditional foods are believed to give strength and health.

There are, of course, personal and cultural differences in how home cooks respond to these cultural constructions of good choices in what to make for dinner. For example, in his study of French cooks, Jean-Claude Kaufmann posits that cooks must choose between abundance and self-control and between pleasure and nutritional value (2010: 241). Nevertheless, he points out that while people may know the nutritional rules derived from expert knowledges on nutrition, they don't necessarily follow them in their cooking and eating practices. He writes, "Ideas come from outside and are stored in a separate mental stratum that may be either active or dormant and which is divorced from our actual practices. They have no immediate effect on the underlying mechanisms that govern our practices which reshape the things that make individuals what they are day to day" (2010: 21). Some people (perhaps a dwindling number in the United States) appear impervious to the discourse of health. They cook and eat what they like and, like Tony in our study, this is often the traditional food of their household cuisine.

Recreating family memories and creating new families

Cooking traditional meals enables the cook to reproduce the taste, appearance, and aromas of meals that connect them to their family of origin. On a day when her office was closed, Linda cooked a special anniversary dinner for her sister and her husband, her niece and her husband, and their two children. She prepared roast chicken, a cheese casserole from her mother's recipe, fried corn, steamed broccoli with garlic, whole grain bread, and ice cream sundaes. She chose the menu to be in her family's tradition, indulgent, comforting, well liked, and to show her personal touch. "It was a terrific success. A nice family gathering with food my sister and I remember from our childhood."

For Janet, cooking a traditional meal can have a therapeutic effect by evoking memories of her late father. She cooks such recipes when stressed: "The only time I don't like helpers is when I am cooking because I am upset and that means I am usually making one of my dad's dishes and cooking alone helps me to remember him and work through what is upsetting me."

Traditional dishes and meals also provide a way for the home cook to infuse their family life with meaning. This may be particularly relevant when the family the home cook is making is differently configured than the one in which they were raised. For many of today's families, which may be smaller and more diverse than yesterday's families, those gathered around the dinner table day to day appear quite different from those gathered around their childhood tables. When Grace prepares and serves a traditional Syrian dinner for just herself and her sisters, putting aside portions for her mother and father to eat when they return from work, she is using the food to recreate the good feelings of her childhood dinners with all the family gathered around the table.

When we allow home cook's "food voices" to tell us about their traditional foods, we can learn a lot about the meaning of making dinner. For example, Jack and Jeremiah are a married gay couple raising a son in a cosmopolitan city geographically and culturally distant from their childhood homes in the Midwestern and Southern United States. Jeremiah is African American and Jack is of Scandinavian heritage: their son is mixed race. Both Jack and Jeremiah grew up in two-parent households with multiple siblings and frequent interactions with extended family members. Making dinner is a site within which home cooks create and sustain their family life: as Lupton (1996) points out, the dinner table is symbolic of ideal family life. Jack and Jeremiah's dinner table today looks quite different from the dinner tables of their childhoods, because their family looks different.

We observed Jack and Jeremiah cooking dinner as part of a pilot research project. The evening we visited, Jack prepared Pillsbury crescent rolls to accompany dinner. This product consists of a sheet of dough, pre-perforated into triangular pieces rolled into a cylinder, in a can. The can is stored in the refrigerator, and preparation involves separating the triangles, rolling them up, shaping them into crescents, and baking them. Jack explained that his grandmother always made Pillsbury crescent rolls, and he fondly recalled her remarking that they were just as good as crescent rolls you could make from scratch. Looking at his and Jeremiah's cooking journal, we can see that the Pillsbury crescent rolls make a regular appearance at their dinner table. Adding the aroma, taste, and visual cue of the rolls to the dinner table makes it "feel like dinner" to Jack. By reproducing the dinners of his childhood in this way, Jack produces the life of his family on a daily basis (DeVault 1991). This mass-produced, industrial convenience food is invested with meaning for Jack by virtue of its role in his childhood family dinners. Pillsbury crescent rolls are the "food of his people," and as a home cook, Jack uses them to make family dinner meaningful and to make memories and traditions for his own family.

8

The Keen Cook: "I Love to Try New Things"

Some kind of light and fresh appetizer possibly including raw ahi tuna,
a small cheese soufflé for a second course, and finally
butter poached lobster with a small portion of perfectly cooked veggies.
For dessert an espresso macchiato with a few macarons. (Andrea)

Dijon crusted rack of lamb,
white asparagus a la hollandaise,
potatoes dauphinoise,
and crème brulee or chocolate mousse for dessert.
(My mouth is watering!) (Kaye)

Bone-in ribeye steak (oscar style),
homemade mashed potatoes,
sautéed baby broccoli,
kale Caesar salad,
pound cake,
merlot. (James)

It would be during the summer
and I would plan a meal around the most delicious produce available.
I would make several different salads –
one a summer salad of melon, cucumber, and avocado;
another of grilled corn and feta; and another with a tomato base,
because summer tomatoes are my favorite food.
I would serve the salads with homemade bread. (Ruth)

Andrea and Kaye wrote the first two menus in response to the question in their cooking journals asking what they would prepare for dinner in an ideal world with unlimited amounts of time, money, and talent. James's steak dinner is his choice for a dinner that would most represent who he is as a cook. (Oscar-style steak is topped with asparagus, crabmeat, and Hollandaise sauce.) Ruth's ode to summer produce is the meal that would most represent who she is as a cook. Andrea, Kaye, James, and Ruth are home cooks whom we have classified as "keen cooks."

Keen cooks: It's about the food

Slightly over one-quarter of the cooks in our study can be classified as "keen cooks." Keen cooks are very interested in food: they enjoy the process of cooking and learning about food and cooking. They express great confidence in their cooking competencies but still seek to gain new knowledge and skills in cooking and food. Of all our home cooks, keen cooks are most likely to view cooking as a hobby or leisure pursuit, at least some of the time, and to enjoy cooking when they have sufficient time. Keen cooks like to challenge themselves by trying new ways of cooking, new ingredients, and new recipes. For example, Emma is a college student who is learning to cook and likes to try new things. She says, "I am a good cook. I like to challenge myself when I cook and when I seek out recipes, I never worry about level of difficulty." James is a family-first and keen cook who cooks for his extended family and also likes a challenge when cooking:

> Yes, I like a challenge. I like to smoke meat and have a pretty good smoker. I do like to try different things different ways. There are a million and one ways to smoke meat, from what I have gathered online. I like that. The challenge is that it can take so long, but there is no guarantee how it will turn out on the other end. Spending five to ten hours smoking something and hoping it will be good is a little bit of a challenge. (James)

James's experience as a keen cook who does not shy away from a challenge is typical. In the cooking journals, keen cooks were less likely to select "easy" as a consideration when deciding what to cook for dinner (42 percent), compared with other cooks (70 percent) ($logit = -1.11$, $X^2 = 7.81$, $p = .005$).

Consistent with their orientation to making dinner, we find that keen cooks are more confident in their skills: keen cooks ($M = 3.75$, $SD = 1.18$) were significantly more confident than other cooks in their heavy cooking skills ($M = 2.52$, $SD = 1.66$) ($F(1,39) = 6.60$, $p = .014$). Keen cooks were also more confident about their ability to plan healthy meals, economical meals, and meals that are liked by their family ($M = 3.00$, $SD = 0.18$) than other types of cooks ($M = 2.60$, $SD = 0.65$) ($F(1,39) = 6.60$, $p = .018$). When making dinner, keen cooks engage in a more positive manner with the task and draw upon greater confidence in advanced skills and planning. Challenges are perceived positively.

Being a good cook is central to keen cooks' self-identity, and they feel their food reflects this. One evening when Joseph was home alone, he prepared and ate tuna salad and saltines for his dinner, a simple meal but nevertheless he felt it "showed his personal touch with spices." James, a keen cook who cooks for his wife, children, and his sister and brother-in-law, checked "shows my personal touch" as a motivation for nearly every meal he cooked during the study period (with the only exceptions being a couple of meals he had to do quickly because he had meetings/other time obligations).

> I would like to think that to some degree everything involves my personal touch because I don't really follow a cookbook when making things. I just take what experience I got growing up from watching my parents and from working in the restaurant industry for a while. Kinda do my own thing. (James)

Similarly, Rebecca feels that her food shows her personal touch because she doesn't use recipes.

> I can cook savory foods without using measurements. Example: mock turtle soup. I know the base flavors and don't need to write down numbers. My personal touch is that I feel confident tweaking spices, etc. (Rebecca)

The dinner that Helen made one night exemplifies how keen cooks' identities are bound up with the food they produce: she prepared two dishes that she refers to as "her" chicken and "her" dessert. Her description of dinner also shows the keen cook's interest in techniques and flavors and the pleasure they take in cooking. On Wednesday, Helen made:

> Wednesday: My Mediterranean chicken (broccoli, olives, feta cheese and my homemade tomato sauce and seasoning)
> My "crustless" apple pie (heated Granny Smith apples—cored, peeled, chopped and cooked with Simply Lemonade, butter, brown sugar, vanilla, cinnamon—over vanilla ice cream)

The difficulties Helen experienced in cooking this menu is that she "had to improvise when I realized I had no lemons, no cider, no apple juice to cook apples with." So instead she used some Simply Lemonade she had on hand. She wanted to use up the apples because they "were close to being non-edible in their raw form," so she used her knowledge of cooking to come up with this method of preparation "on-the-fly." Helen enjoyed cooking this dinner: "It was fun!"

Keen cooks' language regarding food tends to be more precise, more technical, and more evocative of the flavors and textures and taste of food than our other home cooks. When describing a meal she might make representing who she is as a cook, Andrea wrote of a meal not dissimilar from one that was an often-prepared standard for many of our home cooks: chicken with a vegetable and a side dish. For example, family-first, "ok cook" Virginia described a typical meal in her household as "sometimes it is chicken breast with a side and a vegetable." In contrast, Andrea's description of the chicken and vegetables she would prepare in a meal that represents who she is as a cook was more specific and showed a keen interest in flavor, texture, and technique:

> Boneless skinless chicken thighs, well-seasoned and seared and then finished in the oven.
> Cauliflower puree with butter and salt and pepper.
> Roasted brussel sprouts (a little crispy) with shallots.

(Andrea and her partner generally follow a "Paleo" diet, which accounts for the cauliflower puree in place of the more usual potatoes or rice.) Similarly, keen cook Helen described her dinner of chicken, vegetables, and a starchy side as:

Skinless chicken thighs browned and topped with a cranberry/pomegranate glaze
Fresh green beans from our garden
Leftover Yukon gold diced pan-fried potatoes with fresh dill and seasoned salt.

Helen further explained that the green beans were blanched by her husband "prior to my adding them to the chicken pan to finish them off in the juices from the chicken, olive oil and glaze."

When Frances Short (2006) asked her British respondents what made a good cook, they indicated that trying out different recipes, foods, and techniques was a hallmark of a good cook. As Deborah Lupton (1996) points out, the search for new taste sensations and eating experiences can add value and a sense of excitement to everyday life. Current discourses of what makes food "good" emphasize authenticity and exoticism. Writing about food and cooking in American women's magazines has in recent decades emphasized variety and urged home cooks to try new and different foods and dishes (Mennell 1985; Warde 1997).

Most of the home cooks in our study occasionally expressed a desire to introduce more variety in their cooking. This was especially true of family-first cooks with "picky" eaters. Their need to provide an acceptable meal often led them to fall back on a limited repertoire of standard dishes that they knew would be eaten without too much trouble. This prompted a concern with getting into a rut, both due to normative standards of variety and to family members decrying the evening's menu with the familiar complaint of "we're having that again?"

Keen cooks, on the other hand, are more likely to seek out new foods, cuisines, flavors, and techniques as a positive good, not just as a needed change from an otherwise standard repertoire of dinners. Helen says, "I like to try different things, try new things." Mira's ideal meal would include "any kind of ethnic food—Korean, Ethiopian, Indian, Greek, Japanese, etc." Cynthia explained, "Our friend gave us a British vegetarian cookbook and there was this black pepper tofu recipe that looked amazing and I also made homemade ramen broth."

Rebecca is a keen cook who cooks for her husband and teenage daughter. Novelty is definitely important to her when she considers what to make for dinner. Competent in all the cooking skills we asked about, Rebecca is cooking less now that her older child is away at college. This is a "downer" for her. "Unlike me, my family doesn't like leftovers. I don't like waste. This has deterred me from doing more elaborate meals." She likes to experiment with Thai, Vietnamese, and Greek food and other "cultural cuisines" as she finds these a personal challenge that is enjoyable: "If others like it, even better."

As discussed in Chapter 2, cooks may use recipes to try new dishes, flavors, foods, or techniques. Keen cooks often enjoy the challenge of trying out a new recipe. Many collect and read cookbooks and amass large collections of recipes, including cookbooks, recipes cut out from magazines and newspapers, recipes found on the Internet, and recipes from friends and family. They will sometimes seek out recipes for dishes that they've eaten and enjoyed in a restaurant or private home. Kaye, for example, collects recipes from friends, family, cookbooks, magazines, and online. She wrote, "If I have tried something that I really enjoy, then I must have the recipe!" Ruth is a single mother of a teenager who does not prepare "as many nice dinners" as she used to because of a heavier work schedule. She nevertheless continues to use recipes a lot of the time: about 75 percent come from cookbooks and the rest she gets online. She loves cooking. One evening when she was alone, she followed a recipe she'd read in the *New York Times* to prepare a dish of lentils just for herself to eat.

Many keen cooks use recipes for inspiration and to gain insight into and knowledge about food and cooking processes, rather than using them as blueprints to be followed exactly. Cynthia "goes through recipes because we like variety." She and her wife Christina—with whom she shares cooking duties—tend to read a range of recipes to get ideas for a dish they'd like to prepare, rather than selecting and following one recipe closely. Peter uses recipes very rarely and says, "It's extremely difficult for me to follow the recipe exactly." Instead, he uses his knowledge of food and cooking and the taste preferences of those he cooks for (including himself) to adapt recipes so that he achieves the results he wants.

A few keen cooks watch food and cooking programs on television to gain knowledge and for entertainment. For example, Kaye says, "My daughter and I are Food Network Junkies!" Lois is a single mom, who says, "In the last four or five years I have really gotten into cooking shows and so have my kids." She and her twelve- and fourteen-year-old son and daughter like to cook together. She uses recipes about three-quarters of the time and gets them from cookbooks, online, and TV. "My cookbooks are all flagged with things we have cooked or want to cook. I am usually a recipe person and that helps me feel more confident."

In her ethnographic study of amateur, semiprofessional, and professional street and home cooks in Mexico City, Joy Adapon (2008) argues that the skilled, creative practice of cooking creates agency for cooks. The home cooks in her study describe their cooking as the ability "to draw upon a 'stock of knowledge' that is stored in their heads, hearts, hands, noses and mouths" (Adapon 2008: 14). In postindustrial society, acquiring and expressing knowledge are important components of productive leisure (de Solier 2013: 1). Keen cooks seek out knowledge about food and cooking through media, the Internet, and cookbooks. They try new recipes to gain technical skills and experience cooking different types of food. Several spoke of their desire to take formal classes in cooking. If Ruth, a single mom who cooks for herself and her teenage son, had unlimited amounts of time and money, she

> would take a particular cooking class with Harry that is every Wednesday night for three months, with dinner included. It is a very pricey class next door to [a renowned restaurant], and is something that I would like to do with my kid before he leaves home. (Ruth)

Another keen cook, Linda, who shares cooking responsibilities with her husband Tony who is a traditional cook, also expressed her desire to gain more culinary knowledge and skills.

> If money were no object, we've both talked about taking courses in cooking to expand our culinary repertoire. (Linda)

Keen cooks approach cooking as a project and may devote substantial amounts of time and effort to developing the conceptual, perceptual, mechanical, and organizational knowledge and skills needed to perfect a dish. Linda said,

> I've just in the last couple of years gotten into making pot roasts. I mean it is one of the simplest things in the world to make, but I was really hesitant, and the first few times it came out kind of tough. And I was really kind of angry about it and I said why isn't it happening the way it's supposed to … It's just a challenging thing. (Linda)

Linda kept working on the pot roast problem until she achieved the result she wanted. Likewise, Pamela's cooking has been a lifelong project.

> I like to experiment. There were times when I began cooking (quite young) that I made mistakes and learned what not to do. Then I tried to improve by adding things like mushrooms, basil, bay leaves, cheese, etc. (Pamela)

Pamela has developed over time her own recipes that suit her culinary standards and of which she is proud. These include beef stew with shallots and dark beer, pasta sauce, Irish soda bread, and rice pudding.

Keen cooks, when they have the time to devote to cooking, like to cook something challenging to gain new skills, knowledge, and experiences. For example, when deciding what to make for dinner, Peter says that easy is not a consideration for him, in fact "the more complicated the better." He likes a challenge, "either a new ingredient or a new technique that I am not used to." When Lois and her children select recipes to try together, they sometimes look for those that can increase their skills and knowledge.

> Sometimes if it is something that we haven't made before we will pick out something that is rated at a more difficult level to learn a new technique and try something new. We won't try anything that's like super French that we have never done before, but we do like a challenge and have gone out of the box. (Lois)

Rebecca enjoys cooking as a leisure activity when she is "inspired and [has] a craving for a certain type of food" and when she has "plenty of time and good ingredients to work with." She likes the idea that when she wants to eat something, she can make it herself. For example, she went out to a Greek restaurant but was disappointed in the food, which she thought "wasn't very good." In response, she decided she wanted to make her own souvlaki and other Greek dishes and did so when she had the time.

Jack is a family-first and keen cook who had time on a Saturday to make a chicken curry for dinner and very much enjoyed cooking that night. He said, "I kind of enjoy trying things that are challenging. The curry has been taking some time." Joseph is a traditional and a keen cook. He is motivated by a cooking challenge and "loves making authentic Haitian, Italian, and Indian dishes." He has been working on "mastering Haitian cuisine." One weekend evening during the study period, Joseph prepared his grandmother's recipes for rice and beans and peas (Haitian style). He has "spent a great deal of time over about seven years to master the dish as it takes at least seven hours of bean soaking and two hours of cooking time."

Throughout our research, the most important determinant of how much cooks enjoyed cooking was whether they felt they had ample time. This is true for keen cooks as well, but keen cooks also enjoy a challenge in the kitchen. For example, Kaye most enjoys cooking "when I am not under any pressure to prepare something. I like to take my time, to experiment with different food items." Peter most enjoys cooking "in situations where I can be creative and try new things."

Keen cooks or foodies?

> From an early age, food was always integral to everything when I was growing up. I have a deep appreciation of food and enjoy food for more than the sustenance it gives. I enjoy the tastes, the thing as a whole. It is an experience. Don't know if there's a word for that. Food is big. (Helen)

We opened this book with a description of a "French picnic" prepared and served by Peter as a special dinner for a young guest who loves Paris. Peter's menu consisted of salami, cheese, bread, pickles, and fruit. As a keen cook, Peter was able to use his knowledge of what a "French picnic" might be supposed to consist of to create a fun occasion for his daughter's friend and his family. Apparently, there is some consensus among Americans about what the French eat for picnics. For example, on the foodie website Spoon University, Hanna Crea advised readers on "How to Pack the Perfect French Picnic" by selecting the best combinations from the required categories of cured meat, cheese, bread, and fruits and vegetables (Spoon University 2017). These ideas about what might constitute a "French picnic" and the value placed upon this particular configuration of foods are a part of foodie discourse. Keen cooks engage with various discourses on food, including those of foodism or gourmet food. So are keen cooks simply foodies with another name?

Only about one-third of the keen cooks in our study rated themselves above a 5 on a "foodie" scale they completed as part of their cooking journals, which ranged from a 1 representing "not at all foodie" to a 10 representing "totally foodie." Mira, a keen and planful Malaysian cook who cooks for her wife and five-year-old son, rated herself as an 8 on the foodie scale and said that to her, a foodie was "someone who cares about the source of their food, but also someone who is curious about food in terms of its ingredients, history, preparation, and ultimately, its taste." During the study period, she made samosas using the Blue Apron meal kit delivery system (which comes complete with all premeasured ingredients and a recipe) and was pleased with the results: "In the past, samosas have been tricky to make and get right. This recipe was a success!" Mira likes a cooking challenge such as "a French recipe with a lot of parts." She says, "I would say that I am an omnivore. I love trying all new types of food even if I cannot identify with them. I am so curious about it all." Omnivorousness or openness to new foods and eating experiences is part of the foodie experience (Johnston and Baumann 2015;

Nacarrato and Lebesco 2012). According to Naccarato and Lebesco's notion of culinary capital as a status marker, in the contemporary United States, "those who seek out the greatest variety of tastes and are open to the broadest range of experiences emerge as the most culturally capitalized" (2012: 9). The meal Mira chooses to represent who she is as a cook includes Moroccan-spiced ground lamb with pistachios, mint, and peas; naan bread; tzatziki (yogurt) sauce, hummus, and harissa. This meal is "lovely" and a "special treat because it is a favorite of adults and one my son (age five) will eat with little fussing (he is a picky eater)."

To Kaye, a foodie "is just a person who really appreciates food and who seeks out different types of food and who likes to learn about different types of food." She rates herself as a 6 on the foodie scale and told us in her interview:

> I am like an amateur foodie. [Laughs] Because I think that there's a lot about it that I don't know. I mean I've never taken culinary classes or anything. Anything that I learn is pretty much what I see on the Food Network. (Kaye)

Lois is another self-identified foodie.

> I actually live in a town that we call ourselves the foodie town [a large Midwestern city.] I think that it means that you appreciate good, different, and well put together food. Also, that you are open to trying different types of food. I would like to think of myself as a foodie. (Lois)

In her ethnographic research on foodies, Isabelle de Solier highlights the ways in which "it is not just objects [such as food] that are important in self-making; rather, we need knowledge of objects in order to use them in this process: knowledge of how to consume and produce them" (2013: 3). It is, she argues, through the media that we acquire most of this knowledge in the postindustrial world. "Food media are central to foodies' relationships with food and to their self-making through it" (de Solier 2013: 3). Kaye and Lois would seem to fit this model of foodie most clearly.

In their comment on Johnston and Baumann's *Foodies: Democracy and Distinction in the Gourmet Foodscape* (2015), DeSoucey, Demetry, and Fine (2009) note that "foodie" is a multi-valenced identification. Those who self-identify as foodies consider it positively as do those who admire them. For others, it is a somewhat derisive negative term. Ruth expressed this sentiment in her interview when she said:

> I am really uncomfortable with the term foodie. Someone might call me a foodie but I would cringe. I feel that the term is overused. It's a term that is used to elevate people. (Ruth)

In her journal, Ruth elaborated on her ideas about what the term "foodie" means and how she thinks of herself. She rated herself a 5 on a 1–10 scale of being a foodie.

> To me, a foodie refers to people who have a particular interest in food, especially the newest, most different, and most adventurous types of food. I think of foodies

as people who consume food, rather than cook it. I think this term has been way overused and doesn't really mean what it originally meant. I don't like to be called a foodie, although I fit into my own definition of the term. (Ruth)

Emily is a keen cook who rejects the foodie label.

> I like food, but I am not a foodie. I may also be a contrarian. The gluten free thing is going on right now and I actually add more gluten when I make bread because it tastes better. (Emily)

What meaning did the keen cooks in our study ascribe to the term "foodie"? One of our keen cooks, Pamela, who is in her sixties, had not heard of the term. The rest of the keen cooks were fairly evenly split between positive and negative views of self-identified "foodies." The most frequently mentioned characteristics that keen cooks ascribed to foodies were that they keep up with food-related trends and "know what is going on in the food world" (Alice) and that they were interested in trying new things. Alice defined a foodie as "somebody that makes an effort to think about food" and James as "people that enjoy going to many different restaurants in many different cities and trying something new." Foodies were also described as enjoying photographing food and posting the pictures to social media sites and as enjoying watching food-related television.

Cynthia said "I love food and enjoy cooking, but I don't know what label to use" to describe her relationship to food. She said she was an "optimistic and very good" cook. She is a keen cook who distances herself from the foodie self-identity: she rated herself as a 2 on the foodie scale. Cynthia said that "foodie"

> means that someone has a lot to say about food even though their opinion was not invited … Someone who is always on the lookout for new trends in food; loves to talk about and take pictures of food, especially "it" foods; has a sort of "one-upmanship" or "I know best" approach to conversations about food (e.g., "Oh, you used Land O' Lakes butter in that sauce? I only use local, organic butter"). (Cynthia)

Several keen cooks agreed with Cynthia that foodies were "snobby" or "pretentious." For example, Andrea wrote:

> People are starting to back off of it. It's like you just discovered food. It sounds pretentious to me. As if these people have just discovered food. I am not at all a foodie. (Andrea)

Two of our keen cooks once self-identified as foodies but no longer do so. It's not clear whether this is because the meaning they attribute to "foodie" has changed. Perhaps our respondents are interested in distancing themselves from a perceived elitism increasingly associated with "foodies." Peter is a family-first and keen cook who cooks for his wife and young daughter. He defines a foodie as "someone that really appreciates food and is open to trying new things. Someone that really thinks of food and eating food as an experience. Someone who makes food and wine a lifestyle, beyond just sustenance or even appreciation." Peter used to think of himself as a foodie but now "would say maybe gourmand" to describe himself. Rebecca defined foodies as "people who are obsessed with extremely novel, very decadent, farm-raised ingredients. Architectural food. Foams." In her twenties and thirties, she "probably thought" she was a foodie. Now she says, "I am a purist. I now appreciate a really well-thought-out broth, with no showmanship."

Keen cooks, family tastes, and self

Keen cooks may also be family-first cooks, and several of them in our sample are. In general, however, keen cooks' cooking identities, confidence in cooking, and self-assessments of their success in cooking dinner each night are much less contingent upon household members' tastes and reactions to their cooking than we find among other types of home cooks. In the dinners reported in their cooking diaries, keen cooks were less likely to report "liked by my family" as a consideration in choosing what to make for dinner (55 percent) than cooks not typed as keen (74 percent), although this finding was just short of statistical significance ($logit = -.87, X^2(1) = 3.63, p = .057$). This is because keen cooks judge their success and cooking competencies through comparison to reference groups accessed through food media and through self-assessment of their success in achieving goals they have set for themselves in their cooking projects (e.g., perfecting a technique or recipe). In the intersection of cultural, social, material, temporal, and personal dimensions of making dinner, keen cooks' personal self-making as "good cooks" makes the material—the food itself—and the cultural—discourses about what is good food—particularly salient for them.

Kaye, whom we featured in Chapter 6, is a family-first cook who is also a keen cook. She seeks to challenge herself to develop as a cook and likes to try new foods and methods of preparation. She has been working to gain knowledge and skills to cook more healthy meals for her family and is engaging with some of the new discourses related to health and cooking. She emphasizes "whole food" and cooking "from scratch." As a keen cook, Kaye is willing to take some risks as she balances her motivations of achieving healthy, creative, and well-liked cooking. For example, one evening she prepared meatball calzones as the main entrée for dinner. She planned the menu when someone on her Facebook feed mentioned strombolis and it sounded good to her. She made the meatballs and the dough from scratch and used tomato sauce she had made and canned during the summer. Her young children complained about the calzones but ate some of the dish, although one had a sandwich afterward. The only difficulty Kaye reported with making the calzones, which she had not attempted before, was "getting the kids to eat it!" As a family-first cook, Kaye was disappointed that her children didn't eat more of the main dish. But as a keen cook, Kaye was nevertheless happy with the dinner because the calzones turned out according to her standards: "It tasted good, so that was a success, but I wish the kids would have done a little better with it."

Another weeknight Kaye breaded and fried cod fish and served it with oven fries, grapes, and homemade chocolate chip oatmeal cookies. Her children did not eat the cod, and Kaye did not consider the meal a success. For Kaye as well as other family-first cooks, there is an ongoing, daily negotiation between the tastes of those she cooks for and her own food preferences, in this case her goal as a keen cook to prepare a variety of healthy and tasty dinners that satisfy her need for progress and continual improvement as a cook.

> Again, those rotten kids didn't really eat it. My son ate the french fries and half of the fish, and my daughter pretty much just ate ketchup and grapes … I am realizing that what I cook is not always what they'll eat … I'm going to consider that as I go forward, to see if I can satisfy my own cooking desires while also giving them food they'll actually *eat*. (Kaye)

Keen cooks may be less affected by the social in the form of family responses to their cooking and rely more on their personal evaluation of whether their cooking has been successful by judging whether the food they have prepared for dinner is "good" in their own estimation. They use their knowledge of food and cooking to do this. For example, James particularly enjoys smoking meat: he likes the challenge that regulating the temperature of his fire presents and judges the success of the meal on the quality of his product: "It was a success. I didn't burn the meat. The meat came out tender."

Recall that very few of the meals home cooks evaluated for our study were judged by them to be failures. For keen cooks, some dinners were considered to be failures because the cooking did not meet their own standards. For example, Elena considered her beef tacos a failure because they lacked seasoning. Other keen cooks noted technical difficulties they experienced in cooking such as a puree that was too loose, milk that curdled when added to homemade tomato soup, and granola that did not clump. Non-keen home cooks did not express this same level of concern with the quality of the food as they judged whether or not a meal was a success.

On a Friday evening, James prepared seafood gumbo: he indicated in his cooking journal that this was an indulgent special treat in his family's traditions (African American from coastal Alabama) that showed his personal touch and was authentic. His wife, two daughters, brother-in-law, sister-in-law, and nephew were "very eager to taste this meal." Despite difficulties in cooking, James judged the meal a success because the gumbo was delicious and up to his standards.

> The pot I used initially didn't conduct heat evenly, and I burned the roux. I had to use a different pot and start over. [The meal was a success] because after three hours of cooking and having to start over once, the gumbo was delightful to eat. (James)

Keen cooks, as do all home cooks, negotiate family relationships, cooking, and their own values and beliefs about food and family in many different ways. For example, Lois and Chloe are both keen cooks with children at home who enjoy cooking very much. Yet their general approach to cooking and how their children relate to their mother's cooking differ a great deal.

Lois is a single mom of twelve- and a fourteen-year olds. She identifies herself as a "curious home cook." When asked in what situations she most enjoys cooking, she replied, "I love doing dinner because it is not as rushed as breakfast. I love cooking for company like my mother. I think I actually like cooking all of the time." Lois and her children like to watch cooking television programs and cook together. "We really like to cook something easy, but we also like a challenge." Lois says, "I grew up around a lot of food and then even when I had my kids we always tried to find, taste, and make new things." Lois's children cook along with her almost every night: her son even has his own apron and utensils.

Chloe has four children ranging from six to fourteen years old. She identifies herself as a "creative" cook. She is an improvisational cook, and she says she most enjoys cooking "in any situation—whether it's really cooking or just throwing something together." One of the hallmarks of her cooking is "Zero waste. My children never know what to expect." Chloe notes, "Kids want things without green stuff. But you need to appreciate that you never get sick when you eat healthy." She is "trying to teach thinking about what you eat to my kids. Eating healthy has such important effects. From day one, my kids have had to eat what's in front of them." Chloe's two oldest children have "been taught to make certain things: black bean burritos or wraps." They "help me prepare and clean up."

These two keen cooks' general approach to cooking is informed by different cultural discourses: foodism for Lois and healthy eating for Chloe. Lois involves her children in her cooking. Together they choose recipes to try, and the children are involved in all aspects of the food preparation. Through cooking together, Lois and her children learn about food and cooking trends, techniques, and tastes while simultaneously constructing her family relationships. Chloe's children help her with cooking, but their role is secondary. Partially because Chloe doesn't use recipes, she alone holds the knowledge about and power to decide what and how to cook. Chloe is teaching her children about the importance of healthy eating through her cooking and conversation and by teaching them to make specific dishes while simultaneously constructing her family relationships.

The material dimension of making dinner

Cooking as pleasure

As noted previously, most home cooks (with the exception of drudges) can take a great deal of pleasure from making dinner, at least when they are not too pressed for time. The primary source of gratification for family-first cooks is seeing their family members enjoying a nourishing meal that they've prepared for them—what we have termed the social dimension of making dinner. Traditional cooks, as we saw in Chapter 7, take great pleasure in cooking the traditional foods that connect them to their memories and feelings about their families and their cultural heritage, part of what we have termed the cultural dimension of making dinner. Keen cooks take the most pleasure in the material dimension of making dinner. As Lois said, "I love the idea of food, smell, flavor and all types of different things."

Keen cooks take special pleasure in the sensual aspect of cooking: the smell, taste, touch, look, and sounds of food. They enjoy the process of taking fresh, raw ingredients, washing, cutting, stirring, folding and otherwise manipulating them, cooking or combining them, the sounds of searing and simmering, adding flavor through aromatic spices, herbs and seasoning, and combining various dishes to make a meal that has complementary and contrasting flavors, aromas, textures, and colors. They think about the aesthetic qualities of the meals they prepare and make reference to "the plate." They have a developed palate, taste as they go, and adjust the seasoning of the dishes they prepare. They work on their culinary technical and perceptual skills so that they can achieve the right amount of browning, searing, tenderness, or flakiness of the food. They build their knowledge of food and cooking so as to be able to apply their conceptual skills in developing appealing and creative menus for dinners that are tasty and show their personal touch.

Pamela's description of a Sunday dinner she made exemplifies the keen cook's appreciation for food. She made a pork roast with red potatoes, mushrooms and onions, green beans, and brown gravy. She used no recipes, "just followed [her] own way. I used the rest of the beans' water to make the gravy (my mother's way also). It was a dark brown, just the way I like it."

> I was satisfied with myself; the dinner was very good. I've always thought that a roast dinner was the easiest meal to cook. Of course you need a good piece of meat. I had seen the roast in Stop & Shop the previous week, and it looked like a nice piece of pork—very lean and fresh. So I just had to purchase it. The winter is the time to roast, we enjoy the nice smell it gives the house and putting the oven on makes the house very comfy. (Pamela)

Keen cooks pay attention to and take pleasure in the aesthetic qualities of the meal. For example, Jack is a family-first cook who also is a keen cook when he has time to focus on cooking.

> [I enjoy cooking most] when there is something special to make. When it is something out of the ordinary. I like when I can make something that is colorful and has a beautiful presentation in the end. (Jack)

To James, "gourmet" connotes aesthetic appeal.

> [Q: Is "gourmet" an important consideration for you in deciding what to make for dinner?]: A: In a sense yes. Every now and then. I'll cook something aesthetically appealing to the eye. Take a picture of a plate. (James)

Linda is a keen cook who is particularly attuned to the aesthetics of making dinner.

> My friends call me the queen of *garni*. I am great at garnishing foods. I choose foods that will look good together on a plate. I won't put cauliflower with a potato. I'll make sure that there is a color aspect. I choose the plates very carefully. I'm very careful with how things look. (Linda)

Taste and aesthetics are primary considerations for keen cooks. When we asked Lois whether preparing a "well-balanced" meal is a consideration for her when making dinner, she replied that it was important to her. Probing for what "well-balanced" means to her, we found that she was not using the concept of balance in the nutritional sense, but rather as a keen cook, she was using it to mean balance in terms of the tastes and aesthetics of the meal.

> You have to balance between flavor and ingredients and presentation. Even at home I like to have a nice looking plate of food. My daughter really likes to take the towel and wipe the plate down. Balance the colors. Balance is probably very important. (Lois)

Rebecca also said that preparing a well-balanced dinner was important to her and used an aesthetic view of the plate to describe part of what she meant by this.

> Nice variety of colors on the plate. Protein not too fatty. Farm-raised beef, eggs, etc. Good representation of colorful vegetables. (Rebecca)

Keen cooks' affective experiences

Keen cooks' emotional experiences and perceived competencies when making dinner suggest a distinctive quality from that of other cooks: they take more pleasure in cooking. According to the meals reported in their cooking journals, keen cooks felt happier when making dinner than other cooks ($b = -.88$, $X^2 = 4.11$, $p = .043$). Likewise, keen cooks ($b = -1.56$, $X^2 = 9.82$, $p = .002$) felt more creative when making dinner and felt more valued and less taken for granted ($b = -1.19$, $X^2 = 4.56$, $p = .041$). Keen cooks may feel more creative because they are trying something new. They are also likely to modify recipes, and this may feel creative. Keen cooks are likely to feel valued when cooking because those they feed look forward to their good cooking. But why are keen cooks happier when making dinner than other home cooks?

They may take the greatest amount of pleasure in cooking precisely because they seek out situations in which they can spend an extended amount of time working with a constantly changing, ever-increasing level of challenge. When they challenge themselves to cook ambitiously, using a new technique, a new food, or preparing an especially complex menu, keen cooks may be able to enter a state of mind characterized by positive psychology as flow, a state in which they are fully immersed in cooking and experience a feeling of energized focus, full involvement, and deep enjoyment in the process of cooking (Csikszentmihalyi 1990).

Flow is "a state in which people are so involved in an activity that nothing else seems to matter; the experience is so enjoyable that people will continue to do it even at great cost, for the sheer sake of doing it" (Csikszentmihalyi 1990: 4). Mihaly Csikszentmihalyi's influential research and that of others indicate that people may enter into a state of flow by performing activities that are challenging, require skill, have clear and immediate feedback whereby they know whether they are doing the activity properly or not, and have well-defined success or failure metrics. Cooking meets the latter two criteria in nearly every situation. Burning the roux gave James clear and immediate feedback.

The taste, texture, and appearance of the finished gumbo were the metrics of James's success. Although we did not directly ask cooks about it, we would speculate that keen cooks likewise experience a narrowing of attention during an optimal dinner preparation session and may tend to lose track of time, another experiential aspect of flow. In Livert's interviews with professional chefs, such experiences in a crowded, noisy kitchen were frequently reported (Livert and Khabbaz 2016).

Balancing challenge and skills when choosing what and how to cook is a bit trickier. For flow to occur, the activity must be challenging, but the person must feel that they have the skills to meet that challenge. It is a delicate balance between anxiety, where the level of difficulty is too high for the person's skill, and boredom, where the level of difficulty is too low (Csikszentmihalyi 1990). To achieve an optimal cooking experience on occasion, keen cooks must seek out new recipes, foods, techniques, or flavors to achieve the necessary level of challenge in light of their considerable skills, hence their approach to cooking as a project and their continual seeking to gain new knowledge and skills. When the level of challenge is right and there is sufficient time to achieve this mental state, a routine activity such as cooking can be transformed into a transcendent experience. For cooks who have achieved flow experiences in the kitchen, new challenges may be perceived in a positive light and will be engaged in with similar focus and feelings of self-efficacy.

We could also invoke self-discrepancy theory (Higgins 1987) as another explanation for the affective advantage experienced by keen home cooks. Family-first cooks may hold idealized beliefs regarding a home cook (e.g., pleasing every eater with delicious healthy meals within time constraints) as may traditional cooks (e.g., reproducing a meal recalling a family tradition). In everyday life, the ideal may be difficult to attain, leading to negative emotions. On the other hand, the keen cooks idealized self may explicitly incorporate a sense of learning (with attendant frustrations), learning from failures, experimentation, and an orientation to building skills. Given that "failures" are expected by keen cooks, their occurrence may be associated with less discrepancy between ideal and actual selves. From day to day, keen cooks may be better able to realize their aspirations (aside from the ubiquitous temporal constraints faced by most of our cooks).

That keen cooks feel both happier and more creative from day to day when preparing dinner is consistent with evidence from a large-scale study of individuals keeping daily diaries of their activities and emotions (Connor, DeYoung, and Silvia 2017). The researchers found that individuals who engaged in small creative activities each day were happier from day to day than those who did not (statistical analyses demonstrated that activity was affecting happiness rather than vice versa). For keen cooks, cooking dinner on a typical evening provides a number of opportunities for creative reinterpretations, modifications, and tweaks.

Cooking as craftsmanship

Richard Sennett (2008) argues that craftsmanship taps the basic human impulse to do a job well for its own sake. Good craftsmanship involves developing skills and focusing on the work rather than ourselves. Keen cooks approach cooking as craftsmanship, rendering the "making" of making dinner a great source of satisfaction to keen cooks. We found that home cooks—with the exception of the few drudges in our study—enjoy the tactile and sensory experiences of making dinner, at least when they have time to focus on the task. While all the cooks whom Frances Short (2006) interviewed and most of the home cooks in our study found cooking to be a chore at least some of the time, a few keen cooks in our study claimed to always enjoy cooking. Helen, for example, said that if she were cooking in a restaurant, she might find some kitchen tasks tedious, but at home she never feels as if cooking is a chore, although she might be a bit bored chopping onions or deveining shrimp. Andrea works at home and cooks most nights for herself and her partner. She enjoys cooking nearly all of the time, with the exception of big holidays like Thanksgiving. Lois never thinks of cooking as a chore, even when she is "in the weeds." "I like when I have to try and make a lot of different things at one time. I sort of like get a high from that."

The technical challenges and the sensory balm of good smells and sounds, the hands-on tactile pleasure of chopping, stirring, kneading and mixing, the quiet hours of simmering and roasting make cooking a deeply pleasurable, sometimes even transcendent, experience for those whose confidence in their ability to succeed at the task of cooking outweighs their anxiety and fear of failure. For keen cooks especially, when they manage to carve out the time from their busy lives to spend a few hours in the kitchen cooking, they not only transform food into dinner, they transform themselves too. In making good dinners, they make themselves into good cooks and by so doing add meaning and value to their lives.

9

Making Dinner Matters

Cooking is an expression of faith in the idea that cooking matters.
—Bob del Grosso, chef instructor and home cook
(Personal communication, September 8, 2017)

Cooking matters. To the home cooks in this study who let us have a glimpse into their kitchen worlds, and to millions of Americans and others around the world, home cooking matters quite a lot. They affirm this every time they make dinner in their home kitchens. Cooking as a component of everyday life is important to how people think about themselves and their families and how they organize their daily lives. Through their labor, home cooks give shape, form, and order to the everyday lives of their families and themselves. When home cooks make dinner for their families, they make much more than a meal. They also make meaning out of their daily lives as they construct and reconstruct their sense of self and their families through food.

In this book, we have sought to show how cooking is important in making life meaningful on a personal level—as a mode of identification for some—as well as how the work of home cooks creates meaning for those they feed. Making dinner is a site within which the social element of everyday life can clearly be seen as we demonstrate how this personal practice is shaped by the context in which it takes place. Cooks in their home kitchens work at the nexus of the ideals and the quotidian realities of family meals. Home cooks negotiate daily tensions between their own aspirations for their cooking, cultural and social norms and ideologies about family, gender, care, and food, constraints of time scarcity, asynchrony, and material resources, and the expectations and preferences of those they cook for.

Despite these tensions, once they have managed to get the dinner on the table, home cooks almost always feel that their efforts have been successful. While our focus as social scientists has largely been on the constraints and negotiations entailed in home cooking as unpaid and often undervalued foodwork, we do not want to lose sight of the pleasure that many people take in home cooking or the ways in which dinner at home adds meaning to family life and is a way of performing care, sharing time together, and having fun. Home cooking can be, as Alice said of an evening when she, her husband, and their young daughters worked together to prepare sushi and edamame, a "mega-fun family time." Home cooking can also be, in an everyday world where many do not work with their hands, a deeply satisfying experience that affords opportunities for creative expression and sensual gratification.

The journals that cooks completed as part of our research documenting the process of making dinner give us rich insight into their practices, decisions, aspirations, emotions, and perceptions as they go about their daily tasks of preparing the evening meal. Home cooking is a complex, fluid, contingent process that includes planning, provisioning, preparing, and finally serving and eating food at home. Capturing data on multiple dinners made by the home cooks allows us to see patterns in their practices, feelings, and thoughts about cooking and to elucidate the commonalities and differences in how they make dinner, what cooking means to them, and how they negotiate challenges to their ability to achieve their goals in making dinner for their families.

The five dimensions of making dinner: A framework for thinking about domestic cooking

David Sutton reminds us that we "need to pay attention to the contexts in which cooking occurs, both in the sense of social relationships (gendered, generational) that surround cooking, and in the sense of the larger context of cultural values and public and media discourses that frame cooking choices and ideas about what makes for 'proper food' and 'good food'" (2014: 20). As we have seen, the process of making dinner includes more than just cooking as narrowly defined as mechanical skill, but rather this behavior encompasses the entire arc of activities, thoughts, and feelings that constitute the planning, provisioning, and preparing of the evening meal. Our consideration of the aspirations, affect, and practices of home cooks deepens our understanding of the interrelationships of the material and symbolic dimensions of our everyday lives.

Theoretical perspectives and research from the fields of anthropology, sociology, food studies, and women's studies have informed our analysis of the practice, meaning, and social dynamics of home cooking. Our basic conceptual approach derives from classic social psychology's formulation of behavior—the practice of making dinner in this case—as a function of the person, the situation, and the interaction of the two. Consistent with a person–environment or interactionist approach (Funder and Ozer 1983; Ross and Nisbett 1991), we see the cognition, affect, motivations, and behavior of the home cook in preparing dinner as shaped not only by individual factors but also by the physical and social environment, which is made up of situational factors including the material, temporal, cultural, and social. Simply put, cooking in the home kitchen is mediated by the wider contexts in which it takes place.

Making dinner is work, but it is no simple task made up of the available material resources as shaped by the individual cook's skills, motivations, knowledge, and tastes. Dinner is also a physical event, which is bounded by material and temporal considerations and occurs in a social and cultural setting. The setting of the evening meal is a complex interaction situation that is embedded in and both reflects and helps construct family relationships, personal identities, and ideologies of food, family, and gender.

We have used this conceptual framework to trace out the interrelationships of food, identity and family, the social dynamics, meanings and practices of domestic cooking, and the complex interaction situation that is making and eating dinner. We have shown how personal modes of identification, family relationships, ideologies of gender, parenthood and family, discourses of health, nutrition, food and eating, and practices, feelings and goals in producing the evening meal interrelate in the everyday lives of home cooks. We have presented the commonalities and differences in home cooks' culinary confidence and competencies, their use of recipes, how they decide what to cook and how to cook it, their practices of shopping and planning, how they judge their success in the task, how they balance multiple and sometimes contradictory objectives for dinner, and the challenges they face and pleasures they take in making dinner (see Figure 1).

Our research demonstrates that understanding the process of making dinner requires the consideration of five distinct dimensions of home cooking: *personal, material, temporal, social,* and *cultural*. The process of making dinner is shaped by the ways that personal characteristics of home cooks play out within the material, temporal, social, and cultural contexts of their daily lives to make up the particular situation of this home cook, making this dinner, for these diners, on this evening, in this kitchen. Considering the context of cooking is important because behaviors and decisions cannot be understood as acts of individual agency solely but instead are practices affected by the requirements and restrictions or opportunities and constraints of the specific social encounters in which they occur.

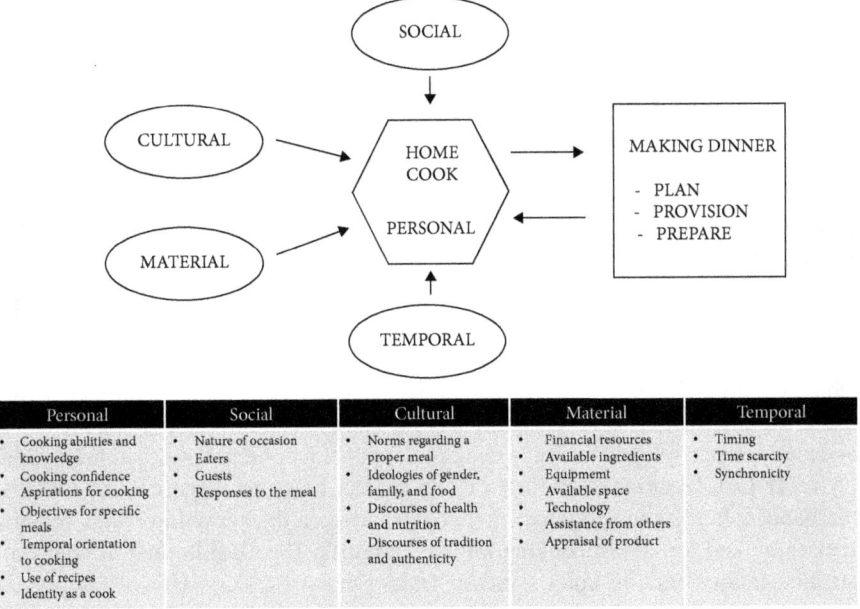

Figure 1 The Five Dimensions of Home Cooking.

The personal factors that most impact home cooks include their cooking abilities and knowledge, confidence in cooking, aspirations for cooking, objectives for specific meals, approaches to planning and the temporal dimension of cooking, use of recipes, and self-identity as a cook. The factors that constitute the material context of making dinner include what resources of money, food, equipment, space, technologies, and assistance from others are available to or utilized by the cook. It also includes the material properties of the food itself: how fresh is the produce, did it stick to the pan? The temporal dimensions of making dinner include getting the dishes and the dinner done on time, fitting the time to cook into the cook's daily life, scheduling dinnertime in busy families, and the ubiquitous problem of time scarcity for working home cooks. The cultural context of making dinner includes how the home cook is situated in regard to norms, ideologies, and discourses that relate to cooking, food, and eating such as ideologies and values of gender, family, and consumption. The cultural dimension includes normative definitions of a "proper dinner" and discourses related to food and cooking such as discourses of health, nutrition, tradition, and authenticity. The social dimension of making dinner includes the social nature of the occasion, who will eat the dinner and what is their relationship to the cook, and how the diners' responses, tastes and needs affect the cook.

The practices of home cooks are not fixed and immutable but rather responsive to changing household and personal circumstances. How home cooks think about, feel about, and do cooking changes in response to the cultural, material, temporal, and social factors in play in any particular home kitchen on any particular evening. Changes in the social context of their cooking—the people and occasions they cook for—over the life course can significantly change how cooks make dinner. For example, as children grow and change, the home cook who feeds them changes what and how they cook for them. Home cooking as an individual practice is always fluid, contingent, and relational.

How home cooks differ

Home cooks vary in how they think and feel about cooking and about themselves as cooks. We identified several different types of home cooks who shared a common general orientation in how they approach, think, and feel about cooking: drudges who dislike cooking and attach little meaning to it; family-first cooks who value their cooking as a means to create, nourish, and sustain their families; traditional cooks whose cooking allows them to make connections and continuities with their family traditions and memories; and keen cooks who strive to continually increase their skills and knowledge regarding food and cooking. The distinct orientations to home cooking of family-first, traditional, and keen cooks impact how they negotiate the material, temporal, cultural, and social factors that make up each day's cooking events and how they think and feel about cooking for their families. The meaning that home cooks attribute to their cooking and the meals that they prepare is shaped by the intersection of their personal self-identities, abilities, and aspirations as home cooks and by the material, temporal, cultural, and social contexts in which their cooking takes place.

How home cooks think and feel about themselves as cooks is in turn shaped by their experiences within these contexts, by how they judge their own success, and by their interactions with those who eat their food.

We find that home cooks (with the exception of the drudges) enjoy cooking, at least when they are not rushed. Family-first cooks particularly enjoy seeing their family members enjoying a nourishing meal that they've prepared for them—what we have termed the social dimension of making dinner. Traditional cooks take great pleasure in cooking the traditional foods that connect them to their memories and feelings about their families and their cultural heritage, part of what we have termed the cultural dimension of making dinner, while keen cooks take the most pleasure in the material dimension of making dinner. The personal dimension of home cooking—exemplified here by type of cook—acts as a mediator through which the home cook filters out from the social, cultural, and material dimensions those aspects of home cooking that are most salient and important to their kitchen lives.

For family-first cooks, cooking is first and foremost an act that expresses and enacts caring for their families. Family-first cooks are particularly focused on how their care is received, or in other words, how much their family members like their food. Cultural factors that contribute to how family-first cooks use food to care for their families include ideologies and discourses of food, family and gender, including intensive motherhood and newer discourses on children's food as a means to protect them from environmental dangers as well as ethical consumption.

Traditional cooks use foods integral to their household cuisine to create and sustain family by recreating dinners based on food memories from their families of origin and by creating new food memories for the families they are making. They may use cooking to express and perform ethnic identity. In comparison to other cooks, they are more calm and less rushed while cooking. Many view traditional food as healthy, and this may elide concerns with healthy cooking.

For keen cooks, being a good cook is a central mode of identification. In comparison to other cooks, they take more pleasure in cooking and express greater feelings of happiness and creativity when cooking. They view cooking as craftsmanship.

Modes of self-identification and other aspects of the personal dimension of home cooking shape how home cooks respond to, engage with, and make meaning of the social, cultural, and material dimensions of their experiences making dinner. For example, the material dimension of cooking, the foods that cooks choose and manipulate, and the dishes that they create and serve, can be linked to the cooks' general approach to cooking. Many home cooks want their cooking to display their personal touch. Traditional and keen cooks were especially likely to say that they wanted their meals to reflect their personal touch, but what "personal touch" means differs for different types of cooks. For family-first cooks, the "personal touch" means Mom's or Dad's cooking. For traditional cooks, the dishes that show their personal touch are dishes that are part of their ethnic or household traditions or cuisines. For keen cooks, the dishes that show their personal touch are dishes that showcase their culinary skills and knowledge.

The diversity of approaches that we found to home cooking existed within a relatively homogeneous sample of respondents. We purposively sampled to select cooks who were employed full-time and who lived with family in order to explore differences between home cooks who face relatively similar structural constraints in planning, preparing, and serving the evening meal. We wanted to understand the practice of making dinner among cooks who had access to most of what is available in the foodscape of the contemporary United States and to kitchen spaces and equipment adequate to engage in any type of preparation of those foods. We also restricted our sample to food-secure households, those that have reliable access to a sufficient quantity of affordable, nutritious food. The challenges and choices of deciding what to cook and how to cook it are strongly related to the resources available. Food insecurity can also limit the variety of food and the likelihood of trying new foods.

Economic class, gender, race, ethnicity, region, nationality, religion, etc., are important factors in shaping the material, cultural, and social dimensions within which the practice of home cooking is embedded. These social structural factors may constrain choices that home cooks make in their everyday practice. However, we did not find that these factors were associated with the personal level of general orientation or approach to planning and preparing the evening meal, nor did they seem to affect the motivations, aspirations, and goals of home cooks for their cooking nor their ways of approaching planning or the time dimension of cooking. We find no clear relationship between ethnic background and becoming a family-first, keen, planful, improvisational, or even a traditional cook. Similarly, although gender shapes cooking in many ways, it does not seem to predict what type of cook one will become: the men in our study who have assumed the role of primary home cook include family-first, traditional, and keen cooks.

Our home cooks were intentionally sampled from middle-class and some upper middle-class households in order to "control" for potential variations in terms of available resources when examining the varying orientations of home cooks to making dinner. In a separate pilot study, we investigated whether home cooks who face severe resource deficits diverged in their thinking about preparing the evening meal. We conducted interviews with thirty-four individuals who collected food for their households from local food banks in a Pennsylvania city. Four out of ten had children under the age of eighteen living with them. Just under two-thirds (62 percent) were on SNAP (food stamps). Nearly three-quarters (71 percent) were classified as food insecure by the USDA's US Household Food Security Module (Bicket et al., 2000) 39 percent received a very low food-security classification.

During our interviews, they responded to the same questions as the cooks in this study regarding the considerations important to them when preparing dinner. The objectives in making dinner among this economically stressed group of home cooks were remarkably similar to those of the relatively affluent cooks described in this book. Cooking a meal the family likes was most important (94 percent), followed by a healthy meal (91 percent), a balanced meal (88 percent), and a meal that was easy (79 percent) and convenient (76 percent). Interestingly, these cooks were more likely than our middle-class cooks to consider it important that the evening meal reflected their personal touch (76 percent), which may suggest a higher proportion of traditional cooks in this sample. The food-insecure families were also more likely than middle-class families to say providing a meal that was comforting was important to them in deciding what to cook (76 percent). Our findings here are similar to those of Priya Fielding-Singh (2017), who has found in her study of parents in Los Angeles that while wealthy and poor parents were similar in their beliefs in the importance of healthy food for their children, they diverged in terms of the meanings that they attached to food, with poor parents using food to buffer against deprivation and provide emotional comfort to their children.

Cooks approach planning and the temporal dimension of cooking differently, as we see in improvisational versus planful cooks. They may hold different general orientations to and aspirations for their cooking, as in traditional versus keen cooks. These personal approaches are important to shaping cooking practices and the meaning of cooking in everyday life and its role in identity work, but because of the limitations of our study, we are not able to understand the process by which individual cooks develop their approach to cooking. It may well be that certain personality traits, such as differences in approaches to time (time urgency) or to challenge (hardiness), may account for some of the variations in approach to cooking.

Issues of food, family, and identity are emotional and complex. In ongoing research, we are investigating the ways in which many young women use food-related identities and related cooking practices in their struggles to establish an independent identity, while others use food and cooking to express their continued identification with family traditions. In the present study, we have the case of Joseph and Monique, a married couple whose parents are from Haiti and Trinidad, respectively. They both cook and are somewhat keen but have incorporated their traditional cuisines into their cooking lives differently. Joseph is a traditional cook who has been perfecting his grandmother's Haitian rice and beans for seven years. In contrast, his wife doesn't often cook traditional food. She did list "baked macaroni and cheese" as the meal most representative of her as a cook, so her identity as a cook is not unrelated to her family background. (Baked macaroni and cheese is a traditional Caribbean dish using evaporated milk that cooks from Trinidad, Jamaica, Haiti, and Barbados may prepare.) An improvisational cook at times, Monique has no favorite recipes from her family but says, "I wish I did. My mother keeps trying to teach me, but they don't stick." Joseph and Monique are similar in many ways, and we don't know why he works to replicate his grandmother's cooking and why her mother's recipes don't play a larger role in her cooking practice. Tracing the trajectories through which individual home cooks develop their approaches to cooking as practice and modes of self-identification over the course of their lives remains a key question to understanding this important aspect of everyday life.

How cooking matters

What role does home cooking play in people's lives? Cooking, for many people, is a mode of self-identification and can be a central part of their narrative of self-identity and how they give meaning to their lives across the years. Cooking is a means through which individuals make meaning of their lives. Being a home cook can figure in how people understand themselves as unique individuals, as a good cook, a keen cook, a traditional cook, etc. Being a home cook can also be a means of understanding oneself as a social being, as one who cooks for others and as one who occupies particular social positions related to life stage, gender, ethnicity, class, and culture. "We come to know ourselves and to know about the world through the stories that we tell, and through the meanings that we construct from these self-defining narratives" (Singer 2004: 454).

The stories we tell of what we cooked, for whom, and how shape the stories of our lives. As an illustration, throughout her cooking journal, Pamela reflected on herself as a home cook, from her youthful experimentations to dinners she made during the study. In the journal she labored over (voluntarily retyping her handwritten version into a word-processing file to send to us), Pamela meticulously recounted a story of how she once made a particular dish for dinner—four decades earlier. That Pamela remembers this story in such detail and that she took the time to write it for us suggests that being a home cook has been part of how she has understood herself, a mode of self-identification for her.

> I only made this once, and it was a hit. I didn't know what I was doing, but when I was young I didn't care, I'd just make a stab at some things that I must have eaten in a restaurant or read about. Anyway, I would start with shrimp cocktails on a bed of lettuce with a thin slice of lemon and a spicy sauce of ketchup and horse radish. After washing a bunch of mussels, I'd simmer them until they opened, put them in a bowl—put washed, peeled, and deveined shrimp in the same bowl with a slice of lemon. Rinse some bay scallops and add to the bowl. Then in a large skillet heat two chopped cloves of garlic in a little olive oil and a few pats of butter, heat the mixture until it thickens a bit and add some white wine. Save the liquid in the bowl. Add the shrimp to the liquid in the skillet, let them simmer a few minutes until they start to be pink, then add the mussels, simmer for a couple of minutes and add the scallops. Simmer everything for a few minutes and remove from the stove. You can add some of the leftover water in the bowl to the butter/wine sauce. Pour the sauce and seafood over the spaghetti and serve with Italian grated cheese, Italian bread, and a glass of white wine, and a small green salad on the side. (Pamela)

Our approach to home cooking and identity adopts MacClancy's modes of self-identification (2004), which emphasizes the roles, motivations, and actions of agents in the process of developing, maintaining, and enacting a sense of self. We find that family-first, traditional, and keen cooks cook and think about food in distinctive manners that produce, perform, and affirm their sense of themselves as good home cooks. Like any other mode of self-identification, it is important to home cooks to succeed, based upon their own criteria, at making dinner, to be a "good" home cook. For those whose self-identity is based in part on being a home cook, their cooking is imbued with moral value. Cooks' overall approach to cooking—whether the ultimate goal of their cooking practice is to nourish and sustain their family (family-first cooks), to continue their family traditions (traditional cooks), or to challenge themselves to produce the highest-quality food they can (keen cooks)—shapes their beliefs, feelings, thoughts, and practices related to cooking.

Home cooks make dinner because it is a way that they express love and care for their families. They make dinner because they care about the continuity, maintenance, and repair of the family and the relationships that constitute it. Planning and preparing the evening meal is a mode of taking care of the family that home cooks take responsibility for. Aspirations for their family life that cooks care about drive the ways in which they organize the feeding of their families.

If cooks care that their families are healthy or carry on family traditions or support community farming, then cooks will try to provision and produce meals, which are consonant with these ways of thinking about food and family. Direct caregiving—actually making dinner—involves continuous and dense time commitments and therefore requires a great deal of responsiveness to the unfolding exigencies of everyday life. Consequently, in the daily expression of their care for their family, making dinner for home cooks often becomes more about the direct caregiving of feeding their family a home-cooked dinner and less connected to other goals they also care about. Thinking about the practice of home cooking through the lens of feminist theories of caring helps us understand why home cooking is so meaningful to those who cook and how it remains so even when cooks must compromise their ideals to get dinner on the table on a daily basis.

What matters to cooks

Family dinner is a complex social interaction. To be successful, family dinner requires the alignment of the goals, feelings, skills, and knowledge of those who cook with the goals, feelings, and tastes of those who eat. These alignments and negotiations take place within the context of structural constraints such as time available to cook, family schedules, and what foods are available in the kitchen at the time that cooking begins. Almost all the meals reported in the cooking journals were considered to be successes by the cooks, with only 3 percent of dinners rated as failures. Different orientations to and feelings about cooking and food resulted in different attributions of failure or success. For some keen and traditional cooks, failure derived from their own assessment of the quality of the dish they prepared. For some family-first cooks, an attribution of failure was based on the reaction—either explicit or implicit—of those who ate the meal. Overall, the most often identified reason for considering a dinner to be a success is that the family liked it, followed by an assessment on the part of the cook herself that the dinner was of good quality in terms of taste and healthiness. Taken together with cooks' self-evaluations, these attributions of success suggest that what is most important to home cooks is getting a dinner on the table that their family will eat.

Why cooking matters

One of the most pleasurable aspects of cooking is the rare opportunity it provides for many in the modern world to create something with one's hands. As production has lost its place in the work life of most contemporary Americans, some argue that it has become more important in home life, specifically in the form of "productive leisure" (Gelber 1999). Productive leisure can include making things, like lemon curd, and it may involve learning things such as mastering a new cuisine or technique. For Andrea, the pleasure of cooking comes from the production or making of food with her hands, a type of producing or making she does not experience in her work life: "I really enjoy the hands-on part of it, especially sitting at the computer all day." Making dinner as craft gives home cooks what may be a rare experience of agency and competency, when they do something and can see the immediate, material result of their actions. Transforming the raw ingredients of the refrigerator and pantry into a beautiful plated meal is about experiencing agency within the constraints of the material qualities of the foodstuffs. Making dinner can satisfy the human need to be creative and to make things with one's hands.

Home cooking can be a way to connect or reconnect with ourselves, our food, and our families and friends. Most Americans don't build houses or make clothes or perform medical care for our loved ones. But we do still cook for them. So while home cooking can and often does, especially for keen cooks, bring pleasure as a form of productive leisure, we argue that it is in fact much more consequential than that.

Home cooking as caring entails paying attention to the needs and desires of those who eat one's food. A home-cooked dinner can be a site that promotes the continuity, maintenance, and repair of family relationships. Home cooks care for loved ones by making their favorite comfort foods, sometimes to celebrate good times and sometimes to alleviate distress. The considerations that home cooks say are most important to them in deciding what to make for dinner are, in order of importance, that the meal be healthy; that the family likes it; that is comforting, well-balanced, and economical; and that is in the cooks' family traditions. Every one of these considerations is an expression of care for their families. Even convenient and easy to prepare dishes, considerations that were also important to our home cooks (although less so), are about caring when choosing these dishes means a cook can manage to make a home-cooked dinner on a day when she would otherwise not be able to.

Making time for dinner

> I just wish I had more time. We eat out so much. I just we had more time to eat at home. (Janet)

In the "About" page of her website, Mommy Hates Cooking, Kristy Still appeals to those suffering from the common dilemma of time scarcity and offers recipes, workbooks, cookbooks, and planning advice to solve their problem.

> Most of us have come to a point in time where we say to ourselves, "I hate cooking!" I'm sure most of the time it tends to be when we are trying to balance a family plus work and so on, right? I mean when you get home from school and immediately

it's time to get homework done before heading out to football practice or dance class, when exactly do you cook? Most of us live very busy lives and there just isn't even enough time in the day to cook a decent meal. That's the dilemma I was running into. I realized that it wasn't that I hated cooking, it was that I had NO time to actually cook. (Mommy Hates Cooking 2017)

As discussed in Chapter 4, temporal challenges are the most significant obstacle that home cooks face in their objective to feed their families a home-cooked dinner. Time scarcity is the primary factor that saps the joy from and attenuates the meaning of home cooking, turning it into a tedious chore when not completely derailing the cook's plan. A lack of time can transform home cooking from an act of caring about and taking care of to simple caregiving.

Our respondents longed for more time in the kitchen. Like Janet's comment above, their cooking journals were full of lamentations about the time pressure that home cooks feel. The home cook has to find the time to make the dinner and must time its completion to suit the schedules of the diners.

Time scarcity and asynchronous family schedules are at least occasional challenges for all the cooks we spoke to. We found that cooks who feel rushed—that they don't have enough time to cook dinner the way they would like to—feel more anxious, less valued, less happy, and more bored while preparing dinner than cooks who felt they had adequate time. Younger children make it hard for some home cooks to find time to focus on their kitchen tasks. The strenuous schedule of older children's organized activities creates challenges for cooks who are trying to get everyone to the table at the same time. While we found ourselves drawn to the discussion of the problem of time asynchrony, problems with time for the home cook are really about time scarcity. And that time scarcity is due to work schedules that leave little time for family life. Almost all of our home cooks worked outside the home and struggled to carve time out of the day to make dinner. As a dual career couple with a young child, time scarcity is a taken-for-granted constraint for us as well, within which we struggle daily to accomplish our family life.

Judith's cooking journal chronicling her experiences making dinner during our study exemplifies the temporal challenges that home cooks face, as well as how they overcome these to make a home-cooked dinner possible for their families. Judith's cooking was affected by both time scarcity and the asynchronous schedules of her household members. She cooks for her husband Bob, her eleven-year-old daughter Avery, and thirteen-year-old son Bill. Her family eats out or gets takeout or delivery food four to six times a month.

Judith works part time as a registered dietician, so she has a large stock of knowledge about nutrition, healthy foods, and cooking. On the nights she checked the box indicating that "shows my personal touch" was important to her in deciding what to cook for dinner, she cooked nutritious foods such as salmon and grilled chicken. Judith collects recipes from newspapers, magazines, and websites: her criteria for selection include healthy, ease of preparation for a weeknight meal, and use of garden vegetables. The menu she chose to most represent her as a cook was salmon with maple glaze, rice pilaf, sautéed fresh spinach, and fruit salad.

In her interview, Judith talked about how she decided what to make for dinner. Time was her first consideration, both in regard to time scarcity and asynchrony.

> I consider the time I have. What I have on hand. Lately, whether something will keep or not because it seems like we are eating in shifts. Someone might eat at 5:30 because he's got something going on at 6 and then my husband might not be home until 7:30. (Judith)

On Tuesday mornings, Judith sits down with the family's calendar and decides what they will have for dinner during the week. She tries to plan as much as possible and buy what groceries she needs for the whole week that morning. Judith's children are involved in multiple activities, including soccer, softball, Boy Scouts, and a handbell choir. She plans her dinner menus "with the specific day in mind. Does Bill have soccer that day, etc.? Will I have an hour to stand there and make dinner?"

Convenience is important to Judith on nights when she works during the day. She will make "something quick or in the crock pot. Doesn't take a whole lot of steps. Just straightforward." She most enjoys cooking "on the weekends or on my days off when I don't have to hurry." She least enjoys cooking "when we're in a hurry. When I've got to feed everyone in shifts because someone's running out at different times or getting home late."

Saturday: Went out to eat because the food in the crock pot wasn't done and it was too late to make something else.

Sunday: *Roasted chicken (cooked in roasting pan with carrots, potatoes and apples), gravy (canned), spaghetti squash with roasted cherry tomatoes, whole wheat dinner rolls, green salad with romaine, red pepper, celery and radishes, salad dressings, margarine.*

Judith had started the chicken and vegetables in the slow cooker on Saturday, but they were not done in time for dinner. The next day, she cut them up and roasted them in the oven. The chicken was from her local farmer's market and the tomatoes from her garden (she sourced the recipe for the tomatoes from the Smitten Kitchen online blog). She chose the menu because it was healthy, comforting, well balanced, and liked by her family. She rated the meal as a success: "Yes, it was healthy, there was plenty to eat, and everyone liked it."

Monday: *Turkey chili, cornbread, bowl of carrot, cucumber and green pepper sticks.* Judith chose this menu because it was "something we could eat at different times when we got home from activities." It was important to her that the meal be fast, healthy, and liked by her family. She got the chili recipe from the newspaper fifteen years ago. All the members of the family ate at different times. "Avery ate at 5:30–6:30 while I was bringing/waiting for Bill at soccer. Bob ate when he got home at 6–7, I ate at 7:20 after bringing Bill to Boy Scouts." Of the meal, Judith wrote, "It was easy and routine; I've made it a hundred times."

Tuesday: *Chicken tetrazzini [baked pasta dish], green salad, baby carrots, leftover spaghetti squash.* Judith chose this menu because it "used up leftover children, could be eaten at different times." Everyone "ate in shifts" this evening. She packed her daughter's tetrazzini in a cup to take in the car. "Avery ate in the car on the way to softball. She liked it but said it was too 'herby.' Bill [son] and I ate together at 6, then I took him somewhere. Bob ate after picking Avery up at 7." In answer to the question about whether the meal was a success, Judith wrote, "Relatively, we ate a healthy meal, it wasn't take-out."

Wednesday: No one ate at home. Judith worked until 8:00 and packed leftovers. Bob took Bill out to a diner. Avery ate at church before handbell practice.

Thursday: *Take-out pizza, tossed salad, bowl of grapes.*

Judith "ran out of time to make homemade pizza because I unexpectedly had to pick up Avery from softball practice."

Friday: *Salmon, jambalaya rice mix, spinach, butternut squash, toasted garlic bread using leftover hamburger buns and English muffins.*

Judith chose this meal because it was healthy, liked by her family, showed her personal touch, and was easy to cook. The personal touch was related to Judith's knowledge of nutrition. As she explained, "It's important to get a source of Omega 3 fatty acids 2x/wk." Everyone was home to eat and enjoyed the dinner. Judith "moderately enjoyed [making dinner.] I had to hold off for a while on the fish because Bob was late getting home." She noted that "timing" was a difficulty in cooking. Judith felt this meal was definitely successful: "Yes, because it was good for us, it turned out well and salmon was cooked perfectly."

Saturday: The family went to a charity spaghetti dinner held at their church.

Sunday: *Marinated grilled chicken breast, tossed salad, pesto, sliced and grilled polenta, toasted tortilla wedges.*

The pesto was homemade from the garden, made on Friday night using a recipe she clipped from *Cooking Light* magazine seven years earlier. Judith chose this menu because it was healthy, something different, well balanced, and showed her personal touch. Everyone was home to eat on Sunday night: "They loved the chicken, didn't love the polenta but ate some of it." Judith thought this meal was successful "because I cooked the chicken perfectly and just about had everything ready at the same time."

Monday: *Turkey stroganoff with ground turkey served over egg noodles, steamed cabbage, lima beans.*

She chose this meal because it was fast, well balanced, convenient, and easy to cook. She used a packet of stroganoff seasoning mix and frozen lima beans in a butter sauce. Everyone was home to eat. Judith did not enjoy cooking this dinner very much because "it was rushed." She felt rushed, rather anxious, and rather bored while making dinner. In answer to the journal query about whether she felt the meal was successful, Judith wrote, "I don't always care whether the meal was a success, just that there is a decent meal available that's relatively healthy."

At the end of the journal, reflecting on her statement from the interview that she was a good cook, Judith wrote, "I am a good cook, I just don't always have the time to cook as well as I would like to." In the section at the end of the journal for any additional comments about home cooking, Judith wrote, "It's difficult to cook the way I'd like to when four out of seven nights a week at dinnertime I have to transport the kids to sports and other activities."

Judith's cooking journal shows how complex family dinner can be in households where time to cook is scarce and time to be together is scarce as well. Time figures in her description of every meal she cooked. On the first night of her journal, the dish she had planned wasn't ready on time to serve for dinner. On two nights, there wasn't time to cook what she had planned. On another two nights, she struggled to get all the dishes ready at the same time (on one of these nights, the trouble was that her husband got home late.) One night, everyone ate at different times to accommodate the children's scheduled activities. Another night, everyone again ate at different times because of asynchronous schedules, and Judith's daughter ate her dinner in the car on the way to softball practice. Despite the formidable temporal and logistical challenges she faces, Judith persists in making the meals that are so important to her: relatively healthy, homemade dinners for her family.

Where is cooking going?

Given the amount of public discourse in contemporary society about the consequences for social, individual, and environmental health of how we shop, cook, and eat food, there is still surprising little empirical data about the practice of cooking in the context of everyday life (Sutton 2014). Public discourse about the current and future state of home cooking in affluent societies tends to posit a continuing decline in the practice and knowledge of home cooking with dire results predicted for the health and wellbeing of individuals, families, and society. Our study of the practice and meaning of home cooking, while idiographic and not generalizable to the American population, nevertheless sheds some light on these public concerns with domestic cookery.

First, persistent concerns that the easy availability of convenience and prepared foods will inevitably result in a loss of cooking skills and kitchen literacy, with a concomitant dependence on industrially prepared foods, seem overstated. Our findings and those of others lead us to argue that the skills and knowledge needed to make dinner may have changed, but they have not been lost. Most of our participants had many basic cooking skills and were confident in the kitchen. Time constraints and family tastes accounted for most of the use of convenience foods among our home cooks, not a lack of cooking skills.

Next, the recurrent charge that, while relatively affluent Americans spend much time consuming old and new media on food and cooking and invest in state-of-the-art kitchens, they no longer regularly cook at home should be put to rest. Our findings and the research on trends in time-use reviewed in Chapter 2 indicate that most Americans continue to cook dinner at home most nights of the week and that the prevalence of home cooking has been relatively stable for the past twenty-five years. Lastly, we address fears of the decline of family dinner and loss of its important dietary, familial, and societal benefits by problematizing what should or may be defined as "family dinner" and as "home-cooked" and by pointing to the valiant efforts of the home cooks in our study to provide a home-cooked dinner for their families despite many challenges and constraints.

One problem with the debate over the decline of the family dinner is that the terms of the debate are not clear. Is it family dinner if family members eat at the same time but eat different meals? To accommodate conflicting likes and dislikes, some families in our study do this. Do "baking off some frozen chicken nuggets" as Judith says and making a salad count as preparing family dinner? Because of time scarcity, some home cooks in our study do this. Is it family dinner if family members eat a home-cooked meal but not at the same time? Because of conflicting schedules, the families in our study sometimes do this. Is it family dinner if everyone eats their home-cooked dinner in the living room while watching a movie? One would guess from the experts and social critics decrying the demise of the family dinner that these alternative practices do not "count" as home cooking. But for our home cooks they do.

For example, on a Friday night, Pauline, who wrote that she has "many advanced cooking skills but I don't always use them due to limited time," made Western omelets with salad with a bottled dressing and whole wheat rolls from the bakery for herself, her husband, and her teenage daughter. She indicated in her cooking journal that she wanted to cook a meal that was fast, healthy, and easy. That night, her cooking journal included the following question and her response:

Q: If this were an ideal world with unlimited amounts of time, money and talent, what would you want to have had for your family dinner tonight?
A: "Cedar plank wild salmon! Some type of soup, roasted baby vegetables, a big salad with lots of veggies, a wild rice pilaf, lemon soufflé."

Although she didn't "really think about it" while cooking the meal and felt "so-so" about it, Pauline considered the meal a success because "it was easy. I didn't have to think too much at the end of the long week." The most important thing to Pauline was to provide a home-cooked meal for her family: "We ate in 'waves' but we all ate at home."

Paradoxically, when it is done well, the work that home cooks do is often unacknowledged and unremarked upon, at least in the public sphere. Anne Murcott (1997) argues that fears of the decline of home cooking are symbolic expressions of concerns about the changing family. As Lupton (1996) points out, the family gathered around the dinner table is a powerful visual symbol of the family. As more households have single parents, same-sex parents, or men as primary cooks, certainly the dinner table of today's families may look rather different than the dinner tables they grew up with. Home cooks use the family dinner to knit families together and to make memories of the dinner table. While various public and private entities and individuals call for more and healthier home cooking to improve the lives, family relationships, and health of Americans, without restructuring the expectations of the workplace, home cooks will continue to struggle to carve out the time to cook and eat dinner with their families.

Home cooks persevere in making dinner because it is a way that they express love and care for their families. The home cooks in our study went to great lengths to preserve the practice of sharing a home-cooked meal, even when this meant preparing in essence two meals to suit family members' divergent tastes or family members eating in parent–child shifts to accommodate the children's schedule of activities. Providing a home-cooked meal for their families is of great importance to our respondents who struggle against significant temporal, logistical, and familial challenges to successfully put dinner on the table. On the last night of her cooking journal, Kaye wrote in response to the question, "Considering what was important to you in preparing tonight's meal, do you feel the meal was a success? Why or why not?"

> After these two weeks of journal writing, I can safely say that *cooking* is what is most important to me, with good, quality ingredients being the runner-up. With that in mind, tonight was a success because I cooked at home. It could have been better with more vegetables, or with more homemade components, but we were home, together, with a home-cooked meal, so ... success. ☺ (punctuated with a hand drawn smiley face) (Kaye)

Not every home cook would be willing to pack their home-cooked dinner into a cup for eating in the car, as Judith did with her daughter's chicken tetrazzini. If we as a society truly want to encourage home cooking and support family dinner, we will need to listen to cooks and hear their struggles with time scarcity and asynchronous schedules. If we heed cooks, we will see that without significant changes in how we organize and prioritize our use of time between work, children's structured activities, and time at home to cook and eat together, home cooks will continue to struggle to carve out time to make the dinners they want to make. Some will give up, as have the drudges, and simply go through the motions, turning to convenience foods when they have to get dinner on the table and don't really care anymore how they do so. Nevertheless, given the centrality of feeding their families home-cooked dinners that they enjoy to home cooks' identities, family relationships, and daily lives, we expect that home cooking—and home cooks—will persist. Home cooks will find the time because it means so much to them. As Kaye told us, a successful dinner is first and foremost just a dinner that is made and eaten at home, together. Home cooks will keep on cooking because, in the apt words of this chapter's epigraph, they keep the faith.

Appendix A: Interview Protocol

First, I need to get a sense of your home and household.

1. Who lives at your house?
    a. Give initials or first names.
    b. [for each:]
        i. How old is ___?
        ii. How is ___ related to you?
        iii. Highest level of educational attainment?
        iv. What type of work does ___ do?
2. As you know, people from different countries and regions of the world have different foods they like to cook. How would you describe the ethnic background or national origin of your household members?
3. Typically, who eats dinner together, and tell me a little about how it works at your house.
4. How much cooking do you do at home? Breakfast, lunch, dinner?
5. If you were to say, I am a "_____" cook, how would you fill in the blank?
6. Have there been times in your life when you have done more or less cooking?
7. How often do you eat out or have food delivered for dinner? How many days a week do you typically cook dinner at home?
8. Who cooks or helps prepare dinner at your house?
9. What kinds of dishes do you typically cook for dinner? What would be a typical dinner menu for you?
10. Do you plan out your menus in advance or have any routines like Taco Tuesday?
11. How do you decide what you will prepare for dinner each night? (After subject completes answer, prompt for: economical, healthy, convenient, easy to cook, fast, novelty [something different], challenging, traditional, comforting, trendy, shows my personal touch, indulgent, family likes, gourmet, well-balanced.) What does each of these mean to you? (For example, ask, "What does 'healthy' mean to you?")
12. Nowadays some people describe themselves as "foodies." What does the term "foodie" mean to you?
13. How would you describe your own relationship to food? For example, some people call themselves "foodies" and some are "vegans." Do you identify with any of these?
    a. Why would you describe yourself as ____?
14. Do you enjoy preparing food and cooking?
15. At what type of occasions do you most enjoy cooking? Least?

16. Are there times when cooking is a leisure activity or a hobby or recreation for you? When?
17. Are there times when cooking feels like a chore to you? When?
18. Does cooking sometimes feel difficult to you? When? What are the difficulties exactly?
19. Do you sometimes have difficulties deciding what to cook for dinner? When?
20. Do you follow recipes when you cook? When? How exact? What appeals to you about using recipes? Where do you get your recipes?
21. Shopping. How often? Where? With list?
22. Do you plan to cook at home for dinner tonight? What are you making?

In the second phase of this project, we are asking participants to keep a brief cooking journal each night for fourteen days. This will involve you answering some questions about what you cook for the evening meal. We will very much appreciate you doing this for us—it should take about five to ten minutes each night, even less if you eat out that night or bring prepared food home. Are you still willing to do that?

Great, we can either send you the cooking journal by standard mail with a return envelope or e-mail it to and you can e-mail the completed form back. Which would you prefer? (Get address or e-mail) _____

And could you recommend a friend or neighbor who you think would like to participate in this study as well? (Get phone or e-mail) _____

Appendix B: Cooking Journal

DAY 1: DAY OF THE WEEK: _____

Nowadays, some people called themselves "foodies." What does the term "foodie" mean to you?

To what degree do you consider yourself a "foodie?" [Place an "X" next to the appropriate number]

    Not at all   Totally

       1   2   3   4   5   6   7   8   9   10

Did you have a home-cooked dinner tonight?

__ NO: WENT OUT TO EAT____ ORDERED IN ____ TAKEOUT _____

Any particular reasons for not cooking at home tonight?

__ YES [Continue below]

Tonight's menu (list all dishes; for example main dish, sides, bread, salad, dessert):

Who cooked or prepared the food for tonight's meal?

When and where did you shop for the main components of tonight's meal?

When did you plan tonight's meal?

Which of the following were most important to you in preparing tonight's meal? "I wanted to cook a meal that was …"
[Put an "X" next to each item that applies.]

__ economical   __ healthy   __ convenient   __easy to cook
__ fast   __ something different __ liked by my family   __authentic

__ in my family's traditions   __ comforting   __ showed my personal touch   __ gourmet
__ indulgent or a special treat __ well-balanced   __ challenging to me as a cook   __trendy

Any other things you considered?

Did you follow any recipes? If so, where did you get them?

Were any components of the dishes preprepared (for example, canned chicken broth)? Please list.

Who was home for dinner tonight? What was their reaction/response to the meal?

How much did you enjoy cooking tonight's meal?

Explain any difficulties you experienced cooking tonight's meal.

Considering what was important to you in preparing tonight's meal, do you feel the meal was a success? Why or why not?

Appendix B: Cooking Journal

DAY 2: DAY OF THE WEEK: _____

| If you had only yourself to cook for tonight, what would you have eaten? |

Did you have a home-cooked dinner tonight?

__ NO: WENT OUT TO EAT____
ORDERED IN ____ TAKE-OUT _____

Any particular reasons for not cooking at home tonight?

__ YES [Continue below]

Tonight's menu (list all dishes; for example main dish, sides, bread, salad, dessert):

Who cooked or prepared the food for tonight's meal?

When and where did you shop for the main components of tonight's meal?

When did you plan tonight's meal?

Which of the following were most important to you in preparing tonight's meal? "I wanted to cook a meal that was ..."
[Put an "X" next to each item that applies.]

- __ economical
- __ fast
- __ in my family's traditions
- __ indulgent or a special treat
- __ healthy
- __ something different
- __ comforting
- __ well-balanced
- __ convenient
- __ liked by my family
- __ showed my personal touch
- __ challenging to me as a cook
- __ easy to cook
- __ authentic
- __ gourmet
- __trendy

Any other things you considered?

Did you follow any recipes? If so, where did you get them?

Were any components of the dishes preprepared (for example, canned chicken broth)? Please list.

Who was home for dinner tonight? What was their reaction/response to the meal?

How much did you enjoy cooking tonight's meal?

Explain any difficulties you experienced cooking tonight's meal.

Considering what was important to you in preparing tonight's meal, do you feel the meal was a success? Why or why not?

Appendix B: Cooking Journal   179

DAY 3: DAY OF THE WEEK: _____

Did you have a home-cooked dinner tonight?

__ NO: WENT OUT TO EAT____ ORDERED IN ____ TAKE-OUT _____

Any particular reasons for not cooking at home tonight?

__ YES [Continue below]

Tonight's menu (list all dishes; for example main dish, sides, bread, salad, dessert):

Who cooked or prepared the food for tonight's meal?

When and where did you shop for the main components of tonight's meal?

When did you plan tonight's meal?

Which of the following were most important to you in preparing tonight's meal? "I wanted to cook a meal that was ..."
[Put an "X" next to each item that applies.]

__ economical	__ healthy	__ convenient	__ easy to cook
__ fast	__ something different	__ liked by my family	__ authentic
__ in my family's traditions	__ comforting	__ showed my personal touch	__ gourmet
__ indulgent or a special treat	__ well-balanced	__ challenging to me as a cook	__ trendy

Any other things you considered?

Did you follow any recipes? If so, where did you get them?

Were any components of the dishes preprepared (for example, canned chicken broth)? Please list.

Who was home for dinner tonight? What was their reaction/response to the meal?

How much did you enjoy cooking tonight's meal?

Explain any difficulties you experienced cooking tonight's meal.

Considering what was important to you in preparing tonight's meal, do you feel the meal was a success? Why or why not?

How did you feel while preparing tonight's meal? *Put an "X" next to each number.*								
	Rushed	1	2	3	4	5	6	7	Relaxed
	Anxious	1	2	3	4	5	6	7	Calm
	Happy	1	2	3	4	5	6	7	Unhappy
	Uncertain	1	2	3	4	5	6	7	Confident
	Valued	1	2	3	4	5	6	7	Taken for granted
	Organized	1	2	3	4	5	6	7	Chaotic
	Creative	1	2	3	4	5	6	7	Bored

Appendix B: Cooking Journal

DAY 4: DAY OF THE WEEK: _____

> Do you watch any television programs on food or cooking? Which ones do you like most? Have you ever cooked any recipes from TV or TV chefs? How did that work out for you?

Did you have a home-cooked dinner tonight?

__ NO: WENT OUT TO EAT____
ORDERED IN ____ TAKE-OUT _____

Any particular reasons for not cooking at home tonight?

__ YES [Continue below]

Tonight's menu (list all dishes; for example main dish, sides, bread, salad, dessert):

Who cooked or prepared the food for tonight's meal?

When and where did you shop for the main components of tonight's meal?

When did you plan tonight's meal?

Which of the following were most important to you in preparing tonight's meal? "I wanted to cook a meal that was ..."
[Put an "X" next to each item that applies.]

__ economical   __ healthy   __ convenient   __ easy to cook
__ fast   __ something different   __ liked by my family   __ authentic
__ in my family's   __ comforting   __ showed my   __ gourmet
   traditions   personal touch
__ indulgent or a   __ well-balanced   __ challenging to me   __ trendy
   special treat   as a cook

Any other things you considered?

Did you follow any recipes? If so, where did you get them?

Were any components of the dishes preprepared (for example, canned chicken broth)? Please list.

Who was home for dinner tonight? What was their reaction/response to the meal?

How much did you enjoy cooking tonight's meal?

Explain any difficulties you experienced cooking tonight's meal.

Considering what was important to you in preparing tonight's meal, do you feel the meal was a success? Why or why not?

DAY 5: DAY OF THE WEEK: _____

> Do any members of your household help you in the kitchen? What do they do? How do you feel about helpers?

Did you have a home-cooked dinner tonight?
__ NO: WENT OUT TO EAT____
ORDERED IN ____ TAKE-OUT _____
Any particular reasons for not cooking at home tonight?

__ YES [Continue below]

Tonight's menu (list all dishes; for example main dish, sides, bread, salad, dessert):

Who cooked or prepared the food for tonight's meal?

When and where did you shop for the main components of tonight's meal?

When did you plan tonight's meal?

Which of the following were most important to you in preparing tonight's meal? "I wanted to cook a meal that was …"
[Put an "X" next to each item that applies.]

__ economical	__ healthy	__ convenient	__ easy to cook
__ fast	__ something different	__ liked by my family	__ authentic
__ in my family's traditions	__ comforting	__ showed my personal touch	__ gourmet
__ indulgent or a special treat	__ well-balanced	__ challenging to me as a cook	__trendy

Any other things you considered?

Did you follow any recipes? If so, where did you get them?

Were any components of the dishes preprepared (for example, canned chicken broth)? Please list.

Who was home for dinner tonight? What was their reaction/response to the meal?

How much did you enjoy cooking tonight's meal?

Explain any difficulties you experienced cooking tonight's meal.

Considering what was important to you in preparing tonight's meal, do you feel the meal was a success? Why or why not?

DAY 6: DAY OF THE WEEK: _____

Did you have a home-cooked dinner tonight?

__ NO: WENT OUT TO EAT____ ORDERED IN ____ TAKE-OUT _____

Any particular reasons for not cooking at home tonight?

__ YES [Continue below]

Tonight's menu (list all dishes; for example main dish, sides, bread, salad, dessert):

Who cooked or prepared the food for tonight's meal?

When and where did you shop for the main components of tonight's meal?

When did you plan tonight's meal?

Which of the following were most important to you in preparing tonight's meal? "I wanted to cook a meal that was ..."
[Put an "X" next to each item that applies.]

__ economical	__ healthy	__ convenient	__ easy to cook
__ fast	__ something different	__ liked by my family	__ authentic
__ in my family's traditions	__ comforting	__ showed my personal touch	__ gourmet
__ indulgent or a special treat	__ well-balanced	__ challenging to me as a cook	__ trendy

Any other things you considered?

Did you follow any recipes? If so, where did you get them?

Were any components of the dishes preprepared (for example, canned chicken broth)? Please list.

Who was home for dinner tonight? What was their reaction/response to the meal?

How much did you enjoy cooking tonight's meal?

Explain any difficulties you experienced cooking tonight's meal.

Considering what was important to you in preparing tonight's meal, do you feel the meal was a success? Why or why not?

How did you feel while preparing tonight's meal? *Put an "X" next to each number.*			
	Rushed	1 2 3 4 5 6 7	Relaxed
	Anxious	1 2 3 4 5 6 7	Calm
	Happy	1 2 3 4 5 6 7	Unhappy
	Uncertain	1 2 3 4 5 6 7	Confident
	Valued	1 2 3 4 5 6 7	Taken for granted
	Organized	1 2 3 4 5 6 7	Chaotic
	Creative	1 2 3 4 5 6 7	Bored

DAY 7: DAY OF THE WEEK: _____

> Congratulations! You are half-way!

Did you have a home-cooked dinner tonight?

__ NO: WENT OUT TO EAT____ ORDERED IN ____ TAKE-OUT _____

Any particular reasons for not cooking at home tonight?

__ YES [Continue below]

Tonight's menu (list all dishes; for example main dish, sides, bread, salad, dessert):

Who cooked or prepared the food for tonight's meal?

When and where did you shop for the main components of tonight's meal?

When did you plan tonight's meal?

Which of the following were most important to you in preparing tonight's meal? "I wanted to cook a meal that was …"
[Put an "X" next to each item that applies.]

- __ economical
- __ fast
- __ in my family's traditions
- __ indulgent or a special treat
- __ healthy
- __ something different
- __ comforting
- __ well-balanced
- __ convenient
- __ liked by my family
- __ showed my personal touch
- __ challenging to me as a cook
- __ easy to cook
- __ authentic
- __ gourmet
- __ trendy

Any other things you considered?

Did you follow any recipes? If so, where did you get them?

Were any components of the dishes preprepared (for example, canned chicken broth)? Please list.

Who was home for dinner tonight? What was their reaction/response to the meal?

How much did you enjoy cooking tonight's meal?

Explain any difficulties you experienced cooking tonight's meal.

Considering what was important to you in preparing tonight's meal, do you feel the meal was a success? Why or why not?

DAY 8: DAY OF THE WEEK: _____

> If this were an ideal world with unlimited amounts of time, money, and talent, what would you want to have for your family dinner tonight?

Did you have a home-cooked dinner tonight?   __ NO: WENT OUT TO EAT____ ORDERED IN ____ TAKE-OUT _____

Any particular reasons for not cooking at home tonight?

__ YES [Continue below]

Tonight's menu (list all dishes; for example main dish, sides, bread, salad, dessert):

Who cooked or prepared the food for tonight's meal?

When and where did you shop for the main components of tonight's meal?

When did you plan tonight's meal?

Which of the following were most important to you in preparing tonight's meal? "I wanted to cook a meal that was ..."
[Put an "X" next to each item that applies.]

__ economical	__ healthy	__ convenient	__ easy to cook
__ fast	__ something different	__ liked by my family	__ authentic
__ in my family's traditions	__ comforting	__ showed my personal touch	__ gourmet
__ indulgent or a special treat	__ well-balanced	__ challenging to me as a cook	__ trendy

Any other things you considered?

Did you follow any recipes? If so, where did you get them?

Were any components of the dishes preprepared (for example, canned chicken broth)? Please list.

Who was home for dinner tonight? What was their reaction/response to the meal?

How much did you enjoy cooking tonight's meal?

Explain any difficulties you experienced cooking tonight's meal.

Considering what was important to you in preparing tonight's meal, do you feel the meal was a success? Why or why not?

DAY 9: DAY OF THE WEEK: _____

Did you have a home-cooked dinner tonight?	__ NO: WENT OUT TO EAT____ ORDERED IN ____ TAKE-OUT _____
	Any particular reasons for not cooking at home tonight?
	__ YES [Continue below]

Tonight's menu (list all dishes; for example main dish, sides, bread, salad, dessert):

Who cooked or prepared the food for tonight's meal?

When and where did you shop for the main components of tonight's meal?

When did you plan tonight's meal?

Which of the following were most important to you in preparing tonight's meal?
"I wanted to cook a meal that was …"
[Put an "X" next to each item that applies.]

__ economical	__ healthy	__ convenient	__ easy to cook
__ fast	__ something different	__ liked by my family	__ authentic
__ in my family's traditions	__ comforting	__ showed my personal touch	__ gourmet
__ indulgent or a special treat	__ well-balanced	__ challenging to me as a cook	__trendy

Any other things you considered?

Did you follow any recipes? If so, where did you get them?

Were any components of the dishes preprepared (for example, canned chicken broth)? Please list.

Who was home for dinner tonight? What was their reaction/response to the meal?

How much did you enjoy cooking tonight's meal?

Explain any difficulties you experienced cooking tonight's meal.

Considering what was important to you in preparing tonight's meal, do you feel the meal was a success? Why or why not?

How did you feel while preparing tonight's meal? *Put an "X" next to each number.*									
	Rushed	1	2	3	4	5	6	7	Relaxed
	Anxious	1	2	3	4	5	6	7	Calm
	Happy	1	2	3	4	5	6	7	Unhappy
	Uncertain	1	2	3	4	5	6	7	Confident
	Valued	1	2	3	4	5	6	7	Taken for granted
	Organized	1	2	3	4	5	6	7	Chaotic
	Creative	1	2	3	4	5	6	7	Bored

DAY 10: DAY OF THE WEEK: _____

> In what situations do you most enjoy cooking? What are your favorite things to cook?

Did you have a home-cooked dinner tonight?

__ NO: WENT OUT TO EAT____ ORDERED IN ____ TAKE-OUT ____

Any particular reasons for not cooking at home tonight?

__ YES [Continue below]

Tonight's menu (list all dishes; for example main dish, sides, bread, salad, dessert):

Who cooked or prepared the food for tonight's meal?

When and where did you shop for the main components of tonight's meal?

When did you plan tonight's meal?

Which of the following were most important to you in preparing tonight's meal? "I wanted to cook a meal that was …"
[Put an "X" next to each item that applies.]

- __ economical
- __ fast
- __ in my family's traditions
- __ indulgent or a special treat
- __ healthy
- __ something different
- __ comforting
- __ well-balanced
- __ convenient
- __ liked by my family
- __ showed my personal touch
- __ challenging to me as a cook
- __ easy to cook
- __ authentic
- __ gourmet
- __ trendy

Any other things you considered?

Did you follow any recipes? If so, where did you get them?

Were any components of the dishes preprepared (for example, canned chicken broth)? Please list.

Who was home for dinner tonight? What was their reaction/response to the meal?

How much did you enjoy cooking tonight's meal?

Explain any difficulties you experienced cooking tonight's meal.

Considering what was important to you in preparing tonight's meal, do you feel the meal was a success? Why or why not?

Appendix B: Cooking Journal

DAY 11: DAY OF THE WEEK: _____

> Do you ever entertain friends or family at dinner? Tell me a little about how you cook when you entertain.

Did you have a home-cooked dinner tonight?

__ NO: WENT OUT TO EAT____
ORDERED IN ____ TAKE-OUT _____
Any particular reasons for not cooking at home tonight?

__ YES [Continue below]

Tonight's menu (list all dishes; for example main dish, sides, bread, salad, dessert):

Who cooked or prepared the food for tonight's meal?

When and where did you shop for the main components of tonight's meal?

When did you plan tonight's meal?

Which of the following were most important to you in preparing tonight's meal? "I wanted to cook a meal that was ..."
[Put an "X" next to each item that applies.]

__ economical   __ healthy   __ convenient   __ easy to cook
__ fast   __ something different   __ liked by my family   __ authentic
__ in my family's   __ comforting   __ showed my   __ gourmet
   traditions   personal touch
__ indulgent or a   __ well-balanced   __ challenging to me   __ trendy
   special treat   as a cook

Any other things you considered?

Did you follow any recipes? If so, where did you get them?

Were any components of the dishes preprepared (for example, canned chicken broth)? Please list.

Who was home for dinner tonight? What was their reaction/response to the meal?

How much did you enjoy cooking tonight's meal?

Explain any difficulties you experienced cooking tonight's meal.

Considering what was important to you in preparing tonight's meal, do you feel the meal was a success? Why or why not?

DAY 12: DAY OF THE WEEK: _____

Did you have a home-cooked dinner tonight?

__ NO: WENT OUT TO EAT____ ORDERED IN ____ TAKE-OUT _____

Any particular reasons for not cooking at home tonight?

__ YES [Continue below]

Tonight's menu (list all dishes; for example main dish, sides, bread, salad, dessert):

Who cooked or prepared the food for tonight's meal?

When and where did you shop for the main components of tonight's meal?

When did you plan tonight's meal?

Which of the following were most important to you in preparing tonight's meal? "I wanted to cook a meal that was …"
[Put an "X" next to each item that applies.]

__ economical	__ healthy	__ convenient	__ easy to cook
__ fast	__ something different	__ liked by my family	__ authentic
__ in my family's traditions	__ comforting	__ showed my personal touch	__ gourmet
__ indulgent or a special treat	__ well-balanced	__ challenging to me as a cook	__trendy

Any other things you considered?

Did you follow any recipes? If so, where did you get them?

Were any components of the dishes preprepared (for example, canned chicken broth)? Please list.

Who was home for dinner tonight? What was their reaction/response to the meal?

How much did you enjoy cooking tonight's meal?

Explain any difficulties you experienced cooking tonight's meal.

Considering what was important to you in preparing tonight's meal, do you feel the meal was a success? Why or why not?

How did you feel while preparing tonight's meal? *Put an "X" next to each number.*									
	Rushed	1	2	3	4	5	6	7	Relaxed
	Anxious	1	2	3	4	5	6	7	Calm
	Happy	1	2	3	4	5	6	7	Unhappy
	Uncertain	1	2	3	4	5	6	7	Confident
	Valued	1	2	3	4	5	6	7	Taken for granted
	Organized	1	2	3	4	5	6	7	Chaotic
	Creative	1	2	3	4	5	6	7	Bored

Appendix B: Cooking Journal 199

DAY 13: DAY OF THE WEEK: _____

Do you have any favorite recipes you inherited from your family? Please list.

Did you have a home-cooked dinner tonight?

__ NO: WENT OUT TO EAT____
ORDERED IN ____ TAKE-OUT _____

Any particular reasons for not cooking at home tonight?

__ YES [Continue below]

Tonight's menu (list all dishes; for example main dish, sides, bread, salad, dessert):

Who cooked or prepared the food for tonight's meal?

When and where did you shop for the main components of tonight's meal?

When did you plan tonight's meal?

Which of the following were most important to you in preparing tonight's meal? "I wanted to cook a meal that was …"
[Put an "X" next to each item that applies.]

__ economical	__ healthy	__ convenient	__ easy to cook
__ fast	__ something different	__ liked by my family	__ authentic
__ in my family's traditions	__ comforting	__ showed my personal touch	__ gourmet
__ indulgent or a special treat	__ well-balanced	__ challenging to me as a cook	__ trendy

Any other things you considered?

Did you follow any recipes? If so, where did you get them?

Were any components of the dishes preprepared (for example, canned chicken broth)? Please list.

Who was home for dinner tonight? What was their reaction/response to the meal?

How much did you enjoy cooking tonight's meal?

Explain any difficulties you experienced cooking tonight's meal.

Considering what was important to you in preparing tonight's meal, do you feel the meal was a success? Why or why not?

DAY 14: DAY OF THE WEEK: _____

> Are you a recipe collector? Where do you get your recipes? What appeals to you in a recipe?

Did you have a home-cooked dinner tonight?

__ NO: WENT OUT TO EAT ____ ORDERED IN ____ TAKE-OUT ____

Any particular reasons for not cooking at home tonight?

__ YES [Continue below]

Tonight's menu (list all dishes; for example main dish, sides, bread, salad, dessert):

Who cooked or prepared the food for tonight's meal?

When and where did you shop for the main components of tonight's meal?

When did you plan tonight's meal?

Which of the following were most important to you in preparing tonight's meal? "I wanted to cook a meal that was …"
[Put an "X" next to each item that applies.]

__ economical	__ healthy	__ convenient	__ easy to cook
__ fast	__ something different	__ liked by my family	__ authentic
__ in my family's traditions	__ comforting	__ showed my personal touch	__ gourmet
__ indulgent or a special treat	__ well-balanced	__ challenging to me as a cook	__ trendy

Any other things you considered?

Did you follow any recipes? If so, where did you get them?

Were any components of the dishes preprepared (for example, canned chicken broth)? Please list.

Who was home for dinner tonight? What was their reaction/response to the meal?

How much did you enjoy cooking tonight's meal?

Explain any difficulties you experienced cooking tonight's meal.

Considering what was important to you in preparing tonight's meal, do you feel the meal was a success? Why or why not?

Please answer these final questions, and then you are done! Thanks so much!

Regarding cooking, I feel confident in my ability to: [Put your initial next to all that apply]

- __ Plan a healthy meal
- __ Plan a meal my family will like
- __ Prepare a dish using a wok or stir fry
- __ Plan an economical meal
- __ Follow a recipe
- __ Sauté meats
- __ Roast meats
- __ Make homemade brownies
- __ Make mashed potatoes
- __ Cook fresh fish
- __ Make homemade bread
- __ Roast a chicken or turkey
- __ Cook a steak
- __ Make stews
- __ Make homemade pizza
- __ Make casseroles
- __ Bake a cake from a mix
- __ Make homemade gravy
- __ Make homemade soup
- __ Make homemade stock
- __ Fry chicken or French fries
- __ Bake a cake from scratch
- __ Make homemade salad dressing
- __ Prepare fresh vegetables
- __ Make homemade tomato/pasta sauce

If you were asked to cook a single dinner that most represented who you are as a cook, what would you make?

In your phone interview, you said you were a/an _____ cook. Would you still describe yourself as a/an _____ cook? If not, please explain:

Congratulations, you have finished your cooking journal!

If you have any additional comments about home cooking you'd like to share with the researchers, please add them here.

References

Abarca, M. (2006), *Voices in the Kitchen: Views of Food and the World from Working-class Mexican American Women*, College Station, TX: Texas A&M University Press.
Adapon, J. (2008), *Culinary Art and Anthropology*, London: Bloomsbury.
Albala, K., and Nafzier, R. (2010), *The Lost Art of Real Cooking: Rediscovering the Pleasures of Traditional Food One Recipe at a Time*, New York: Perigree.
Arvola, A., Vassallo, M., Dean, M., Lampila, P., Saba, A., Lähteenmäki, L., and Shepherd, R. (2008), "Predicting Intentions to Purchase Organic Food: The Role of Affective and Moral Attitudes in the Theory of Planned Behavior," *Appetite*, 50(2): 443–454.
Askegaard, S., Ordabayeva, N., Chandon, P., Cheung, T., Chytkova, Z., Cornil, Y., Corus, C., Edell, J., Mathras, D., Junghans, A., Kristensen, D., Mikkonen, I., Miller, E., Sayarh, N., and Werle, C. (2014), "Moralities in Food and Health Research," *Journal of Marketing Management*, 30(17–18): 1800–1832.
Avakian, A. (1997), *Through the Kitchen Window: Women Explore the Intimate Meanings of Food and Cooking*, London: Bloomsbury.
Avakian, A., and Haber, B. (2005), *From Betty Crocker to Feminist Food Studies: Critical Perspectives on Women and Food*, Amherst: University of Massachusetts Press.
Bandura, A. (1986), *Social Foundation of Thought and Action: A Social Cognitive Theory*. Englewood Cliffs, NJ: Prentice-Hall.
Bartels, J., and Reinders, M. J. (2010), "Social Identification, Social Representations, and Consumer Innovativeness in an Organic Food Context: A Cross-national Comparison," *Food Quality and Preference*, 21: 347–352.
Baudrillard, J. (1998), *The Consumer Society: Myths and Structures*, London: Sage.
Bava, C, Jaeger S., and Park J (2008), "Constraints upon Food Provisioning Practices in 'Busy' Women's Lives: Trade-offs Which Demand Convenience," *Appetite*, 50: 486–498.
Beagan, B., Chapman, G., Johnston, J., McPhail, D., Power, E., and Vallianatos, H. (2015), *Acquired Tastes: Why Families Eat the Way They Do*, Vancouver: UBC Press.
Began, B., Chapman, G., D'Sylva, A., and Bassett, B. (2008), "'It's Just Easier for Me to Do It': Rationalizing the Family Division of Foodwork," *Sociology*, 42(4): 653–671.
Beardsworth, A., and Keil, T. (1997), *Sociology on the Menu: An Invitation to the Study of Food and Society*, London: Routledge.
Beck, U. (1992), *Risk Society: Towards a New Modernity*, London: Sage.
Beck, U., and Beck-Gernsheim, E. (2001), *Individualization: Institutionalized Individualism and Its Social and Political Consequences*, London: Sage.
Belasco, W. (2008), *Food: The Key Concepts*, London: Berg.
Benny, H. (2012), "When Traditions Become Innovations and Innovations Become Traditions in Everyday Food Pedagogies," *Australian Journal of Adult Learning*, 52(30): 595–616.
Berge, J., Wall, M., Hsueh, F., Fulkerson, J., Larson, H., and Neumark-Sztainer, D. (2015), "The Protective Role of Family Meals for Youth Obesity: 10-year Longitudinal Associations," *Journal of Pediatrics*, 166(2): 296–301.

Berger, J., and Heath, C. (2007), "Where Consumers Diverge from Others: Identity Signaling and Product Domains," *Journal of Consumer Research*, 34(2): 121–134.

Bianchi, S., Sayer, L., Milkie, M., Robinson, J. (2012), "Housework: Who Did, Does or Will Do It, and How Much Does It Matter?" *Social Forces*, 91(1): 55–63.

Bickel, G., Nord, M., Price, C., Hamilton, W.L., and Cook, J.T. (2000), *Guide to Measuring Household Food Security. Revised 2000*. USDA, Food and Nutrition Service. Available at: http://www.fns.usda.gov/fsec/files/fsguide.pdf/ Retrieved April 22, 2018.

Biltekoff, C. (2013), *Eating Right in America: The Cultural Politics of Food and Health*, Durham, NC: Duke University Press.

Bisogni, C., Connors, M., Devine, C., and Sobel, J. (2002), "Who We Are and How We Eat: A Qualitative Study of Identities in Food Choice," *Journal of Nutritional Education and Behavior*, 34: 128–139.

Bittman, M. (2014), *How to Cook Everything Fast: A Better Way to Cook Great Food*, Boston, MA: Houghton-Mifflin-Harcourt.

Bittman, M. (2017), *Cooking Solves Everything: How Time in the Kitchen Can Save Your Health, Your Budget, and Even the Planet*. [ebook] Available at: https://www.amazon.com/Cooking-Solves-Everything-Kitchen-Health-ebook/dp/B005OKGVT0 [Accessed September 8, 2017].

Blake, C. E., Wethington, E., Farrell, T. J., Bisogni, C. A., and Devine, C. M. (2011), "Behavioral Contexts, Food-choice Coping Strategies, and Dietary Quality of a Multiethnic Sample of Employed Parents," *Journal of the American Dietetic Association*, 111(3): 401–407.

Blount, S., and Janicik, G. (2002), "Getting and Staying In-pace: The "In-Synch" Preference and Its Implications for Work Groups," *Research on Managing Groups and Teams: Toward Phenomenology of Groups and Group Membership*, Volume 4, 235–266, New York: Elsevier Science.

Bourdieu, P. (1984), *Distinction: A Social Critique of the Judgment of Taste*, Cambridge, MA: Harvard University Press.

Bowen, S., Elliott, S., and Brenton, J. (2014), "The Joy of Cooking?" *Contexts*, 13(3): 20–25.

Bracken, P. (1960), *The I Hate to Cook Cookbook*, Robbinsville: Fawcett Publications.

Brannen, J., O'Connell, R., and Mooney, A. (2013), "Families, Meals and Synchronicity: Eating Together in British Dual Earner Families," *Community, Work and Family*, 16(4): 417–434.

Brown, N. (2017), *Why We Love Comfort Food: A Sensory Experience Tied to Memory*. [online] Fix.com. Available at: https://www.fix.com/blog/why-is-comfort-food-so-tasty/[Accessed September 23, 2017].

Bugge, A., and Almås, R. (2006), "Domestic Dinner: Representations and Practices of a Proper Meal among Young Suburban Mothers," *Journal of Consumer Culture*, 6(2): 203–228.

Bryon, Lord. (George Gordon), *Don Juan*, Canto, 13. Urbana, IL: Project Gutenberg. Avalible at: www.guhtenberg.org/files/2/700/21700-h/21700-h.htm retrieved April 22, 2018, 99.

Cairns, K., and Johnston, J. (2015), *Food and Femininity*, London: Bloomsbury.

Cairns, K., Johnston, J., and MacKendrick, N. (2013), "Feeding the 'Organic Child': Mothering through Ethical Consumption," *Journal of Consumer Culture*, 13(2): 97–118.

Caraher, M., Dixon, P., Lang, T., and Carr-Hill, R. (1999), "The State of Cooking in England: The Relationship of Cooking Skills to Food Choice," *British Food Journal*, 101(8): 590–609.

Carrigan, M., and Szmigin, I. (2006), "'Mothers of Invention': Maternal Empowerment and Convenience Consumption," *European Journal of Marketing*, 40(9/10): 1122–1142.

Carrigan, M., Szmigin,I., and Leek, S. (2006), "Managing Routine Food Choices in UK Families: The Role of Convenience Consumption," *Appetite*, 47(3): 372–383.

Carrington, C. (1999), *No Place like Home: Relationship and Family Life among Lesbians and Gay Men*, Chicago, IL: University of Chicago Press.

Chan, J., and Sobel, J. (2011), "Family Meals and Body Weight: Analysis of Multiple Family Members in Family Units," *Appetite*, 52(2): 517–524.

Charles, N., and Kerr, M. (1988), *Women, Food, and Families*, Manchester: Manchester University Press.

Colwin, L. (1988), *Home Cooking: A Writer in the Kitchen*, New York: Vintage Books.

Comstock, G. (2012), "Ethics and Genetically Modified Food," in D. Kaplan (ed), *The Philosophy of Food*, Berkeley, CA: University of California Press.

Connor, T., DeYoung, C., and Silvia, P. (2017), "Everyday Creative Activity as a Path to Flourishing," *Journal of Positive Psychology*, Advance online publication. doi:10.1080/17439760.2016.1257049[Accessed September 23, 2017].

Counihan, C. (1988), "Female Identity, Food, and Power in Contemporary Florence," *Anthropological Quarterly*, 61(2): 51–62.

Counihan, C. (2010), *A Tortilla Is Like Life: Food and Culture in the San Luis Valley*, Austin, TX: University of Texas Press.

Coveney, J. (2006), *Food, Morals and Meaning: The Pleasure and Anxiety of Eating*, London: Routledge.

Csikszentmihalyi, M. (1990), *Flow: The Psychology of Optimal Experience*, New York: Harper Perennial.

De León, D. (2003), *Actions, Artefacts and Cognition: An Ethnography of Cooking*, Lund, Sweden: Lund University Cognitive Studies, 104.

De Solier, I. (2013), *Food and the Self*, London: Bloomsbury.

Dean, M., Raats, M., and Shepherd, R. (2012), "The Role of Self-identity, Past Behavior, and Their Interaction in Predicting Intention to Purchase Fresh and Processed Organic Food," *Journal of Applied Social Psychology*, 42(3): 669–688.

Del Grosso, R. (2017), Personal Communication.

DeSoucey, M., Demetry, D., and Fine, G. (2009), "The Foodie's Dilemma: Snobbery No More," Comment on "Tension in the Kitchen: Explicit and Implicit Politics in the Gourmet Foodscape," by Josée Johnston and Shyon Baumann. *Sociologica*, p. 1, doi: 10.2383/29567.

DeSoucey, M., Demetry, D., and Fine, G. (2009), "Comment on Josee Johnston and Shyon Bumann/2. The Foodie's Dilemma: Snobbery No More," *Sociologica*, (1): 1–5.

DeVault, M. (1991), *Feeding the Family: The Social Organization of Caring as Gendered Work*, Chicago, IL: University of Chicago Press.

Doré, L. (2015), "The Top Ten Comfort Foods that Cheer Britain Up," *The Independent*. Available at: http://www.independent.co.uk/life-style/food-and-drink/news/the-top-ten-comfort-foods-that-cheer-britain-up-10303269.html [Retrieved April 22, 2018].

Doré, L. (2017), *These Are the Country's Top 10 Comfort Foods*. [online] *The Independent*. Available at: http://www.independent.co.uk/life-style/food-and-drink/news/the-top-ten-comfort-foodsthat-cheer-britain-up-10303269.html [Accessed September 23, 2017].

Douglas, M. (1966), *Purity and Danger: An Analysis of Concepts of Pollution and Taboo*, New York: Praeger.

Douglas, M. (1972), "Deciphering a Meal," *Daedalus*, 101(1): 61–82.

Ekstrom, M., and d'Orange Furst, E. (2001), "The Gendered Division of Cooking," in U. Kjaernes (ed), *Eating Patterns: A Day in the Lives of the Nordic Peoples, Report* Number 7, 213–234, Lysaker: National Institute for Consumer Research.

Endrijonas, E. (2001), "Processed Foods from Scratch: Cooking for a Family in the 1950s," in S. A. Inness (ed), *Kitchen Culture in America: Popular Representations of Food, Gender and Race*, 157–173, Philadelphia, PA: University of Pennsylvania Press.

Engler-Stringer, R. (2010), "The Domestic Foodscapes of Young Low-income Women in Montreal: Cooking Practices in the Context of an Increasingly Processed Food Supply," *Health Education and Behavior*, 37(2): 211–226.

Ers.usda.gov. (2017), *USDA ERS—Food Security in the U.S.* [online] Available at: https://www.ers.usda.gov/topics/food-nutrition-assistance/food-security-in-the-us/[Accessed September 23, 2017].

Escalas, J., and Bettman, J. (2005), "Self-construal, Reference Groups, and Brand Meaning," *Journal of Consumer Research*, 32(3): 378–389.

Farb, P., and Armelagos, G. (1980), *Consuming Passions: The Anthropology of Eating*, New York: Houghton Mifflin.

Featherstone, M. (1991), *Consumer Culture and Postmodernism*, London: Sage.

Fielding-Singh, P. (2017), "A Taste of Inequality: Food's Symbolic Value across the Socioeconomic Spectrum," *Sociological Science*, 4(17): 424–448.

Finch, J., and Groves, D. (1983), *A Labour of Love: Women, Work and Caring*, London: Routledge and Kegan Paul.

Fine, G. (1996), *Kitchens: The Culture of Restaurant Work*, Berkeley, CA: University of California Press.

Fischler, C. (1979), "Gastro-nomie et Gastro-anomie," *Communications*, 31: 189–210.

Fisher, B., and Tronto, J. (1990), "Toward a Feminist Theory of Caring," in E. Able and M. Nelson (eds), *Circles of Care: Work and Identity in Women's Lives*, 35–62, Albany, NY: SUNY Press.

Fisher, M. (1942), *How to Cook a Wolf*, New York: North Point Press.

Flagg, L., Sen, B., Kilgore, M., and Locher, J. (2014), "The Influence of Gender, Age, Education and Household Size on Meal Preparation and Food Shopping Responsibilities," *Public Health Nutrition*, 17(9): 2061–2070.

Fmi.org. (2017), *FMI | Food Marketing Institute | Supermarket Facts*. [online] Available at: https://www.fmi.org/our-research/supermarket-facts [Accessed September 8, 2017].

FoodAnthropology. (2017), *New Zealand Symposium of Gastronomy Deadline Extension*. [online] Available at: https://foodanthro.com/2017/08/02/new-zealand-symposium-of-gastronomy-deadline-extension/[Accessed September 8, 2017].

Foucault, M. (1988), "The Technologies of the Self," in L. H. Martin, H. Gutman, and P. H. Hutton (eds), *Technologies of the Self: A Seminar with Michel Foucault*, 16–49, Amherst, MA: University of Massachusetts Press.

Fulkerson, J., Larson, N., Horning, M., and Neumark-Sztainer, D. (2014), "A Review of Associations between Family or Shared Meal Frequency and Dietary and Weight Status Outcomes across the Lifespan," *Journal of Nutrition Education Behavior*, 4(1): 2–19.

Funder, D., and Ozer, D. J. (1983), "Behavior as a Function of the Situation," *Journal of Personality and Social Psychology*, 44: 107–112.

Gabaccia, D. (1998), *We Are What We Eat: Ethnic Foods and the Making of Americans*, Cambridge, MA: Harvard University Press.

Gatley, A., Caraher, M., and Lang, T. (2014), "A Qualitative, Cross Cultural Examination of Attitudes and Behavior in Relation to Cooking Habits in France and Britain," *Appetite*, 75: 71–81.

Gelber, S. (1999), *Hobbies: Leisure and the Culture of Work in America*, New York: Columbia University Press.
Gevers, J. M. P. Claessens, B. J. C., Van Eerde, W., Rutte, C. G., and Roe, R. A. (2006), "Beyond Conscientiousness: Testing the Predictive Validity of Pacing Styles." Paper presented at It's About Time! Increasing the Temporal Focus in Organizational Research Symposium. University of Maastricht, The Netherlands.
Giard, L. (1998), "Doing-cooking," in M. De Certeau, L. Giard, and P. Mayol (eds), *Practice of Everyday Life, Volume 2: Living and Cooking*. Minneapolis, MA: University of Minneapolis Press.
Giddens, A. (1991), *Modernity and Self-identity: Self and Society in the Late Modern Age*, Cambridge, MA: Polity Press.
Goody, J. (1982), *Cooking, Cuisine, and Class: A Study in Comparative Sociology*, Cambridge, CA: Cambridge University Press.
Graham, H. (1983), "Caring: A Labour of Love," in J. Finch and D. Groves (eds), *A Labour of Love: Women, Work and Caring*, London: Routledge and Kegan Paul.
Hauck-Lawson, A. (1998), "When Food Is the Voice: A Case Study of a Polish-American Woman," *Journal for the Study of Food and Society*, 2(1): 21–28.
Hays, S. (1996), *The Cultural Contradictions of Motherhood*, New Haven, CT: Yale University Press.
Heldke, L. (2012), "Let's Cook Thai: Recipes for Colonialism," in C. Counihan and P. Van Esterik (eds), *Food and Culture: A Reader*, New York: Routledge.
Herndon, A. (2010), "Mommy Made Me Do It: Mothering Fat Children in the Midst of the Obesity Epidemic," *Food, Culture, and Society*, 13(3): 331–349.
Higgins, E. (1987), "Self-discrepancy: A Theory Relating Self and Affect," *Psychological Review*, 94: 319–340.
Higgins, E., Roney, C., Crowe, E., Hymes, C. (1994), "Ideal Versus Ought Predilictions for Approach and Avoidance Distinct Self-regulatory Systems," *Journal of Personality and Social Psychology*, 66: 276–286.
Highet, G. (2003), "Cannabis and Smoking Research: Interviewing Young People in Self-selected Friendship Pairs," *Health Education Research*, 18(1): 108–118.
Hobsbawm, E., and Ranger, T. (1983), *The Invention of Tradition*, Cambridge, MA: Cambridge University Press.
Hochschild, A. (2012), *Second Shift*, New York: Penguin.
Holm, L. (2001), "Family Meals," in U. Kjaernes (ed), *Eating Patterns: A Day in the Lives of Nordic Peoples*, 159–212, Lysaker: National Institute for Consumer Research.
Inness, S. (2001), *Dinner Roles: American Women and Culinary Culture*, Iowa City, IA: University of Iowa Press.
Jabs, J., Devine, C., Bisogni, C., Farrell, T., Jastran, M., and Wethington, E. (2007), "Trying to Find the Quickest Way: Employed Mothers' Constructions of Time for Food," *Journal of Nutritional Education Behavior*, 39: 18–25.
Jackson, P., and Viehoff, V. (2016), "Reframing Convenience Food," *Appetite*, 98: 1–11.
Johnston, J., and Baumann, S. (2015), *Foodies: Democracy and Distinction in the Gourmet Foodscape*, New York: Routledge.
Jones, P., Comfort, D., and Hillier, D. (2003), "Retailing Fair Trade Food Products in the UK," *British Food Journal*, 105(11): 800–810.
Jones, S. A., Walter, J., Soliah, L., and Phifer, J. T. (2014), "Perceived Motivators to Home Food Preparation: Focus Group Findings," *Journal of the Academy of Nutrition and Dietetics*, 114(10): 1552–1556.
Julier, A. (2013), *Eating Together*, Champaign, IL: University of Illinois Press.

Kaufmann, J. (2010), *The Meaning of Cooking*, Cambridge, MA: Polity Press.
Kaufman-Scarborough, C., and Lindquist, J. (2003), "Understanding the Experience of Time Scarcity: Linking Consumer Time-personality and Marketplace Behavior," *Time and Society*, 12(2/3): 349–370.
Kerner, S., Chou, S., and Warmind, M. (2015), *Commensality: From Everyday Food to Feast*, London: Bloomsbury.
Kobasa, S. (1979), "Stressful Life Events, Personality, and Health: An Inquiry into Hardiness," *Journal of Personality and Social Psychology*, 37(1): 1–11.
Kopelman, P., Caterson, I., and Dietz, W. (2010), *Clinical Obesity in Adults and Children*, Hoboken, NJ: Wiley-Blackwell.
Kuhn, M. H., and McPartland, T. S. (1954), "An Empirical Investigation of Self-attitudes," *American Sociological Review*, 19: 68–76
Kwik, J. (2008), "Traditional Food Knowledge: A Case Study of an Immigrant Canadian 'Foodscape,'" *Environments Journal*, 36(1): 59–74.
Landy, F., Rastegary, H., Thayer, J., and Colvin, C. (1991), "Time Urgency: The Construct and Its Measurement," *Journal of Applied Psychology*, 76(5): 644–657.
Larson, N. I., Story, M., Eisenberg, M. E., and Neumark-Sztainer, D. (2006), "Food Preparation and Purchasing Roles among Adolescents: Associations with Sociodemographic Characteristics and Diet Quality," *Journal of the American Diabetic Association*, 106(2): 211–218.
Laska, M., Larson, N., Neumark-Sztainer, D., and Story, M. (2012), "Does Involvement in Food Preparation Track from Adolescence to Young Adulthood and Is It Associated with Better Dietary Quality? Findings from a 10-year Longitudinal Study," *Public Health Nutrition*, 15(7): 1150–1158.
Laudan, R. (1996), "A Plea for Culinary Modernism: Why We Should Love New, Fast, Processed, Foods," *Gastronomica*, 1(1): 36–44.
Laurence, J. (2001), "Notes on an Eighteenth-century Manuscript Recipe Book," in H. Walker (ed), *Proceedings of the Oxford Symposium on Food and Cookery 2000*, 145–156, Blackawton, UK: Prospect Books.
Leech, R. M., McNaughton, S. A., Crawford, D.A., Campbell, K. J., Pearson, N., and Timperio, A. (2014), "Family Food Involvement and Frequency of Family Dinner Meals among Australian Children Age 10–12 Years. Cross-sectional and Longitudinal Associations with Dietary Patterns," *Appetite*, 75: 64–70.
Levi-Strauss, C. (1962), *The Savage Mind*, Chicago, IL: University of Chicago Press.
Levi-Strauss, C. (1970), *The Raw and the Cooked*, London: Jonathan Cape.
Lewin, K. (1947), "Frontiers in Group Dynamics: II. Channels of Group Life; Social Planning and Action Research," *Human Relations*, 1(2): 143–153.
Lincoln, Y., and Guba, E. (1985), *Naturalistic Inquiry*, Newbury Park, CA: Sage.
Livert, D., and Khabbaz, T. (2016), "Flourishing in the Kitchen: Finding Well-being Amid Controlled Chaos," Paper presented at the annual meeting of the Eastern Psychological Association. New York.
Locher, J., Yoels, W., Maurer, D., and Van Ells, J. (2005), "An Exploratory Journal into the Social and Emotional Significance of Food," *Food and Foodways*, 13: 273–297.
Locher, J., Yoels, W., Maurer, D., and Van Ells, J. (2015), "Comfort Foods: An Exploratory Journey into the Social and Emotional Significance of Food," *Food and Foodways*, 13(4): 273–297.
Loureiro, M., and Lotade, J. (2005) "Do Fair Trade and Eco-labels in Coffee Wake up the Consumer Conscience," *Ecological Economics*, 51(1): 129–138.
Lupton, D. (1996), *Food, the Body and the Self*, London: Sage.

MacClancy, J. (2004), "Food, Identity, and Identification," in H. Macbeth and J. MacClancy (eds), *Researching Food Habits: Methods and Problems*, 63–74, New York: Berghahn Books.

Mackendrick, N. (2014), "Foodscape," *Contexts*, 13(3): 16–18.

Meah, A. (2013), "Reconceptualizing Power and Gendered Subjectivities in Domestic Cooking Spaces," *Progress in Human Geography*, 38(5): 671–690.

Meah, A., and Jackson, P. (2017), "Convenience as Care: Culinary Antinomies in Practice," *Environment and Planning*, 49(9): 2065–2081.

Mennell, S. (1985), *All Manners of Food: Easting and Taste in England and France from the Middle Ages to the Present*, Oxford: Basil Blackwell.

Mercille, G., Receveur, O., and Potvin, L. (2012), "Household Food Insecurity and Canadian Aboriginal Women's Self-efficacy in Food-preparation," *Canadian Journal of Dietetic Practice and Research*, 73(3): 134–140.

Merriam, S. (2009), *Qualitative Research: A Guide to Design and Implementation* (2nd ed.), San Francisco, CA: Jossey-Bass.

Metcalfe, A., Dryden, C., Johnson, M., Owen, J., and Shipton, G. (2009), "Fathers, Food, and Everyday Life," in P. Jackson (ed), *Changing Families, Changing Food*, 93–117, London: Palgrave.

Milliken, P. (2010), "Grounded Theory," in N. Saldkind (ed), *Encyclopedia of Research Design*, 549–554, Thousand Oaks, CA: Sage.

Mills, S., White, M., Brown, H., Wrieden, W., Kwasnicka, D., Halligan, J., Robalino, S., and Adams, S. (2017), "Health and Social Determinants and Outcomes of Home Cooking: A Systematic Review of Observational Studies," *Appetite*, 111: 116–134.

Mommy Hates Cooking. (2017), *Mommy Hates Cooking*. [online] Available at: https://www.mommyhatescooking.com [Accessed September 11, 2017].

Moisio, R., Arnould, E., Price, L., (2004), "Between Mothers and Markets: Constructing Family Identity through Homemade Food," *Journal of Consumer Culture*, 4(3): 361–384.

Moon, S., Dillon, D., and Sprenkle, D. (1990), "Family Therapy and Qualitative Research," *Journal of Marital and Family Therapy*, 16(4): 357–373.

Murcott, A. (1982), "On the Social Significance of the 'Cooked Dinner' in South Wales," *Social Science Information*, 21(4/5): 677–695.

Murcott, A. (1983), "'It's a Pleasure to Cook for Him': Food, Mealtimes and Gender in Some South Wales Households," in E. Gamarnikow, D. Morgan, J. Puvis, and D. Taylorson (eds), *The Public and the Private*, London: Heinemann.

Murcott, A. (1995), "Raw, Cooked and Proper Meals at Home," in D. W. Marshall (ed), *Food Choice and the Consumer*, 219–236, Glasgow: Blackie and Academic.

Murcott, A. (1997), "Family Meals – A Thing of the Past?" in P. Caplan (ed), *Food, Health, and Identity*, 32–48, New York: Routledge.

Naccarato, P., and Lebesco, K. (2012), *Culinary Capital*, London: Berg.

Nestle, M. (2007), *What to Eat*, New York: North Point Press.

Nestle, M. (2010), *Safe Food. The Politics of Food Safety*, Berkeley, CA: University of California Press.

Nestle, M. (2013), *Food Politics: How the Food Industry Influences Nutrition and Health. Revised and Expanded Tenth Anniversary Edition*, Berkeley, CA: University of California Press.

Oakley, A. (1974), *Housewife*, London: Allen Lane.

O'Connell, R., and Brannen, J. (2016), *Food, Families and Work*, London: Bloomsbury.

OED Online. (2017), Oxford University Press. http://www.oed.com/viewdictionaryentry/Entry/11125 [Accessed September 10, 2017].

Parkin, K. (2006), *Food Is Love: Advertising and Gender Roles in Modern America*, Philadelphia, PA: University of Pennsylvania Press.

Penzeys Spices. (2017), *Penzeys Spices*. [online] Available at: https://www.penzeys.com/ [Accessed September 11, 2017].

Pillsbury, R. (1998), *No Foreign Food: The American Diet in Time and Place*, Boulder, CO: Westview Press.

Pollan, M. (2006), *The Omnivore's Dilemma: A Natural History of Four Meals*, New York: Penguin Books.

Pollan, M. (2009a), *Out of the Kitchen, Onto the Couch*. [online] Nytimes.com. Available at: http://www.nytimes.com/2009/08/02/magazine/02cooking-t.html?mcubz=0 [Accessed September 11, 2017].

Pollan, M. (2009b), *Food Rules: An Eater's Manual*, New York: Penguin.

Pollan, M. (2013), *Cooked: A Natural History of Transformation*, New York: Penguin Press.

Poortman, A., and Van Der Lippe, T. (2009), "Attitudes toward Housework and Child Care and the Gendered Division of Labor," *Journal of Marriage and Family*, 71(3): 526–541.

Pratt, M., Pradies, C., and Lepisto, D. (2013), "Doing Well, Doing Good, and Doing with: Organizational Practices for Effectively Cultivating Meaningful Work," in B. Dik, Z. Byrne, and M. Steger (eds), *Purpose and Meaning in the Workplace*, Washington, DC: American Psychological Association.

Preisendörfer, P., and Wolter, F. (2014), "Who Is Telling the Truth? A Validation Study on Determinants of Response Behavior in Surveys," *Public Opinion*, 78(1): 126–146.

Probyn, E. (2000), *Carnal Appetites: FoodSexIdentity*, London: Routledge.

Rachel Laudan. (2017), *Rachel Laudan*. [online] Available at: http://www.rachellaudan.com/blog [Accessed September 11, 2017].

Rahman, M. (2017), "The Advantages and Disadvantages of Using Qualitative and Quantitative Approaches and Methods in Language 'Testing an Assessment' Research: A Literature Review," *Journal of Education and Learning*, 6(1): 102–112.

Rawlins, R. (2014), "The Mother's Club of Cambridge, 1878–1904: Reappropriating, Reconfiguring and (Re)presenting Expert Knowledge of Mothering," *Journal of the Motherhood Initiative*, 5(1): 172–184.

Rawlins, R., and Livert, D. (2014), "The Dilemma of Dinner," in T. Conroy (ed), *Food and Everyday Life*, Lanham, MD: Lexington Books.

Ray, K. (2004), *The Migrant's Table: Meals and Memories in Bengali American Households*, Philadelphia, PA: Temple University Press.

Rose, N. (1990), *Governing the Soul: The Shaping of the Private Self*, London: Routledge.

Ross, L., and Nisbett, R. (1991), *The Person and the Situation: Perspectives on Social Psychology*, New York: McGraw-Hill.

Rousseau, S. (2012), *Food Media: Celebrity Chefs and the Politics of Everyday Interference*, London: Berg.

Rozin, P. (1999), "Food Is Fundamental, Fun, Frightening, and Far-reaching," *Social Research*, 66(1): 9.

Ruhlman, M. (2017), *Grocery: The Buying and Selling of Food in America*, New York: Abrams Press.

Sayer, L., England, P., Bittman, M., and Bianchi, S. (2009), "How Long Is the Second (Plus First) Shift? Gender Differences in Paid, Unpaid, and Total Work Time in Australia and the United States," *Journal of Comparative Family Studies*, 40(4): 523–544.

Scholliers, P. (2015), "Convenience Foods. What, Why, and When," *Appetite*, 94(1): 2–6.

Schwartz, B. (2004), *Paradox of Choice*, New York: Harper Perennial.
Sealy, Y. M. (2010), "Parents' Food Choices: Obesity among Minority Parents and Children," *Journal of Community Health Nursing*, 27(1): 1–11.
Segal, L. (2007), *Slow Motion: Changing Masculinities, Changing Men*, Basingstoke: Palgrave Macmillan.
Sennett, R. (2008), *The Craftsman*, New Haven, CT: Yale University Press.
Short, F. (2006), *Kitchen Secrets: The Meaning of Cooking in Everyday Life*, Oxford: Berg.
Singer J. A. (2004), "Narrative Identity and Meaning-making across the Adult Lifespan: An Introduction," *Journal of Personality*, 72: 437–459.
Singleton, W. (1978), *The Study of Real Skills. Vol. 1. The Analysis of Practical Skills*, Lancaster: MTP Press.
Sliwa, S. A., Must, A., Perea, F., and Economos, C. (2015), "Maternal Employment, Acculturation, and Time Spent in Food-related Behaviors among Hispanic Mothers in the United States, Evidence from the American Time Use Survey," *Appetite*, 87: 10–19.
Smith, D. (1987), *The Everyday World as Problematic: A Feminist Sociology*, Boston, MA: Northeastern University Press.
Smith, L., Ng, S., and Popkin, B. (2013), "Trends in US Home Food Preparation and Consumption: Analysis of National Nutrition Surveys and Time Use Studies from 1965–1966 to 2007–2008," *Nutrition Journal*, 12(1): 1–10.
Sobal, J. (2005), "Men, Meat, and Marriage: Models of Masculinity," *Food and Foodways*, 13(1/2): 135–158.
Southerton, D., Diaz-Mendez, C., and Warde, A. (2012), "Behavioral Change and the Temporal Ordering of Eating Practices: A UK-Spain Comparison," *International Journal of Sociology of Agriculture and Food*, 19(1): 19–36.
Spence, C. (2017), "Comfort Food: A Review," *International Journal of Gastronomy and Food Science*, 9: 105–109.
Spoon University. (2017), *How to Pack the Perfect French Picnic*. [online] Available at: https://spoonuniversity.com/how-to/how-to-pack-the-perfect-french-picnic [Accessed September 10, 2017].
Stats.oecd.org. (2016), *Average Annual Hours Actually Worked per Worker*. [online] Available at: https://stats.oecd.org/Index.aspx?DataSetCode=ANHRS [Accessed September 11, 2017].
Storfer-Isser, A., and Musher-Eizenman, D. (2013), "Measuring Parent Time Scarcity and Fatigue as Barriers to Meal Planning and Preparation: Quantitative Scale Development," *Journal of Nutrition Education and Behavior*, 45(2): 176–182.
Supski, S. (2006), "It Was Another Skin: The Kitchen as Home for Australian Post-war Immigrant Women," *Gender, Place and Culture*, 13(2): 133–141.
Sutton, D. (2014), *Secrets from the Greek Kitchen: Cooking, Skill, and Everyday Life on an Aegean Island*, Berkeley, CA: University of California Press.
Symons, M. (2000), *A History of Cooks and Cooking*, Urbana, IL: University of Illinois Press.
Szabo, M (2011), "The Challenges of 'Re-engaging with Food': Connecting Employment, Household Patterns and Gender Relations to Convenience Food Consumption in North America," *Food, Culture and Society*, 14(4): 547–566.
Szabo, M. (2012), "Foodwork or Foodplay? Men's Domestic Cooking, Privilege and Leisure," *Sociology*, 47(4): 623–638.
Szabo, M., and Koch, S. (2017), "Introduction," in M. Szabo and S. Koch (eds), *Food, Masculinities, and Home: Interdisciplinary Perspectives*, 1–28, London: Bloomsbury.
Tannahill, R. (1989), *Food in History*, New York: Crown Publishers.

TheHarrisPoll.com. (2017), *Kitchen Creations: Nearly 4 in 5 Americans Say Dinners at Home Mean Cooking from Scratch*. [online] Available at: http://www.theharrispoll.com/health-and-life/Cooking-Dinners-At-Home.html [Accessed September 16, 2017].

Thompson, C. (1996), "Caring Consumers: Gendered Consumption Meanings and the Juggling Lifestyle," *Journal of Consumer Research*, 22: 388–407.

Thompson, C., Cummins, S., Brown, T., and Kyle, R. (2016), "Contrasting Approaches to 'Doing' Family Meals: A Qualitative Study of How Parents Frame Children's Food Preferences," *Critical Public Health*, 26(3): 322–332.

Tourangeau, R., Rips, J., and Rasinkski, K. (2000), *The Psychology of Survey Response*, New York: Cambridge University Press.

Trubek, A., Carabello, M., Morgan, C., and Lahane, J. (2017), "Empowered to Cook: The Crucial Role of 'Food Agency' in Making Meals," *Appetite*, 116: 297–305.

Tumin, R., and Anderson, S. (2017), "Television, Home-cooked Meals, and Family Meal Frequency: Associations with Adult Obesity," *Journal of the Academy of Nutrition and Dietetics*, 117: 937–945.

Turkle, S., and Papert, S. (1990), "Epistemological Pluralism: Styles and Voices within the Computer Culture," *SIGNS: Journal of Women in Culture and Society*, 16(1): 28–156.

USDA. (2012), "U.S. Household Food Security Survey Module: Six-item Short Form. Economic Research Service.

Vincent, C., and Ball, C. (2007), "'Making Up' the Middle Class Child: Families, Activities and Class Dispositions," *Sociology*, 41(6): 1061–1077.

Virudachalam, S., Long, J. A., Harhay, M. O., Polsky, D. E., and Feudtner, C. (2013), "Prevalence and Patterns of Cooking Dinner at Home in the USA: National Health and Nutritional Examination Survey (NHANES) 2007–2008," *Public Health Nutrition*, 17(5): 1022–1030.

Waller, M., Conte, J., Gibson, C., and Carpenter, M. (2001), "The Effect of Individual Perceptions of Deadlines on Team Performance," *Academy of Management Review*, 26(4): 586–600.

Walzer, S. (1996), "Thinking about the Baby: Gender and Divisions of Infant Care," *Social Problems*, 43(2): 219–234.

Wang, M. C., Naidoo, N., Ferzacca, S., Reddy, G., and Van Dam, R. (2014), "The Role of Women in Food Provision and Food Choice Decision-making in Singapore: A Case Study," *Ecology of Food and Nutrition*, 53(6): 658–677.

Warde, A. (1994), "Consumption, Identity-formation and Uncertainty," *Sociology*, 28(4): 877–898.

Warde, A. (1997), *Consumption, Food and Taste*, London: Sage Publications.

Warde, A. (1999), "Convenience Food Space and Timing," *British Food Journal*, 101(7): 518–217.

Warde, A. (2014), "After Taste: Culture, Consumption and Theories of Practice," *Journal of Consumer Culture*, 14(3): 279–303.

Warde, A., Cheng, S., Olsen, W., and Southerton, D. (2007), "Changes in the Practice of Eating: A Comparative Analysis of Time-Use," *Acta Sociologica*, 50(4): 363–385.

Warde, A., Martens, L., and Olsen, W. (1999), "Consumption and the Problem of Variety: Cultural Omnivorousness, Social Distinction and Dining out," *Sociology*, 33(1): 105–127.

Wansink, B. (2003), "Profiling Nutritional Gatekeepers: Three Methods for Differentiating Influential Cooks," *Food Quality and Preference*, 14(4): 289–297.

Wansink, B., and Sangerman, C. (2000), "Engineering Comfort Foods," *American Demographics*, 22(7): 66–67.

Williams, L., and Germov, J. (2017), "From 'The Missus Used to Cook' to 'Gt the Recipe Book and Get Stuck Into It': Reconstructing Masculinities in Older Men," in M. Szabo and S. Koch (eds), *Food, Masculinities, and Home: Interdisciplinary Perspectives*, 108–125, London: Bloomsbury.

Williams-Forson, P. (2006), *Building Houses out of Chicken Legs: Black Women, Food, and Power*, Chapel Hill, NC: University of North Carolina Press.

Wills, W. (2012), "Using Spoken and Written Qualitative Methods to Explore Children's and Young People's Food and Eating Practices," *Sociological Research Online*, 17(3): 1–10.

Wolfson, A., Bleich, S., Smith, K., and Frattaroli, S. (2016), "What Does Cooking Mean to You?: Perceptions of Cooking and Factors Related to Cooking Behavior," *Appetite*, 97: 146–154.

Wrangham, R. (2010), *Catching Fire: How Cooking Made Us Human*, New York: Perseus.

Wright-St Clair, V.W., Hocking C., Bunrayong W., Vittayakorn S., and Rattakorn, P. (2005), "Older New Zealand Women Doing the Work of Christmas: A Recipe for Identity Formation," *Sociological Review*, 53(2): 332–350.

Index

Abarca, M. 19
Acquired Tastes: Why Families Eat the Way They Do (Beagan, Chapman, et al.) 62
Adapon, J. 145
Almäs, R. 28, 97
Armelagos, G. 129
Avakian, A.V. 17, 18–19, 20

Baumann, S. 148
Beagan, B. 62
Beardsworth, A. 21, 136
Belasco, W. 63
Biltekoff, C. 62
bricoleurs 94–5
Bugge, A.B. 28, 97

Cairns, K. 19, 120, 121
care 23–7, 80, 97, 112, 161, 162–3, 165–6
  components of 26
  and convenience foods 61, 84
  and division of labor 34
Catching Fire (Wrangham) 18
Chapman, G. 62
Charles, N. 21
children
  childcare 34, 80, 84, 111–12, 116–17, 167
  cooking for 36, 69, 92, 113, 115–17, 120–1, 161
  extra-curricular activities 80–1, 167
  as helpers 37–8, 125
  taste preferences 68–9, 71, 91, 107, 113, 116
  teaching 37–8, 71, 130, 152
Colwin, L. 50
comfort food 132, 138, 162–3
  as goal 73–7, 166
  perceptions of 73–4
community supported agriculture 41, 89, 125

convenience foods 3, 46, 61, 83–6, 166, 171
Cooking, Cuisine and Class (Goody) 18
cooking, home
  as chore 54, 56, 57, 79, 81–2, 115, 116, 118, 120, 156
  as craft 19, 55, 155–6, 161, 165–6
  cultural meaning 20–2
  decline of 3, 22–3, 24, 84 (*see also under* family meal)
  defined 3–4
  dimensions of 158–60, 162
  and economizing 40–1
  as enjoyable 55–7, 68, 81, 91–2, 93, 113, 120, 135, 146, 152–6, 157, 160–1
  goals of 13–14, 64–78
  as leisure 55, 142, 146, 166
cooking shows 3, 48, 145
cooking skills 41–4
  confidence in 43–4, 93, 98–100, 122–3, 135, 142, 150
  decline of 3, 22–3, 84, 171 (*see also* deskilling)
  defined 5–6
  home *vs.* professional cooks 42, 79–80, 155
  and recipe use 46–7
  and self-identity 13–14, 98–100, 107, 142, 146
Counihan, C. 19
Coveney, J. 22, 62–3, 112, 119, 137
craftsmanship. *See under* cooking, home
creativity 101, 145, 154–5, 157, 161, 165
Csikszentmihalyi, M. 55, 82, 154
cuisine 129, 132, 144, 161
culinary antinomies 61
culinary capital 28, 147

Deciphering a Meal (Douglas) 3
De Léon, D. 79

deskilling 23, 84, 171. *See also under* cooking skills
de Solier, I. 28, 148
DeVault, M. 4, 17, 22, 59, 119–20
dinner parties. *See* entertaining
division of labor 31–4, 35, 36–8, 39, 118, 124
Douglas, M. 3, 17, 18, 21
drudges
  defined 16, 54
  self-identity 54, 102

Eating Together (Julier) 17
economic resources 7, 19, 24–5, 40–1, 60, 63, 162
emotions 58, 102, 114–15, 119–20, 134–6, 154–5, 161
  anxiety 93, 113, 121, 136, 167
  comfort 73–4, 113, 132, 138
  flow (*see* psychological flow)
Endrijonas, E. 19
entertaining 48–9, 50, 56
ethnicity
  of study participants 13, 130
  and traditional cooking 76, 128, 130, 132, 161, 163
Everyday World as Problematic, The (Smith) 15

family-first cooks 111–26, 161
  defined 16, 112–13
  and dining alone 50–1
  emotions 114–15
  and self-identity 27, 112–13
family meal
  decline of 22–4, 121, 136, 170–2 (*see also under* cooking, home)
  ideal of 24–5, 69, 138, 171–2
  incidence 170
  as interaction 105, 116, 132, 164, 166
family schedules 80–1. *See also under* time constraints
Farb, P. 129
Feeding the Family (DeVault) 17–18, 22, 59, 119–20
feeding work 4, 22, 26–7, 59, 119–20, 122, 166
feminism
  and cooking 18–19, 165

  in data analysis 15
  and food studies 17
Fine, G. 79
Fischler, C. 21, 136
Fisher, B. 26
Fisher, M.F.K. 61, 93
food agency 80, 145
Food and Femininity (Cairns and Johnston) 120
food choice 57, 58–9, 61–3, 136. *See also under* meal planning
foodies 147–50
Foodies: Democracy and Distinction in the Gourmet Foodscape (Johnston and Baumann) 148
food insecurity 7, 162–3
food memories 128, 129, 138–9, 161
Food, Morals and Meaning: The Pleasure and Anxiety of Eating (Coveney) 62–3
food rules 21, 48, 136
food studies 17–19
food television. *See* cooking shows
food voice 28, 129, 138
food waste 41

gastro-anomie 136
gender
  and care 26, 120
  and cooking 19, 20, 118–24, 161
  and division of labor 32–4, 118, 121
  and meal planning 35–6
Giard, L. 4, 25, 28
Giddens, A. 27–8
"good" food 61–2, 63, 136–8, 144, 153–4, 158
Goody, J. 18

Haber, B. 17, 18–19, 20
Hauck-Lawson, A. 28, 129
healthy food. *See also* nutrition
  and distinction 72
  as goal 64–6, 71–2, 108, 114, 125–6, 150–1, 166
  perceptions of 41, 61, 62, 72–3, 136–8, 161
  shopping for 41
  "well-balanced" as type of 74–5
helpers 36–8

Herndon, A. 121
hierarchical linear models (HLM) 15–16
Higgins, E.T. 29, 155
History of Cooks and Cooking, A (Symons) 25
Holm, L. 25

identity. *See* self-identity
improvisational cooks 90, 92–6, 163
    defined 16, 79, 90
    emotions 93–4

Jabs, J. 96
Jackson, P. 84
Johnston, J. 120, 121, 148
Julier, A. 17

Kaufmann, J.C. 17, 20, 27, 81, 137
keen cooks 141–56, 161
    confidence 142–3
    defined 16, 142
    and dining alone 51
    emotions 152–5
    and recipes 45–6, 144–5
    and self-identity 27, 142
Keil, T. 21
Kerr, M. 21, 24
Kitchen Secrets (Short) 4, 5, 20, 25, 144, 156

Laurence, J. 131
Lebesco, K. 28, 148
Levi-Strauss, C. 17, 94
Lewin, K. 58, 61
life-course transitions 115–18, 160
lifestyles 28
Lupton, D. 22, 28, 138, 144, 171

MacClancy, J. 27, 109, 164
MacKendrick, N. 120, 121
Meah, A. 84
meal kit delivery service 86, 147
meal planning 5. *See also* improvisational cooks; planful cooks
    as care 26
    confidence in 44
    division of labor 31–5
    and enjoyment 91–2
    and entertaining 49–50
    and food cost 40–1

and food shopping 38–40
as mental load 60
menu selection 56, 59–64, 70
patterns 87–90, 91, 96, 163
and time scarcity 80
meals, family
    decline of 22–4
    as ideals 61, 171
    incidence 23–4, 32
mechanical skills 42, 46
men as cooks 33–4, 35
mental burden 67
modernity 27–8
modes of identification. *See* self-identity
motherhood, ideologies of 62, 63, 118–22, 161
Murcott, A. 4, 21, 171

Naccarato, P. 28, 148
National Health and Nutritional Examination Survey (NHANES) 24, 32
No Foreign Food: The American Diet in Time and Place (Pillsbury) 129
nutrition 24, 62, 71–3. *See also* healthy food
    and cooking skills 42
    and discourses of power 22, 62–3, 119, 137
    and food cost 41
nutritional gatekeepers 58, 61

Oakley, A. 118
obesity 121
"Out of the Kitchen, Onto the Couch" (Pollan) 3, 48

Paradox of Choice, The (Schwartz) 59, 62
Parkin, K. 62
performance of cook 29, 104–6, 155
Pillsbury, R. 129
planful cooks 90, 91–2, 163
    defined 16, 79, 90
planning. *See* meal planning
Pollan, M. 3, 48, 137
power 19, 22, 28, 35, 131
prepared food. *See* convenience foods
"proper" meals 21, 26, 48, 59–61, 98, 137, 158

provisioning. *See* shopping, food
psychological flow 82, 102, 154–5
Purity and Danger (Douglas) 18

Raw and the Cooked, The (Levi-Strauss) 18
recipes
    and cooking confidence 46–7
    and food cost 40
    sources of 47–8
    traditional 130–1
    use of 31, 44–6, 144–5

same-sex couples 32–4
Scholliers, P. 97
Schwartz, B. 59
self-discrepancy theory 29, 155
self-identity 128, 132, 157, 161, 164
    and consumption 28
    and cooking 16, 19, 24, 27–9, 97, 118, 129
    and cooking skills 43–4, 98
    ethnicity 132
    as "foodies" 147–50
    and performance 98, 103–4, 142–3
self-perception. *See* self-identity
Sennett, R. 155
shopping, food 4, 38–41
Short, F. 4, 5, 20, 25, 144, 156
Smith, D. 4, 15, 18
Smith, L. 24
social psychology 3, 14, 29, 58, 98, 109, 158
study design
    characteristics of participants 8–12, 13
    construction of ideal types of cooks 16
    hierarchical linear modeling (HLM) 15
    interviews and journals 13–14, 31–2, 64, 94, 98, 158
    mixed methods 6
    qualitative data analysis 15
    quantitative data analysis 15–16
    sample 6–7, 161–2
success, perceptions of 57, 104–8, 111–12, 150–1, 157, 164, 165
Sutton, D. 20, 130, 158
Symons, M. 25
Szabo, J. 34

taste preferences
    of cooks 50–1, 61, 70, 90, 153
    of family members 5, 7, 56, 59, 66, 69, 71, 90, 91, 100, 103–4, 111, 113, 116, 123–4, 150, 165
    satisfaction as goal 67–71, 100, 106–7, 113, 114, 150, 166
Thompson, C. 69, 91
time constraints 16, 23–4, 122, 147, 166–7, 170
    and cooking skills 42, 79–80
    emotional implications of 83, 134–5, 167
    and food shopping 38–9
    and helpers 37
    synchronicity 80–1, 82, 167
    time scarcity 24, 55–6, 57, 60, 79, 80–3, 111–12
    time-urgency 96
    and traditional cooks 134–5
traditional cooks 127–39, 161
    defined 16, 76, 128
    emotions 134–6
    recipe use 45
    and self-identity 27, 132
traditional food 75–6, 127, 132, 166
Tronto, J. 26
Trubek, A. 4, 5, 64–5, 80, 94
types of cooks 162
    construction of 16
    definitions of 16, 109, 160

Virudachalam, S. 24, 32

Warde, A. 61, 80, 83
women
    and care 26, 120
    and feeding work 22, 118–19
    gendered roles of 37, 118–20
    and generosity 25
    as primary cooks 31–3, 34, 35–6
women's studies. *See* feminism
work–life balance 16, 80, 166–7
    and family meals 24, 122
    and gender 33–4, 122
Wrangham, R. 18

CPSIA information can be obtained
at www.ICGtesting.com
Printed in the USA
LVHW080917061120
670848LV00008B/84